Chicken Soup for the Soul: Dreams and the Unexplainable
101 Eye-Opening Stories about Premonitions and Miracles
Amy Newmark & Kelly Sullivan Walden

Published by Chicken Soup for the Soul, LLC www.chickensoup.com
Copyright ©2017 by Chicken Soup for the Soul, LLC. All Rights Reserved.

The publisher gratefully acknowledges the many publishers and individuals who
granted Chicken Soup for the Soul permission to reprint the cited material.

Front cover artwork courtesy of iStockphoto.com/Ljupco (©Ljupco)
Front cover and back cover space background artwork courtesy of iStockphoto.
com/bestdesigns (©bestdesigns)
Interior illustration courtesy of iStockphoto.com/GeorgePeters (©GeorgePeters)
Photo of Amy Newmark courtesy of Susan Morrow at SwickPix
Photos of Kelly Sullivan Walden courtesy of Carl Studna

Cover and Interior by Daniel Zaccari

Distributed to the booktrade by Simon & Schuster. SAN: 200-2442

Publisher's Cataloging-In-Publication Data
(Prepared by The Donohue Group, Inc.)

Names: Newmark, Amy, compiler. | Walden, Kelly Sullivan, compiler.
Title: Chicken soup for the soul : dreams and the unexplainable : 101 eye-
    opening stories about premonitions and miracles / [compiled by] Amy
    Newmark [and] Kelly Sullivan Walden.
Other Titles: Dreams and the unexplainable : 101 eye-opening stories about
    premonitions and miracles
Description: [Cos Cob, Connecticut] : Chicken Soup for the Soul, LLC,
    [2017]
Identifiers: ISBN 978-1-61159-971-8 (print) | ISBN 978-1-61159-271-9
    (ebook)
Subjects: LCSH: Dreams--Literary collections. | Dreams--Anecdotes. |
    Precognition--Literary collections. | Precognition--Anecdotes.
    | Miracles--Literary collections. | Miracles--Anecdotes. | LCGFT:
    Anecdotes.
Classification: LCC BF1091 .C45 2017 (print) | LCC BF1091 (ebook) | DDC
    135/.302--dc23

Library of Congress LCCN 201794798

PRINTED IN THE UNITED STATES OF AMERICA
on acid∞free paper

25 24 23 22 21 20 19 18 17   01 02 03 04 05 06 07 08 09 10 11

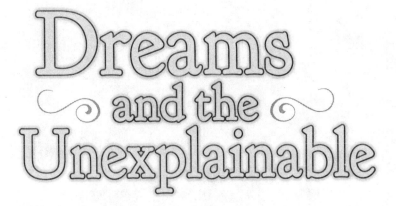

101 Eye-Opening Stories
about Premonitions and Miracles

Amy Newmark
Kelly Sullivan Walden

Chicken Soup for the Soul, LLC
Cos Cob, CT

Chicken Soup for the Soul

Changing lives one story at a time®
www.chickensoup.com

Table of Contents

❸

~Prophetic Premonitions~

❹

~Life Changing Guidance~

❺

~The Miracle of Finding Love~

6

~Dreams that Saved Lives~

7

~Amazing Coincidences and Synchronicity~

8

~Comfort and Closure~

9

~Listening to That Little Voice~

We dedicate this book to our good friend Julie Isaac (@WritingSpirit), the "godmother" of this book and our previous collection of stories on this topic, *Chicken Soup for the Soul: Dreams and Premonitions*. Thank you, Julie, for introducing Amy and Kelly to each other in a most synchronistic and magical way.

Introduction

I t was 2015 and I'd taken on so many creative projects that I felt like a juggler who was dropping balls left, right, and center. As I tried to keep up with my deadlines, I felt I was letting everyone down. I found myself snapping at my husband, yelling at my mother, slamming doors on my sister, even exploding at my dogs for giving me a look that implied they wanted more from me than I could give them.

And then I had a dream, and everything changed for me.

In my dream, I'm walking into a dark, unfamiliar living room and a terrifying alien with menacing eyes jumps out from behind a couch. She has flowing dreadlocks and a Medusa look. I gasp in fright... until I realize there is something familiar about her.

"Don't I KNOW you?" I say.

She is thrown off by my question — disappointed her scare tactics aren't working on me. Then, it dawns on her... she knows me, too.

Our hearts melt as we realize how much we know and love each other — dear friends reunited after a long time of no contact. With this recognition she begins to soften and morph before my eyes into a soft, crystalline blue alien... with the sweetest upside down teardrop-shaped head. Her beauty is so stunning I can barely breathe.

This version of her is completely the opposite of the monster she showed herself to be just moments before. The love she now beams at me feels alien, but also comforting, as if I'm floating in a warm bubble bath.

When I journaled about this dream I struggled to find the words to describe the profound feeling of peace it gave me. The only word that came close was "fleece." The dream left me feeling like I was surrounded by the softest, most cushiony baby blanket… protected from harm and cradled in love… a shock absorber to keep my life smooth amid all the chaos and stress in my waking reality.

My dream was a gift from my subconscious sleeping self to my awake self. It revealed to me how I had been "alienating" people when I really had a deep desire to connect and love. Reconciling these conflicting needs felt impossible until this dream came to my emotional rescue. Now I had my cushiony, soft fleece to protect me as I navigated my impossible deadlines, and I could do so with joy instead of stress.

Shortly after this dream, I found myself on the phone with Amy Newmark, my co-author and publisher for this book and for our previous book, *Chicken Soup for the Soul: Dreams and Premonitions*, which was about to be released at the time of our call.

Over the year that I'd worked with her, most of our conversations revolved around practical matters pertaining to our book. I never shared my daily dream report with her. I'm not sure why, but that day I decided to share my "Blue Alien" dream with Amy.

As the dream slipped out of my mouth, I immediately wished it hadn't because all I heard was silence from her end of the line. I guessed she was figuring out how to break our contract and run as far away from me as she possibly could.

You see, here in Southern California, conversations about aliens and fringy, "new age" topics are normal. But, Amy, being from the more conservative East Coast… I thought, *Now I've done it… I've alienated Amy… she's going to write me off.*

To my surprise, during the very long silence that followed, Amy was actually texting me a photograph of her bright blue car's personalized blue license plate that read ALIEN in blue letters.

What? Why? You live in Connecticut! What are you doing with a blue license plate on your blue car that says ALIEN in blue letters?

She proceeded to tell me that there's a running joke in her family that she is an alien. She said that one day twenty years earlier, when she and her family were sitting around the kitchen table, her seven-year-old son, Mike, asked her, "Mommy, what are we?" She knew what he was asking: He had heard his friends talking about their parents' religions and diverse backgrounds.

But Amy spontaneously assumed a serious demeanor and said, "Mike, I think you and Ella are old enough to know the truth." It sounded like she was about to tell them they were adopted. Mike later told her that he was excited that he might not be biologically related to his annoying five-year-old sister.

"Your father is Catholic... and I am an alien. So, you are half Catholic and half alien." The kids' mouths were hanging open.

She continued to improvise: "In alien families, there is a marker person in each generation so that all the aliens will be able to recognize each other. My father's name is Allan, and that name is spelled almost like 'alien.' In *my* generation, I am the marker since my initials are ALN and if you say A-L-N really fast it sounds like 'alien.' Ella, your middle name is Anne. If you say 'Ella Anne' really fast, what does it sound like? It sounds like 'alien.'"

By then, the children had caught on to the fact that she was kidding. But, she had started a wonderful new family tradition with her kids, even ordering that ALIEN license plate from the Connecticut DMV. Soon, everyone at the elementary school knew that Mike and Ella's mom drove the "AlienMobile."

My jaw would not come off the floor at her telling me this story. What a bizarre coincidence!

Now, with my Blue Alien fleece, no matter how intimidated I might be by people or deadlines, I feel the warmth and comfort of my dream... further strengthened by that synchronicity with Amy, who represented one of those people and one of those deadlines that used to intimidate me. Synchronicities, which I interpret as being in the right place, with the right people, at the right time, doing the right thing, are another focus of my work, along with premonitions and all those other unexplainable, but life affirming things that happen to us if we just keep our minds and eyes and ears open. We cover all of them in this new collection of *Chicken Soup for the Soul* stories, and I am so excited to present them to you.

As I write this introduction, my eyes are blurry and swollen from the tears I've shed reading the final 101 stories that we chose from the thousands of submissions for our book. These are tears of awe, inspiration, and gratitude, because each of these stories is a dramatic reminder that we live in a friendly universe in which miracles abound, no matter what hardships we may endure.

Some of these stories are even ones that I personally experienced! You'll read Amanda Lee's story, for example, about her preteen son, Andrew, who was desperate to meet his skateboarding idol on a trip to Los Angeles from Australia. In a city of four million people, because of his strong intent (and a little help from the angels in the city of angels) he ran into his hero in a most magical and unexplainable way, and I had the privilege of being there to watch it happen.

No matter what your religion or spiritual path is (or even if you don't have one) you will be convinced through reading these stories that there is more going on here on Planet Earth than our five senses report. After her husband passed away, Loreen Broderick was desperate to make her husband's special pasta sauce for her grown children for Christmas dinner. The handwritten recipe was nowhere to be found until, just in time, the family dog woke her at 3:30 a.m. What was that folded piece of white paper at her feet? The recipe.

These 101 stories of dreams, premonitions, synchronicities, and the unexplainable also demonstrate that magic happens when we listen to the still, small voice within, even if it diverts us from our original plans. The detours we take are divinely orchestrated and lead us to the most incredible people, places, and situations. In "Destined to Detour," Ferna Lary Mills shares how after losing her best friend to a drunk driver, and moving to another state, she found her car inexplicably sputtering and stopping on the side of the road. It sputtered and stopped intermittently for miles until it finally gave out at a gas station in the middle of nowhere. Who did she find there, watching the place for "just a few minutes for his brother," but her friend's father, renewing a connection that had been lost for years.

When we pay attention to these mysterious navigation nudges, whether in waking life or in dreams, we can not only avert disaster, but we find love, happiness, fulfillment, joy, and even... hidden treasures. You'll read about Patricia Miller, whose grandmother led her through her dreams to find a gorgeous crystal chandelier left behind in a box in the back of a dark cellar — just days before the house was scheduled to be torn down. And you'll find plenty of love stories in this collection. Prepare to be wowed by Jake Aller's story. He dreamt of a beautiful Asian girl for more than eight years, even joining the Peace Corps and moving to Korea in his quest to find her. She finally appeared in front of him one day, after he had been in Korea for many years, and they fell in love instantly. Jake's still married to the girl in his dreams, thirty-five years later.

I've learned that the solutions we seek and the miracles we've been praying for occur most often when we listen to the GPS that comes from our own consciousness. One of the themes particularly close to my heart in this book is the occurrence of a dream or vision that gives hope to survive (and even thrive) after the devastating loss of a loved one. Aurora Winter's young husband died suddenly of a heart attack right in front of her, and she understandably had a hard time moving on until two years later when she received a dream where her late husband asked her "Three Questions" that transformed her, and gave her a new lease on life. Grieving people from around the world caught wind of her dream, and to date, Aurora has coached thousands of people from "Heartbreak to Happiness."

In addition to being entertained by these stunning short stories of premonitions, dreams, and miracles, one of the benefits of reading this book is the fact that it is a "wake-up call" to live the life you were meant to. No story illustrates the awakening power of a dream more than Judy Dykstra-Brown's. She dreamt of a woman approaching her in a bar, throwing a drink in her face, and hitting her on the head with the glass, as she shouted, "Wake Up!" As jarring as that dream was, Judy changed her life on a dime and is no longer living a safe distance from the creative life she always longed for, but is now truly pursuing her passion.

So, you may be reading this, thinking, *That's great for those lucky people who have premonitions and remember their dreams, but I'm not that kind of person!*

My response to you is this: The wisdom of your subconscious communicates with you all the time, whether you are asleep or awake, whether you listen or not. You might want to pay more attention now, to your daytime premonitions and intuition, and to your nighttime dreams—maybe even get a dream journal and write down those dreams the moment you wake up before they fade away.

Surprising as it may seem, even ordinary people can have these extraordinary experiences, as evidenced by the stories in this book from people who thought "it would never happen" to them! All that ability is inside you, whether it seems strange to you or not. As I like to say, "It's our *personal power* that is most *alien* to us." The stories in this book will help guide you to using that power!

~Kelly Sullivan Walden

Chapter 1

Dreams and the Unexplainable

Divine Intervention

Miracle at the Oscars

Pregnancy is a process that invites you to surrender
to the unseen force behind all life.
~Judy Ford

I sat in the limo next to my husband, Sebastian, nervously adjusting my navy blue sequined gown and staring out the tinted window. Hollywood Boulevard looked like a slow-moving river of limousines. Spectators pushed against the chain-link fences at the sidewalk edge. Some screamed for us to roll down the windows. Others held signs that said, "God hates you." The crowds thickened as we neared the Kodak Theatre. Finally, the limo stopped, and the doors opened. "This is it," Sebastian whispered. "We're at the Oscars."

It was the final event of a long awards season for Sebastian's first documentary film, but for us it was the beginning of a season of miracles.

Walking down the red carpet was a miracle in itself. I grew up in Bulgaria under communist rule, five of us in a one-bedroom apartment that had no hot water or central heating. I was eighteen when, after the fall of communism, I watched my first Oscars. And here I was now, nearly twenty years later, walking into the Kodak Theatre, my family in Bulgaria gathered in front of the television hoping to catch a glimpse of me among the stars at the Academy Awards ceremony.

I remember when Sebastian, an author and war journalist, first told me that he wanted to bring a camera on his next trip to Afghanistan. He was going to make a documentary about the American soldiers in one of the remote outposts there. Tim Hetherington, an acclaimed international photojournalist, joined him a few months later. Their film, *Restrepo*, won the Grand Jury Prize for a documentary at the Sundance Film Festival in 2010 and was now nominated for an Academy Award. The four of us — Tim, his girlfriend Idil, Sebastian, and I — flew out to Los Angeles for a week of parties and events that culminated with Oscars night.

The trip to Los Angeles was a much-needed distraction from our six-year battle with infertility. We had done countless intrauterine inseminations and six in-vitro cycles before finally resorting to using donor eggs. But that failed, too, just two months prior to the Oscars. It had been our last hope.

Restrepo didn't win an Oscar, but we returned to New York with a far greater prize than the gold statuette of a bald man. A home pregnancy test two weeks later confirmed the miracle. After all of the treatments and invasive procedures, we had gotten pregnant naturally.

Miscarriages are common in the first trimester, and with our history, we didn't want to get too excited. But as the weeks went by and the pregnancy progressed normally, I allowed myself to believe that perhaps it was finally happening for us. At seven weeks, we cried as we heard the baby's heartbeat at our reproductive endocrinologist's office. Everything looked good, and he released us into the care of an obstetrician. We sighed with relief. We even began indulging in speculation about the gender of the baby. If it were a boy, we joked, we would have to name him Oscar.

The Academy Awards ceremony was the final event of a three-year project that had begun with Sebastian and Tim embedding with the American soldiers in a remote outpost in Afghanistan. While we were in Los Angeles, going from one awards party to another, the Arab Spring was in full swing. Sebastian and Tim felt restless. Before we had even returned to New York, they'd begun formulating their plan to cover the civil war in Libya. As the time neared, I felt the familiar tug before Sebastian went to a war zone. But something was different this time. I was pregnant, and all I could think about was the life growing inside me. I felt so protective of it that I couldn't possibly excite myself by putting up a fight, arguing that going to Libya was dangerous.

I didn't have to. Sebastian decided to stay with me. He didn't want to take chances either and jeopardize the prospect of finally becoming parents. We'd waited for a baby for so long and would do anything to protect it.

We were excited to go to our first appointment with the obstetrician. Finally, we had joined all other pregnant couples. "Now is the moment of truth," the doctor said as he inserted the magic wand that would project a black-and-white image of the uterus onto the screen. Sebastian held my hand as we both looked expectantly at the ultrasound machine. The doctor kept adjusting the wand, trying different angles. "I'm not seeing the heartbeat," he said finally.

I stared at the screen. Sebastian was crushing my hand in his. I kept staring at the little, dark blob that was to be our baby, as if by sheer will I could wake it up, and we'd suddenly see the flicker of a heartbeat. But the image remained brutally still.

It was the first sunny, warm day of the year. Sebastian and I walked silently from York Avenue to Central Park where we sat on a bench, gutted with grief. Around us, children ran, birds sang, and the forsythia bushes bloomed bright yellow. The heartless excitement of spring was around us.

A week after our visit to the obstetrician, I had a D&C procedure to remove the dead fetus. Back from the hospital, I crashed on the couch, looking forward to a long, dreamless sleep after the anesthesia. The phone rang. Sebastian answered it, listened for a moment, and hid his face in his hands.

Tim had been killed in Libya.

The days and weeks that followed were a blur. At Tim's funeral, I cried inconsolably. Together with Tim, I was burying — if not a child — the promise of one. Tim's girlfriend Idil sat in front of me. As I noted her heaving shoulders, pangs of guilt pushed through the mountain of grief inside me. Guilt that I was sitting next to my man, my hand sweating inside his, while Idil sat alone at the edge of the church pew.

I couldn't know for sure, but had Sebastian gone to Libya with

Tim, he would have been on the same street, in the blast radius of the same mortar that had killed Tim and another photojournalist, Chris Hondros.

What if I hadn't gotten pregnant when I had?

Eight weeks after the miscarriage, the doctor called me with the results of the genetic report. The pregnancy had been doomed from the moment of conception because of a rare chromosomal abnormality.

I never conceived again. Not even with medical intervention. But that new life Sebastian and I had created in Los Angeles had lasted just long enough to protect my husband from losing his own.

~Daniela Petrova

A Divine Delay

You are not just waiting in vain. There
is a purpose behind every delay.
~Mandy Hale

The plan was to drive five hours from the Napa Valley to a northern coastal town for a little weekend vacation. I had invited my best friend, Paula, to take that weekend trip with me. The day before our departure, she called to say that she wouldn't be able to make the journey because she had been asked by her boss to attend a meeting the very evening we were supposed to leave. I told her we could just pack the car and take off when her meeting was over.

I waited in the car while the meeting we assumed would take one hour stretched into three. When Paula finally came out, she only opened the car door long enough to say, "I'm so sorry." That's when her boss stuck his head out the door and asked her to come back in. At that point, a thought struck me: *God must be delaying us for a purpose.*

When Paula returned fifteen minutes later, profusely apologizing, I told her not to worry. We started out on our big adventure, but before we even reached the "Thanks for Visiting" sign at the end of town, we both decided that we should get an ice cream cone. We pulled into the last open ice cream stand and went in to order.

"Oh, I'm sorry, but we just turned off the machine! But I'll turn it back on," the cheery waitress said. We waited twenty minutes for that ice cream to get hard enough to put into a cone. Paula and I just looked at each other.

When we were finally back in the car and on our way, we were stopped at a train crossing… by a very, very long train.

"What is going on?" Paula moaned.

"God is delaying us, Paula," I responded happily.

An hour from our destination, Paula had fallen asleep, and I was driving on the deserted freeway. Well, deserted, except for the one car in front of me in the slow lane, going very, very slow. I pulled into the passing lane, and as I passed the car, I heard it go *putt, putt, putt.* Then it pulled over to the side of the road.

THIS is why I delayed you, I heard. *Turn around and help.* I felt this so strongly that I simply obeyed without hesitation. Paula woke up while I was turning the car around and asked me what I was doing. I explained and she complained, but I was determined. I pulled up beside the broken down car.

"Do you need some help?" I shouted across Paula to the young man, now standing on the side of the road.

"Yes! I ran out of gas. I didn't think anyone was going to come by!"

Paula crawled into the back seat, giving me "the eye" before she did. The young man sat in the passenger's seat. We chatted and then I asked him his name.

"Andy Lane."

Okay, that sounded familiar. "My last name is Lane, too! What's your mom's name?"

Puzzled, he said, "Mae."

I took a deep gulp. "What's your dad's name?"

"Doug."

At that point, I screamed, slapped him on the back, and pulled the car over.

"I'm Stan Lane's daughter! Our fathers are brothers!"

Because of a divorce in their family, I had last seen this cousin when he was a year old. He was now eighteen. I turned on the car light, and we looked at each other… yup, we were both Lanes.

We were both astonished by this encounter! It encouraged Andy, and gave him some much-needed faith that God was watching over him. Some plans just need to be set aside for the greater one.

~Brenda M. Lane

The Most Perfect Timing

Impossible situations can become possible miracles.
~Robert H. Schuller

Things were not going well at all. I was laid off from my job and the next day my teenage daughter broke her foot. Then, when I took my children to the playground, my two-year-old ran in front of my daughter on the swing and got hit by the heavy boot on her foot.

He was laid out flat, but he finally got up and wanted to play again, so I thought at least that was going to be okay!

Unfortunately, when we got home, he asked if he could go lie down. That was weird.

He went to bed and tossed and turned and moaned. He finally got back up and said he couldn't sleep. Then he threw up. It was pink.

I called his doctor, and he advised me to go to the closest pediatric trauma center. Three doctors converged on my daughter to grill her on what happened. She was terrified. I knew why they were doing it. If there was a chance we were beating up this kid, they didn't want to give me a chance to coach her on what to say. But I watched a piece of her childhood float away, knowing this moment would be one of the most traumatic moments of her life.

They did some scans and told us my son had massive internal bleeding. I started to feel faint.

"But it was just a playground accident. How can this have happened?" I said.

They looked at me with pity and could only offer this: "These things sometimes happen."

They decided we needed to go downtown to the medical district where there was a pediatric hospital better equipped to deal with internal bleeding. They were going to take him by ambulance right away. I would have to take my other three kids home, find someone to watch them, and then race downtown to the hospital.

For two days, my son fought a fever and did not so much as sit up. I thought he was dying. My father, whom I had not spoken to in years, showed up for comfort. I needed him.

Finally, on the third day, my boy sat up. His fever had broken. Relief all around! They sent us home, telling us to come back in a month to make sure the bleeding had stopped.

The next month, we were all smiles when we came back. My son was happy, awake, alert, energetic and back to his old self. He was fine.

We did the scans and were told we'd get the results in two days. A friend of mine advised, "Good news comes slowly." So I comforted myself that waiting would be a good thing.

The next morning, however, the doctor called. "Are you sitting down?" he asked. What they had thought was massive internal bleeding was actually a cancerous tumor on his kidney. It was about the size of a small melon. They'd have to remove it and what remained of the kidney. "There's a ninety percent survival rate, so that should be a relief," he told me. They would be expecting us at the hospital and we should go right away.

My whole world disintegrated. My ears started ringing. I fell to my knees and sobbed.

We got to the ER, and my son, feeling fine, was happily running up and down the hall through the chairs. Parents holding feverish, rash-covered children scowled at me for being there with a well child when their kids were obviously sick.

My kid was about to leave with one less organ. But all those parents saw was a family cutting the line for no apparent reason.

We stayed overnight, as they were going to do the surgery bright and early in the morning. I recited a prayer I always say when I'm worried about my kids. "Dear God, please send your very best guardian angels to watch over and protect my child." I've said it before first days of school, plane flights, slumber parties, and any time I'm feeling anxious about my kids facing something without me. But this was the biggest thing we'd ever faced.

The next morning, as we prepared for surgery, a man sat down in front of me. He was French. He said, "Listen. Your surgeon is the very best surgeon you could have possibly hoped for. He specializes in this rare tumor, and he's here. In Houston. At this hospital. You're very lucky. But he's worried about this one. So he called me. Because I'm the very best anesthesiologist. I'll be watching over your son through the entire surgery. So think of me as…" he looked up for the right word, "his guardian angel."

I felt a blast of endorphins as I turned to look at this man.

"What did you just say?"

He laughed. "His guardian angel."

At that moment, I knew my baby was going to be okay. God had sent two of his very best guardian angels to look after him. Then I thought back. If my daughter hadn't broken her foot, she wouldn't have hit my son with her boot. We wouldn't have found his tumor for a few more years, and by then it might have metastasized all over his body. Because I was laid off the day before my daughter broke her foot, I could get unemployment and take time off to care for my son after his surgery.

The good luck continued. I got a new job shortly thereafter, and a year later my son was declared cancer free.

Everything happened with the most perfect timing. Ever since, I've made sure to list every single thing I'm grateful for when I pray.

~Heather McMichael

Purely Providential

With each new experience of letting God be in control,
we gain courage and reinforcement for daring
to do it again and again.
~Gloria Gaither

I awakened with a smile on my face. Sunbeams danced across the bedroom wall. "Wake up, sleepyhead!" I said. "It's the first day of our vacation!"

John reached over, enfolding me in his strong arms. "I had the strangest dream," he said. "We were driving along a country road, and every sign we spotted had the number 39 on it!"

"Hmmm… that is kinda strange. Maybe it was something you ate!" Tossing my pillow in John's direction, I headed off to the kitchen to start the coffee. Several minutes later, we were sipping the hot beverage while John Googled driving directions.

"We've actually got our choice of two routes to the camping site we'll be staying at tonight. We need to decide which one."

Suddenly, John gasped. I looked up from the list I'd made of provisions I'd already loaded in the RV the night before.

"Take a look at this!" I hurried to the computer, leaning over John's shoulder.

"This is the shortest route, which would get us there before dark. But now take a look at this other route!" It was my turn to gasp as I spotted the number 39 posted all along a mountain highway.

"Guess we know which one we'll be taking! What can it mean?"

Silently, we studied each other's puzzled expression as the printer noisily hummed away.

An hour later, we were officially on vacation, wreathed in smiles.

The ride was pleasant as we listened to soft music and pointed out various points of interest along the way. The warm sun caressed my face, and I nodded off to sleep, awakened much later by John's soft whistle.

"Route 39 coming up!" With each mile, the traffic increased.

"Looks like we made a mistake," I murmured, spotting a bustling town up ahead.

Colorful shops lined the busy highway, including several restaurants and a daycare center. For years, I'd been a professional caregiver. Early childhood education was my passion. "Lord, be with the children there," I whispered, as I often did when I spotted a daycare center. Suddenly, I spotted something darting out the front door of the establishment. A little girl, no more than three, ran out into the busy, oncoming traffic. Frantic and sobbing, she weaved her way between cars. No one seemed to notice.

"John, pull over there!" I cried, pointing toward a parking lot and then flinging myself out the door. I raced after the toddler, scooping her into my arms as she lost her lunch down the front of my white sweater.

"It's okay, sweetie! I've got you now. It's going to be okay!" I held her closer as traffic suddenly came to a halt. We made our way safely back inside the daycare center, greeted by two hysterical adults.

"Do you have any idea what could have happened to this child?" I exclaimed.

Tears formed in the director's eyes as she apologized over and over. The child offered her arms to the woman, and I relaxed somewhat. A policeman arrived, and John and I answered his questions, leaving our contact information if needed.

With grateful hearts that all was well with the little girl, we climbed back into our "home away from home," anticipating the continuation of our journey. But before we started the engine, there was something more important on our minds.

Clasping each other's hands, we bowed our heads, thanking God for being our Savior, for being Divine... for sending John dreams about Route 39.

~Mary Z. Whitney

Angel on Board

An angel can illuminate the thought and mind of
man by strengthening the power of vision.
~St. Thomas Aquinas

Little voices chattered in the back seat — a mix of nonsense, songs, and the unique communication that occurs between young children that only they understand. The day was bright and sunny, and the usual traffic was moving along the four lanes headed south on California Highway 101.

For this young mother at the wheel, it was a good day so far — no one was fighting or crying yet. I pushed the "On" button, flooding the red-and-white Suburban with music. I always liked to sing along. Sometimes, the kids would try to join in, kicking their little feet or clapping their chubby hands in time to the funky beat of the music that characterized Marin County in the early 1980s. We were headed to the medical clinic for a well check for one of the kids. Life was good.

Motherhood had always been my fondest dream, and I was acutely aware of that little slice of time that makes up the tender years of one's children. I knew my good fortune, and I cherished it. The only unease that lurked below this happy surface had to do with their father; our relationship was not good. But today I didn't want to think about any of that.

All three of my children were delightful in their own precious ways. The oldest and youngest had always been easygoing; they ate heartily, nursed to sleep, and slept well. The middle child was different.

I couldn't put my finger on quite what it was, but she had some kind of connection with the unseen, even as an infant. If ever I happened to open even one eye while in my bed (in a separate room), she knew I was awake and cried or called out to me. She was very "tuned in," you might say, and had a unique way of being in the world.

As we cruised along with the traffic, this middle child piped up with a question. "Mommy, where do we go when we die?"

Oh, my! Quickly, I asked myself, *What are my beliefs on that? And how to explain them to a three-year-old in a way she might understand?* The kids went to Sunday school and were learning something about the concept of God. They said prayers every night with me. But I wasn't really prepared for questions about death.

"Well, honey, you know how you learn about God at Sunday school? When we die, many people believe we go to heaven to be with God."

"Oh, that's good," her cheerful little voice replied. "Because we're going there right now!"

My hands froze on the wheel. My heart stopped. *What can she mean?* I checked my speed and carefully applied the brakes. Then, out of the corner of my eye, I saw it: a blue car careening across three lanes of traffic, heading right for us. I hit the brakes harder, and the vehicle roared across our lane, just in front of us! I heard the squealing of tires and watched pieces of black rubber fly through the air.

The orderly lanes of traffic were now a confused jumble of vehicles, each trying to avoid a crash. Everything screeched into slow motion as drivers carefully made for the side of the road or continued bravely on their way. The distressed vehicle came to rest in the middle median, stopped by the large oleander bushes. Miraculously, no cars had collided with it or with each other.

If I had not braked when my daughter spoke up, the out-of-control car would have broadsided us at high speed. I shuddered at the thought, at the tragedy our lives could have become in that lightning flash of time. Deep breathing helped me regain control, but I kept a tight grip on the wheel.

How are the kids? I glanced in the rearview mirror. They continued to chatter and play, buckled safely in their car seats. Then my foresighted daughter caught my eye and gave me what can only be described as a knowing smile. We had a guardian angel on board that day!

Did she have a special connection with God and the angels? Or was she herself the angel? All I can say for sure is this: That was not the only day when, as a small child, she received a message from God.

~Sallianne Hines

A Dreary Saturday

*I would maintain that thanks are the highest form
of thought; and that gratitude is happiness
doubled by wonder.*
~G.K. Chesterton

Even though I loved watching the *Snorks* cartoon series on Saturday mornings, I loved candy even more. The bank handed out Dum Dums lollipops, so I always wanted to go to the bank with my mom.

However, for some reason, one dreary Saturday morning I refused to go the bank with my mother. I kicked. I screamed. I threw the biggest fit I could. My mother wasn't going to make it to the bank before it closed, so she had to make a decision. She would only be gone for fifteen minutes, maximum. What could happen in fifteen minutes?

She took my little brother and rushed off to the bank, and for the first time in my eight years, I was home alone. It didn't seem like a big deal. I sat back down in front of the television, but something drew me to the back window. I went into the dining room and looked into my back yard. The gray sky opened up and it poured. As I watched the rain hit the water in our family pool, a sudden and violent jolt took me by surprise. To this day, I'm still not sure what it was.

I gathered my bearings, and something inside told me to get dressed and ready to go. I ran upstairs to my room and flung open my dresser drawer. I grabbed the most accessible pair of sweatpants and put them on under my nightgown. My mother was still in the habit of dressing me, so picking out what to wear wasn't on my mind. I just knew I needed pants. After that, I needed shoes. My fuzzy bunny slippers would suffice. After I was dressed to my best ability, the same voice inside told me to watch out the window for the police.

I stood in my family room's front picture window, waiting and watching. Maybe three minutes passed until I saw the brown sheriff's vehicle come flying around the corner and onto my street, complete with lights flashing. I went to the front door and was coming out before the sheriff had even put the car in Park.

My brother met me halfway to the car and told me, "We were in a crash, and Mommy's hurt."

All I could say was, "I know."

I walked to the car, opened the door, and crawled into the sheriff's back seat. I can't imagine how much my behavior must have puzzled the officer. How could I have known? We didn't have a cell phone back in 1987. I rode quietly in the back seat while my younger brother sobbed in the front.

Once we arrived at the accident scene, the ambulance was waiting, and paramedics were still getting my mother stabilized. A kind police officer handed my brother and me each a stuffed teddy bear. I hugged mine gently as I saw my mother in the ambulance, lying on the gurney in a cervical collar. The police officer lifted my brother into the ambulance, and just before he lifted me, I saw my mother's small, four-door sedan. She had been rear-ended by a lifted Jeep, the kind built for off-road fun. The force of the impact crushed the trunk, and the Jeep, having a higher clearance, ran up onto the back end of my mother's car. The damage was severe, but my eyes were transfixed on the back seat — or what remained of it. It was crushed. If I had gone, either my brother or I would have been in that back seat, and one of us would have been crushed and most likely killed.

Someone or something saved me that day, and I continue to be grateful thirty years later.

~Heather M. Cook

Black Dog

What seems to us as bitter trials are
often blessings in disguise.
~Oscar Wilde

As we lowered the skinny body of what had been my big, fluffy, platinum-blond dog, Woofie, into his grave, I erupted in primal sobs. I didn't know a dog could make her way so deeply into the center of my heart and soul. I swore I'd never have another dog again... I didn't think I could live through the heartache of losing another one.

Six months later, I was invited to speak at a conference in New Mexico — state slogan the "Land of Enchantment" — spearheaded by our dear friends George and Sedena Cappannelli. To sweeten the pot of an already sweet opportunity, they offered my husband and me the opportunity to stay in their lovely guesthouse for the weekend. How could we resist?

We drove the long but scenic fourteen hours from Los Angeles to Santa Fe. We arrived the night before I was to speak so we could experience the acclaimed mythologist, author, and storyteller Michael Meade.

He strutted onto the stage with a conga drum. The lights went dim, and a faint spotlight found him. He told us a story in rhythm with his drum. I was transported back in time to a grassy field, starry sky, and open fire. He mesmerized us with this raspy, staccato fable (allow me to paraphrase):

*There's an old woman… as old as time… long, gray hair…
lives in a cave… with her black dog sitting by her side… all day
and night… she rocks in her chair and weaves… the most beautiful weave you've ever seen… blending all the fabric of time and
space from the far reaches of this universe… She's been weaving
since the beginning of time… and it's now almost finished… and
it's beautiful.*

*Just a few stitches left, and it will be perfect… but she can
smell the aroma of her hearty stew that's been brewing in a pot
in the back of her cave… All that weaving made her hungry…
She lays her weave down on her rocking chair while she hobbles
to the back of her cave to feast on her delicious stew.*

*While she's enjoying her feast, her black dog sniffs around
at her weave, and begins playing and pulling on the string with
his teeth and paws… it's a toy, a game, it's having a great old
time… and by the time the old woman returns to her rocking
chair, the entire weave — the one that has taken millions of years
to perfect — is completely destroyed.*

*So, what does the old lady do? She sits back down in her
rocking chair, picks up her needle and pieces of string, and resumes
her weaving.*

He paused dramatically, stopped drumming, and asked the audience point blank:

Who is your black dog?
*Who or what in your life gets in the way, just when everything
is going perfectly? Just when everything is exactly the way you
want it, just when you're at the finish line of an important plan
or project, when you're so close you can taste it?*
Everyone has a black dog.
*Is it a person, an injury, a political leader, a parent, a child,
your job that rips it all into shreds?*
*And you might think it strange, but be grateful for your
black dog.*

When something is perfect, in Latin, it also means finished. Complete. Done. No more. If the old lady had finished her weave, it would mark the end of time, perhaps the end of the world, and maybe the universe, for that matter.

Thank God for the black dog — that troublemaker, saboteur, nuisance we blame for our problems. But, in fact, if we looked at the situation differently, we'd see that it's the black dog that keeps us in the game, that triggers our passion, keeps us going, engages and challenges us to be more creative and alive than we ever were before.

I was in tears as we drove through the high desert with the sky brightly lit by more stars than I'd ever seen. I thought about the legions of "black dogs" that lined my path. I saw so many of what I deemed horrible interruptions to my life's "perfect" path: almost getting the starring role in a TV series back in my acting days — subverted by a producer who wanted a relationship with me I wasn't willing to have; nearly adopting a child who mysteriously died the day before the adoption would be finalized; and the business deals my husband had been involved in that would have made us a fortune — sabotaged by a person or situation that was a "black dog" in disguise.

We made it "home" to our guesthouse situated amid red rocks and cacti, and our friend/host George yelled out to us, "Welcome home. Hey, don't be scared of the BLACK DOG sitting on your porch. She's a stray. She has been hanging around the guesthouse for the past few weeks. We don't know where she came from, but she's friendly."

Sure enough, a beautiful, shiny Black Lab was sitting on our porch, waiting for us, with her pink tongue out and tail wagging.

George was right. She was friendly. I asked her to sit, and she sat. I asked her to shake, and she lifted her right paw to shake my hand. I asked her to lie down, and she did. After fumbling with the keys, we opened the door, and she walked right in like she owned the place. I had a few bites in a "doggy bag" left from dinner that I fed her. She seemed very happy.

We slept that night with the black dog curled up in a ball on the rug right next to our bed.

Without going through all the details, suffice it to say, Shadow has been our dog now for the past six years. And as adorable and loveable as she is, true to the "black dog" story, she has been a force of destruction in our lives as well. She refuses to be left alone, and we've nearly gone broke paying for "doggy day care" every time we want to go on a date or out of town. She's made the interior of two of our cars look like Freddy Krueger and Edward Scissorhands had a fight inside.

But, on a positive note, she's also managed to rip my heart open in a whole new way. Despite the challenges that come from our black dog, Shadow, I love her with my entire heart and wouldn't trade her for all the perfectly well behaved dogs on the planet.

My dear friend and world-class fusion artist, Rassouli, is famous for saying: "There can be no creation without destruction. Destruction always precedes creation!"

About a month after Shadow entered our lives, my stepdaughter, Meesha, was moving into a new apartment that did not allow dogs. She asked if her dog, Lola (a Chiweenie — half Chihuahua, half Dachshund) could live with us.

Before my heart had been opened by Shadow, I would have never been open to such a proposition. Add to it the fact that my stepdaughter and I had a strained relationship at that point.

But with my now opened heart, I surprised myself by responding, "Why not? Let's take her. She'll be a playmate for Shadow, and it will help Meesha — a win-win all around."

Lola and Shadow, despite being an "odd couple," are the best of friends. In fact, I could not imagine Shadow without Lola, or Lola without Shadow.

Little did I know the ripple effect of embracing our black dog into our lives would be the catalyst for my stepdaughter becoming a wonderful part of my life and a healing balm being released throughout my husband's family. Where there once was anger and resentment, there is friendship and warmth… and it all started with the unexplainable trail of coincidences (synchronicities) that all led back to our black dog.

Every day, I hug her big, fluffy black self, and she reminds me not to cry over the near-perfect plans I weave that get thwarted. Instead I embrace the "black dogs" that life brings me as the source of untold blessings in disguise.

~Kelly Sullivan Walden

Dreams of Yesterday

Timing in life is everything.
~Leonard Maltin

Over the years, I have met many people through my family, neighbors, church, and various workplaces. Some I have been lucky to keep in touch with or run into once in a while. Many, like Dorothy, a former boss, I haven't seen in years. That is why I was totally surprised to dream about working for her.

She had been one of my supervisors when I was a young administrative secretary working in our local school district. A vivacious, no-nonsense executive, she was highly organized and managed a department of twenty-six employees for a large company. Even though she had a husband and several children, she also volunteered her time as the president of the district school improvement team. The district team was comprised of two parent volunteers and the principal from each school. They met once a month with the superintendent at an evening meeting. As her secretary, it was my responsibility to reserve the boardroom, schedule the set-up of tables, chairs and equipment, and record the minutes.

The officers of this team also attended a second night meeting to discuss and plan the next month's agenda. Most of them worked a full-time job, too, so it was not unusual for each of us to bring something to eat while we worked. For Dorothy, it involved quite a few more hours because she personally visited many of the schools and was frequently invited to attend special school assemblies and events. But she loved students and education, and often insisted, "This is a fun job to me."

Dorothy and I looked forward to the monthly meetings. She would always try to present an interesting and informative program highlighting students, teachers, curriculum, and administrators. She gave me the responsibility of selecting a group of students to perform or present their talents in music, art, drama, and academics. At the end of the workday, we always felt fortunate to work with so many talented people. Even though Dorothy was my supervisor, she had also been a mentor and a friend.

In my dream, she stood down the hall from my cubicle quietly observing me. I was busy taking directions and answering questions from my main boss, who was meticulous and a workaholic. After she left and went back to her office, Dorothy came to my desk and whispered in my ear, "Bravo. If you learn to work for that person successfully, you will be able to work for anyone on the planet."

I must admit that, after all these years, she was absolutely right. Several nights later, I dreamed about Dorothy again.

This time, we were at one of our meetings where a high school song-and-dance group of about sixteen students performed. They were a favorite of everyone in the community. After a long meeting about graduation require-ments, Dorothy and several of the parents invited me to meet them at a local restaurant for pie and conversation. We had such a good time. Everything was in vivid detail and seemed so real, even after I woke up.

As I wondered why I kept dreaming about a former boss whom I hadn't seen in fourteen years, I got ready to go grocery shopping with my husband. When he drove our car into an open parking space, I looked over and could not believe my eyes. In the car next to me, Dorothy was backing out. Without thinking, I quickly opened my door, ran to the back of our car, and put up my hand for her to stop. Rolling down the driver's side window, Dorothy asked, "What did I do wrong?"

"You didn't do anything wrong. Do you remember the secretary you had many years ago as the president of the school improvement team?"

Looking at me closely, she smiled in recognition and said, "I do remember you because you were one of my best secretaries."

Leaning into her car window, I gave her a little hug and told her, "And you were one of my best bosses."

We reminisced a few minutes until a truck pulled up behind her and honked. Then we held hands and reluctantly said goodbye. Going into the grocery store, I couldn't help but marvel at the fact that I had just seen Dorothy again after all these years. Even though she looked the same, I rationalized that if I hadn't dreamed about her, I might have missed her.

I didn't dream or think about Dorothy again until a couple of months later. In the Sunday paper, I was shocked to read in the obituaries that Dorothy had died. It didn't seem possible. When I had seen her, she was in good spirits and didn't look sick.

At her funeral, the minister told us that Dorothy and her family had known for a while she was ill. To celebrate her illustrious life, the family held an unforgettable service. On a big screen they shared many cherished pictures of her as a child, teenager, bride, young mother, grandmother, and friend to hundreds in our community. We laughed at the funny stories told about her, and we sang her favorite songs as a child and as an adult. Reciting the Lord's Prayer before leaving, tears of gratitude blurred my vision because I now knew in my heart that heaven had arranged our final farewell in that parking lot.

~Brenda Cathcart-Kloke

The Lifeguardian Angel

The bravest are surely those who have the clearest
vision of what is before them, glory and danger alike,
and yet notwithstanding, go out to meet it.
~Thucydides

I put the youngest of my four children down for bed. Whew! Abby was a handful. At eighteen months old, she was a bundle of youthful energy. Everything fascinated her. Earlier that day, she had been toddling through the fresh cut grass chasing a tiny butterfly.

My oldest daughter, Alison, was starring as "Annie" in her school's fifth grade play. She spent hours singing "The Sun Will Come Out Tomorrow" to Abby. Her other siblings had lost interest after hearing it for the umpteenth time, but little Abby loved it. She clapped her chubby, little hands after every performance. I slathered some sunscreen on her plump arms and managed to dab a drop on Alison's freckled cheeks.

"Don't stay out here too long. You will burn," I warned.

"I know, Mom…" Alison barely missed a note and returned to practicing.

That night, I told my husband about the day as I pulled down the bed sheet. "I hope the girls didn't get too much sun today."

"You worry too much," my husband reassured me. That was true. With four children under the age of eleven, I was a masterful worrier.

I recited my checklist. "I bathed Abby, administered Austin's eye drops, wrapped a Band-Aid on Ansley's injured finger, and remembered Alison's allergy medicine."

"Good grief!" Allen mimicked his best Charlie Brown.

"I don't mean to worry, but it just comes with the job," I sighed.

"You are great at it!" he reassured me before I collapsed into bed.

Now was not the time to discuss my recent recurring nightmare. I turned out the light, hoping for a good night's sleep.

Then the nightmare returned. I could see her at the bottom of the water. My little Abby was trapped under the water, staring at me with her bright, blue eyes full of fear. I looked around, trying to scream for help, but my voice wouldn't work.

But someone else was there, too. He always showed up during this dream. He was so beautiful and calm. I wasn't afraid to follow him, but I didn't know where we were going, and I had to get my baby. She was drowning.

I sat up in the bed.

"Amy, what is wrong?" Allen shook me gently.

"Abby. Where is she?" I tossed back the covers, jumping to my feet.

"She is asleep. This is the third night in a row. Stop worrying about the kids." He turned over.

"I am just going to peek at them," I whispered. My heart was racing as the image from my dream replayed in my head.

I gently touched the top of her soft, little head. I placed my palm lightly on her chest to make sure she was breathing. I think all moms do that on occasion just for reassurance.

She was not underwater. She was safe.

I quietly checked the others. All were safe and sound.

The clock beside my bed read 3:40 a.m.; I needed to go back to sleep. I tossed and turned. The image of my baby trapped underwater kept resurfacing. I wanted to find the calm man. I couldn't remember much about him, but when he was near me, I wasn't afraid. Maybe he would help me… I drifted back to sleep.

"BZZZZZZ!" the alarm clock shattered my peace.

"Did you go check on the kids again?" my husband whispered.

"I can't help it. I've had this nightmare three nights in a row. Abby is underwater," I mumbled.

"It's just a dream. The kids are safe." He sighed.

That morning, I sipped coffee, prepared lunches, packed book bags, and went over the daily schedule. "Mom, I have rehearsal until 5:00 today," Alison noted.

"I'll be there. Gabrielle will watch the kids for a few hours after school." My neighbor offered to babysit anytime. She had three little boys.

I ironed costumes and played with Abby, my nightmare almost forgotten. I was looking forward to actually wearing make-up and real clothes when I attended Alison's rehearsal. Most days, I am in sweats.

The rehearsals went well and Alison sounded beautiful. I enjoy being at the Performing Arts Centre, but I couldn't shake my anxiety. I needed to see my other children.

"You ready, kiddo?" I gathered Alison's costumes.

"Yep, let's go." We headed to the car.

We chatted about her music on the twenty-minute ride home. As soon as I turned into Gabrielle's driveway, I saw the man from my dream. I instantly got goose bumps.

"Look!" I pointed toward the man standing near the driveway.

"What?" Alison looked. "Mom, that's a tree."

I looked again, and she was right. It was just a tree. I really needed more sleep.

The kids were playing in the swimming pool. Austin was happily splashing in the shallow end with Ansley. Gabrielle's three boys ran around, jumping in and out of the pool. Abby was sitting near Gabrielle, fully dressed.

"She didn't want to swim. She cried when I put her feet in the water," Gabrielle laughed.

"It's okay." I bent over to pick her up.

Gabrielle's youngest son ran toward the driveway, forcing his mother to chase him.

"Come on, kids. We have to go." I put down Abby and gathered up Austin in a towel.

Abby toddled off, following the other kids. As I dried Austin, I heard a splash.

"MOM!" Alison screamed.

I ran toward the deep end of the pool and looked down to see Abby sinking deeper and deeper into nine feet of water. Her saucer-blue eyes stared up at me. Just like my dream...

I jumped in feet first, fully clothed, jewelry and all. I grabbed her shirt. She was so heavy. I pulled harder. I threw her up on the side of the pool. Alison grabbed her. Abby started crying... melodic music to my ears. She was scared, but perfectly safe. We didn't even have to do CPR.

The commotion brought Gabrielle and the other kids running.

"I didn't mean to bump her," her oldest son apologized. He was as scared as Abby. "We were just playing."

"It's okay. I was standing right here, too." I assured him it was an accident.

Gabrielle handed me a towel. I was shaking, but managed to dry myself off.

"Thank you for watching them," I offered as we left. But I knew she wasn't the only one watching...

At home, my children shared the excitement of the day with their dad.

"Mom jumped in with all of her clothes on and grabbed Abby!" Alison laughed.

At bedtime, I whispered a silent "thank you" to my guardian angel. He visited my dreams so I would be prepared, and I know he was in Gabrielle's driveway that afternoon. It wasn't "just a tree."

~Amy McCoy Dees

A Voice in the Dark

*Therefore we must pay much closer attention to what
we have heard, lest we drift away from it.*
~Hebrews 2:1

"Get up and go to Ginny's!" A resounding voice jolted me awake in the cold, dark hours of the early morning. I closed my eyes again. As a counselor at the summer aquatic camp, I had been allotted a lumpy dorm room bed. Not having slept well, I was not ready to leave my warm blanket behind.

The voice sounded again with commanding authority. "Get up and go to Ginny's!"

Shocked, I bolted upright, my heart pounding and my head clearing.

"Lord, is that you?" I asked.

"Get up and go — now!"

Without stopping to ask why, I rushed into action. "Okay, okay," I answered. "I hear you!"

Quickly, I scanned the stark, tomb-like room for my clothes and a hairbrush. The icy tile beneath my feet sent me scurrying for the bathroom. Disoriented, I screeched to a halt. *Where was the bathroom?*

The previous afternoon had been filled with orientation to the campus and a review of the week's activities, so I had not fully unpacked. I scrambled to stuff a few loose items into my suitcase while I worried over a believable excuse to give the camp director for leaving. I felt certain that telling him the Lord had woken me up and told me to go to my daughter's house would brand me as certifiably crazy.

Understandably, the director was disgruntled as I mumbled a few words of apology for leaving him in the lurch. I rushed across the college campus, determined but still asking myself, *What are you doing? Did you really hear a voice?*

My daughter had a two-year-old daughter and a three-month-old son. To her great chagrin, she was pregnant again. She had called the previous Friday to tell me the news, but expressed concern because she had experienced a couple of fainting spells that she could not explain.

She described how she had collapsed the first time in the grocery store. Suddenly feeling lightheaded, she slumped to the concrete floor. Her children were in the grocery cart, unattended, while she lay in a heap. Help came quickly, of course, but she was confused, embarrassed, and terrified by the realization that she had left her children alone in a public place, even for a few minutes. A day later, she almost fainted again while getting out of her car.

Ginny had never fainted before in her life, so of course she was afraid it might have something to do with the pregnancy. I agreed and suggested she talk with her doctor right away. When she called the doctor's office to discuss her concerns, a nurse chided her about the fainting spells, saying they could be the result of a hormonal imbalance caused by becoming pregnant again so quickly.

"Call back if the problem continues," she said briskly, putting an end to the conversation. Her abruptness seemed to imply that Ginny was overly excitable and wasting the nurse's precious time.

After driving for an hour in the pre-dawn, I arrived at Ginny's apartment and knocked on the door. It was 7:00 a.m. Shocked to see me standing there, my son-in-law asked, "Ann, what are you doing here?"

"I'm here to take care of the children while you take Ginny to the doctor," I said firmly. Then I whispered, "All I know is the Lord woke me up and told me to come. So, here I am."

Ginny padded into the living room looking rumpled and pale. Confused, she echoed her husband's question. As I repeated my story, I began to feel very foolish. *Had I just imagined the voice?*

Ginny's typical no-nonsense response was, "If the Lord told you to come so I could go to the doctor, then I guess I'd better go!"

Dressing quickly, they gave me instructions on where to find bottles, formula, and diapers, then rushed off to the doctor's office without even calling for an appointment. I waited anxiously as I comforted my hungry and confused granddaughter, sterilized bottle parts, and soothed the baby. Doubts assailed me again. *Was there really a serious issue, or had I disrupted their routine for nothing?* I almost felt embarrassed, but not quite.

Several hours later, Robert called to say that Ginny had been admitted to the hospital. She had passed out again on the way to the doctor's office. After examining her, the doctor determined that Ginny was bleeding internally from an ectopic pregnancy. Ginny's condition was so precarious that the doctor would not even allow them to drive across the parking lot to the hospital. She called an ambulance to deliver her the few hundred yards to the emergency room.

"The emergency room doctors said Ginny might have died if they hadn't seen her when they did," Robert told me over the phone. "They were amazed at how lucky she was to have come to the doctor's office this morning."

As the words "she could have died" sank in, I looked at her babies and realized how much they might have missed in life. I cried. Shaking with relief, I silently acknowledged the true source of our "luck."

Following surgery and a night in the hospital to monitor her blood pressure, Ginny was sent home for some bed rest. My camp clothes were perfect for taking care of two small children — children who still had a mother because I listened and acted when a voice said, "Get up and go to Ginny's!"

~Annette Geroy

Chapter 2

Dreams and the Unexplainable

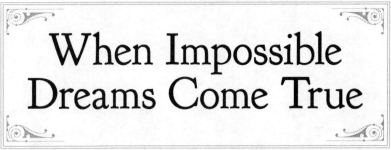

When Impossible Dreams Come True

The Hidden Room

A house is made with walls and beams;
a home is built with love and dreams.
~Ralph Waldo Emerson

Ever since I was a small girl, I've been fascinated with houses. I used to dream about what my house would be like when I grew up. I loved decorating my dollhouses. Even when playing the game *Clue*, I planned my dream floor plan — the library, the conservatory, the billiard room, the lounge. I watched the Saturday afternoon mystery movies and was enthralled by the hidden staircases and secret rooms behind bookcases. I didn't always remember the plots or whether or not the butler did it, but I always remembered those rooms.

When I bought my first home, it was significantly larger than any of my previous dwellings. The first few nights after getting the keys to my new kingdom, I was there all alone. I walked around what then seemed like a vast empty space. Not yet used to the layout, I got a little lost a couple of times.

Each night, I settled down on my temporary mattress, exhausted from the work of painting and cleaning. I fell into dream-filled slumbers. One dream in particular kept repeating.

I was wandering through the house, and I came upon a hidden room. Sometimes, it was like an abandoned attic filled with various objects. Other times, it was just an empty space. But, either way, the new room was a welcome surprise.

I'd experienced a couple of the standard recurring dreams in my life, and they were easily traceable to my daytime experiences. At university, I often dreamed about a surprise test or not being able to find my classroom. When I started a new job, I often dreamed of repeatedly doing the tasks I had learned during that day or of being late for work. So I just chalked up this new recurring dream of a hidden room to the stress and excitement of moving into my new home and being unfamiliar with the floor plan.

Not long after, the moving and decorating complete, I settled down into the routine of daily living. The house didn't seem so vast once it was filled with all my belongings, and I certainly didn't get lost anymore. Yet every now and then, I still experienced the hidden-room dream.

A dozen years after moving in, it was time to replace the tiled roof. That spring, the roofers came and began the task of removing the old and laying down the new. One day, when the basic framework was in place, but before the insulation and tiles were installed, the lead roofer casually said to me, "That room sealed off behind your bedroom—do you want me to insulate that?"

I smirked at him, thinking he was in cahoots with my spouse, teasing me about my secret-room fascination.

"You know about that room, right?"

"Yeah, sure," I said, sarcastically. "I'm going to make that into the library."

"Okay, so you want me to insulate it then?" he pressed.

At this point, I was thinking he was taking the joke too far. So to end it, I said, "Well, show me the space so I can decide."

I walked out onto the balcony off the master bedroom, climbed up his ladder, and looked where he pointed. And, sure enough, behind the wall that our headboard sat against was a fully contained 8x12 room. It was unfinished and completely empty, but it was there nonetheless—a bona fide secret room.

My jaw dropped, and I just stared. When the shock wore off, I asked if he could make a small entrance to the area.

And that is how I came to have a small, cozy library years after I moved into my house.

I do miss those hidden-room dreams, though.

~Donna L. Roberts

A Walk with My Son

Where there is great love, there are always miracles.
~Willa Cather

I was raised in the Roman Catholic faith, making my Communion and Confirmation while adhering to the church doctrine as best one can. During my high-school years, my parents divorced, and I had stopped attending Sunday mass altogether by the time I entered the military. Though I drifted far away from structured religion, I always fancied myself a spiritual person, whatever that meant. I justified my purposeful distance from religion by living a righteous and moral life, guided by the non-denominational "Golden Rule" of doing unto others as you would have others do unto you.

An amazing woman came into my life serendipitously, culminating in a whirlwind marriage. We lived blissfully for many years, sharing an identical spiritual philosophy and an uncomfortable, yet rarely spoken, distrust of organized religion. We had three beautiful daughters over the course of thirteen wonderful years. My wife and I were approaching forty, our children were healthy, and our careers were steady. As much as we loved our family and life, we decided the time had come to officially "close the baby shop," and my wife proceeded to have a tubal ligation. We had given up on our dream of having a boy.

Several equally wonderful years passed, and our lives remained blissfully full of dances, soccer games, track meets, and myriad activities that would fuel our memories for the rest of our lives. On August fourth, my thirty-ninth birthday, I was awakened around 2:00 a.m.

by the most evocative dream I had ever experienced. I sat straight up in bed, rubbed my eyes and pinched myself hard enough to leave a quarter-sized bruise on my arm. I glanced over at my sleeping beauty and tried my best to let her lie. I could not. Almost as if she could sense my excitement, my wife grabbed my hand, and I recounted my vision right then and there.

The dream began in a rather pedestrian manner, with me walking alone on a nondescript beach on an overcast day. The lack of sun must have kept the usual throngs away as the beach was completely abandoned. I stopped and knelt down to examine a variegated conch shell and noticed what appeared to be a man and boy walking hand in hand in the distance. The pair was coming toward me, and as they drew closer, they began to come into focus, leaving no doubt as to who was approaching. Jesus Christ was walking toward me, clasping the hand of a small, blond, blue-eyed boy. One look at the lad, and I knew this was the son I would have had were circumstances different.

No words were exchanged as my son and Jesus arrived. I locked eyes with Jesus, and with silent affirmation, he replaced his hand with mine, leaving me holding the hand of the boy. I looked down at the boy; he looked up and offered a reassuring smile. I held my son's hand firmly but gently, determined to never let go. The dream ended.

As I finished describing this palpable vision to my wife, she took my hand, rubbed it on her cheeks and brushed away the small trail of tears trickling down her face. She leaned over, pulled my head closer and whispered in my ear two very small yet unforgettable words, "Me, too."

We didn't speak of our simultaneous and identical dreams the next day. There were no words to explain our experience, and we had no earthly idea what it meant, if anything. I thought perhaps it was some manifestation of our longing for a son, possibly a message of closure, a symbolic missive from God. We took care of our daily duties, and several uneventful weeks had passed when I received a most unlikely surprise in my lunch bag. I opened my lunch and found a laminated copy of the famous biblical poem "Footprints in the Sand." My wife had included it as a reference to our shared dream, but also to tell me that an impossible dream had come true.

While tubal ligations have a ninety-nine percent efficacy rate, did you ever wonder about the remaining one percent? Neither did we… until we became members of this elite group. My wife was pregnant. Eight months later, we were cradling our miracle baby boy.

After our son's birth, my wife and I agreed to revisit our long-held mistrust of organized religion and re-examine our personal commitment to God. We began attending church more regularly and learned to accept the imperfections of Catholicism. There is no denying some otherworldly force was at work, alerting us so vividly to the pending arrival of our son. The dream lives on every time I see my son, attend a mass, or take a walk on the beach. While "miracle" is a word that is often overused, in our family we believe in them wholeheartedly.

~Michael Hausser

13

Charming Treasure

Those we love and lose are always connected
by heartstrings into infinity.
~Terri Guillemets

I grew up running through fields and playing with kittens in a red barn on my grandparents' farm, which was right next to our home. My grandfather died before my first birthday, but I was lucky enough to have my kind grandmother, Rose Baker, into my teenage years.

After Rose's passing, my family cleared her belongings from the farmhouse and rented it out. Tenants came and went, hauling their worldly possessions behind them as they left.

While I was in university, my parents retired and moved farther north. I missed the day that the moving truck carted my folks' boxes to their new home overlooking a pond inhabited by fish, frogs and, to my disgust, pits of snakes!

The buildings where I'd grown up held wonderful memories—baking my first apple pie at age eight, working in the shop with my dad at age seventeen, my first real boyfriend who fixed up my "rust bucket" car, and countless Christmas dinners with my aunts, uncles, and cousins. Now the buildings stood empty, their fate left to the developers who bought the land to build a subdivision.

All of my gram's lifetime possessions had been removed. Or so we thought!

The first time I had the dream, I chalked it up to nostalgia. In the dream, I was merely walking through Gram's house, through the mudroom, kitchen and living room, surveying the bare walls and floors. There was nothing there. When I woke, I reasoned that I was simply sad because I'd never get to set foot inside Gram's home again.

I carried on with my student life. I attended lectures by day and ate pizza with my friends at night.

Then the dream returned.

The scene was similar. Again, I walked through Gram's house, but this time, I ventured into the small pantry off the kitchen. Then, I went up the steep staircase to the second floor where the bedrooms were located. I ventured through the rooms one by one: the blue room that was my dad's, Gram's room, and the spare room with the weird angled ceiling. I looked inside the cubby hole above the stairs that once stored wool socks needing darning and stacks of old paperback books.

All of these spaces were empty. I was definitely searching, but for what?

I woke with a start. Deep down, I knew the dream wasn't merely nostalgia. I was on a mission — looking for a forgotten object! I was certain of it and phoned home.

My mom answered.

"Hi, Mom, I have news," I said.

"You didn't quit school, did you?"

I laughed. "No! I've been having odd dreams where I'm walking through Gram's house searching for something we left behind."

"Oh, honey, dreams are just that — dreams. Gram's house is empty. You know how many times it's been rented since she died. We cleared out everything. I bet you're just missing her."

I grew defensive. "Yes, I miss Gram. But this isn't about my feelings. This is different. Something of Gram's is still in her house."

"Well, I don't know what to say, Patricia. Dad and I left nothing behind. Now, tell me about university. How's it going?"

That night, the dream made its third and final appearance.

It picked up where the last dream had ended.

I was upstairs in the hall outside the bedrooms. I turned and walked downstairs to the kitchen, and then headed straight to a door in the corner that led to the cellar.

I never liked Gram's cellar. It was one of those spooky spaces with a dirt floor, damp cement walls, a low ceiling, and spiders. I had only been in the cellar a few times. Once, I had ventured down and spotted a pair of black rubber boots resting on the floor without a person in them. I was scared silly. I ran back to the safety of tea and walnut-date cookies with Gram, slamming the door behind me. But in this dream, I took a deep breath and went down, unafraid.

I walked through the dim space to a large rectangular recess in the wall, a cool spot once used to store jars of preserves. I looked into the hole and felt the sadness of the dreams slip away, replaced by euphoria, because I saw a cardboard box!

Then I woke. I sat straight up in my bed, relieved.

I called my mom in the morning. I felt silly, but I had no choice. The dream was vivid. I couldn't let it go.

My mom was busy when she answered the phone. "What can I do for you, honey? I'm baking quiches for the bridge club, and your dad's on his way in from his shed for a coffee break."

"I'll be quick," I said. "When do the land developers take possession of Gram's property?"

"Later this week, before the weekend," she said. "Why?"

"Shoot! I won't be home before then. You and dad have to go to Gram's. I had that dream again."

"Oh, Patricia," Mom said.

"Mom, I mean it. You have to go. I know where it is," I said.

"Where what is?" she asked.

I realized I sounded crazy, but I wasn't deterred. "I know it's a strange request. I don't know what it is, but I know where it is. You have to find it. If you don't, I'll have to skip class, drive home, and go myself."

"You're serious?" I heard the disbelief in her voice.

"Dead serious," I said.

I heard my mom sigh. "I'll talk to your dad. We'll go."

"It's in the cellar. Check the wall for a cardboard box."

"Fine. But I don't want you to be disappointed. We cleared out everything."

"Will you call me afterward?" I said.

"Sure will. Love you, sweetie."

"I love you, too. And Mom?"

"Yes?"

"Thanks."

I hung up.

Mom phoned me right after they visited Gram's.

"Did you find it, Mom?" I asked.

There was a short pause before she spoke. "We went to the cellar. There was a box right where you said it was, but way at the back. It was hard to spot. Your dad used his flashlight."

"I knew it!" My body relaxed. "What was inside?"

"A crystal chandelier. The one Gram had hanging in her living room. It's awfully pretty."

A sense of calm washed over me.

When I saw the chandelier a week later, my eyes welled with tears. My mom dusted off its leaf-shaped metal sides and its many sparkling, teardrop-shaped crystals.

We hung the charming fixture in my parents' new home.

Gram's chandelier will be displayed in a special spot wherever our family lives. When a recurring dream defies explanation and leads to treasure in a musty nook, there's nothing left to do but admire its mysterious beauty!

~Patricia Miller

14

Puppy Love

I don't like dreams or reality. I like when dreams
become reality because that is my life.
~Jean-Paul Gaultier

My husband Roy was driving. He was the Commodore of the Houston Canoe Club and we were taking flyers for the San Marcos River Clean-Up to Whitewater Experience, a business run by Don Greene. "I had a dream last night," I began hesitantly. "I never had one that seemed so real. I saw every detail."

"Yeah? What was it about?" he replied, getting interested.

"I dreamed that we were getting a little black and tan puppy. In the dream, we got it from a business that was run out of a house."

We had not been married very long and been talking about getting a puppy, but the time never seemed right.

"That's nice. What kind of dog was it?" Roy was almost parked in front of Whitewater Experience.

"I'm not sure," I replied. "But it was small and energetic, and we both just adored it."

"Well, maybe after we get through today, we'll visit the SPCA and see what they have for adoption," Roy responded. "I don't want a frou-frou dog. It's going to have to be a dog that will camp and go canoeing with us."

We parked and got out of the car, and as we approached the building, I couldn't believe my eyes. Whitewater Experience was doing business out of a refurbished old house. *No, it couldn't be,* I thought, yet it looked vaguely familiar. Roy grabbed the flyers, and we walked through the front door. I stared and grabbed Roy's arm.

"This is the place in my dreams, Roy, right down to the Indian blankets on those old Army footlockers."

About this time, Don Greene greeted us and Roy introduced him to me. After exchanging niceties, I couldn't stand it any longer. "I know this is going to sound strange, but you wouldn't happen to have a small black and tan puppy for sale, would you?"

Just as I posed this question, a small Yorkie puppy emerged from under Don's desk. He ran directly to me and gave me puppy kisses.

"It's him, Roy. This is *our* puppy." It *was* the puppy I had seen in my dream the night before.

Don looked confused by our exchange, so we explained my dream to him. He was mesmerized. "Well, I wasn't going to sell this one. I was going to keep him for myself. You see, he shouldn't even be here. I call him Gordo the Magnificent because he was the first puppy born in his litter. He was so big that his head was stuck in the mother's birth canal. I had to hold open the birth canal and drive a stick shift twenty miles to get them to the vet for an emergency operation to save the litter. The vet was successful, and four puppies were born. The rest of the litter has been sold, but Gordo is something special. He has even been with me on several canoe and raft trips."

Don said that Gordo never approached strangers. But he ran directly to me. He *was* the dog I had seen in my dream, and I was crestfallen when Don said he was going to keep the puppy.

Don saw the sadness in my eyes as I played with Gordo. "Well, I have the mother and the father. There will be more puppies. You folks are good folks and would take him in the outdoors with you. I guess I can let you have this one," Don said.

I was ecstatic. Now the big question… "How much do you want for him?"

"I got $250 for the other puppies," Don said. "Guess I'll ask the same for him."

Now I was saddened for the second time. There was no way we could afford that.

"But for you guys, I would let him go for $225."

Don agreed to a payment plan. We made the first payment and got ready to take the pup home. Then Don said there was one stipulation—that he keep Gordo long enough to teach him how to eddy turn in moving water before we took him home. We agreed, and two weeks later, Gordo was ours.

Most dogs only respond to one person, but from the beginning, Gordo was always *our* dog. He was smart, friendly and not afraid of anything—except thunder. We registered him with the AKC with a name that fit our lives—George Mutt. George because I always wanted a dog named George, and Mutt (Roy's contribution) because this was the first registered dog Roy had ever owned. George went on many adventures with us and was indeed a water dog. He had his own life jacket and understood currents. He loved to "fish" in the shallows, and when he got hot on a summer canoe trip, he would jump into whatever body of water we were paddling.

George Mutt brought us joy for fifteen years. We have owned other dogs since, but none of them was a "dream" dog, and none measured up to George. His pictures are still in our living room and bedroom, and Roy still carries a picture of him in his wallet. He will be with us always—if only in our dreams.

~Janice R. Edwards

15

The Next Chapter of My Life

*Don't give up on your dreams, or your
dreams will give up on you.*
~John Wooden

I was living above my tiny antique shop when I dreamt that I won the lottery. Even after I woke up, the event felt real, which was odd because I knew I hadn't bought a lottery ticket.

I did need some sort of miracle, however, because my business was failing.

Later that day, I bought a lottery ticket. I didn't know which of the lottery games to choose, so I just decided to ask for two Lotto tickets and then went home to watch the drawing on TV. When the announcer pulled the winning balls from the tumbler, I didn't hit a single number.

I went back to my antique shop to work and try to think of new ways to make money. The fact was, on most days, my shop didn't make any money at all. If it did, it was often less than I'd spent to refurbish the furniture. The more days I was in business, the more worried I had become. My savings were nearly gone, and I was bored and unhappy with the work. As I sat polishing a dresser, my thoughts returned to the dream of winning the lottery. "If I won," I said to myself, "I'd follow my real dreams."

The day I'd bought the lottery tickets I knew I was gambling, but

I told myself, "Believing in dreams and miracles is a good thing," and justified buying two, even though I know that two tickets insignificantly improves the odds over buying one ticket. I told myself, "It's not like I buy lottery tickets every day, and if I win it will be a miracle." Two dollars just felt luckier than one.

I should mention that a few of my dreams have come true. As a girl, I'd dreamt that my thirty-four-year-old uncle died from a heart attack by the Snohomish River. When I'd told my father about the frightening dream, he had reassured me that dreams weren't real. But when my uncle didn't come home, my father went searching for him at the river. To everyone's surprise, he had died as I'd dreamt. No one could explain it. Over time, there were other premonitions about auto accidents, meeting the partner that I would spend eight years with and then, sadly, the dream of his infidelity that ended our romance. These special dreams were few and far between, and the older I'd become, they had become fewer, although my overall intuition was quite good.

What I wasn't good with was money. Everything I had was tied up in the antique shop, and it wasn't earning enough to pay the bills. My savings had already run out. I knew I would have to close shop. I took out an ad to find someone to take over the lease, since my one-year-in-business anniversary was approaching. I figured that would be a good time to turn the shop over to someone with greater resources.

To tell you the truth, I regretted opening the store. Selling antiques was never my dream. It was my mother's dream. She loved antique shopping and had cultivated a beautiful collection that she and my father enjoyed. I only thought that I'd wanted it because it reminded me of the fun I had antique hunting with my family growing up.

My true dream wasn't in sales or refurbishing furniture at all. I wanted to be a writer. If anyone ever asked, "What's your dream job?" I always said, "Writer," and I'd always acted like one. I kept journals since kindergarten and was an avid reader. I tested at a college reading level in fifth grade, and wrote and bound my first poetry chapbook before I reached junior high.

For all practical purposes, I should have become a writer, but my life was riddled with hardships along the way. I was bullied in elementary school for being "too smart." Later, in high school, I fell into the wrong crowd. And, since trouble begets trouble, my twenties and thirties became about drinking, a hopeless search for love, and a series of dead-end jobs. I still wanted to be a writer, but I didn't know how to get there. I no longer wrote in journals, but still dreamt of literary success.

After I lined someone up to take over the shop, I held a closeout sale, but even with a big red-and-white "Going Out of Business Sale" banner draped across the front of the shop, I sold little. I remember sitting at my empty cash register with my eyes closed, apologizing to God for making so many bad choices.

The apartment I lived in was connected to the shop, so I had to move out of there, too. I didn't have enough money to rent a new place, which meant I would have to be a middle-aged couch surfer who relied on the generosity of family and friends to survive until I saved enough to start over. All of it depressed me. I regretted the years I'd wasted partying in bars and I cried about not having found true love. Most of all, I regretted not pursuing my dream job.

On the second to the last night in the shop, I wrote in a journal for the first time in years. Afterward, I accepted that I would have to ask friends and family for help and felt genuinely grateful to have people who would help me. When I fell asleep, I dreamt I won the lottery again.

This time, I saw a specific grocery store, the QFC on 45th St. in Seattle's Wallingford neighborhood. Inside the store, I also saw the clock on the wall behind a specific clerk. It said 9:50 a.m. I heard myself ask the cashier, "Is there a game called Lucky for Life?"

When I woke up, I knew I had to go to the QFC in Wallingford. As I stepped up to the counter, I felt a surge of energy shoot through me when I saw the sign advertising the game from my dream. The clerk said, "It's a two-dollar ticket." I smiled, remembering I'd felt compelled to buy two one-dollar lottery tickets after my first lottery dream.

Afterward, I went home to finish packing. I was excited, even though I knew that the odds of winning the lottery were incredibly small. It felt good to be hopeful even if it was silly. It gave me something to fantasize about while I finished packing up the shop's inventory and my apartment.

The Lucky for Life drawing was held the night before I had to be out of the antique store. I decided, win or lose, that I would go back to college and finish my bachelor's degree. It seemed the wise choice for someone who wanted to be a writer.

I couldn't watch the Lucky for Life drawing on TV because everything I owned was packed or given away. The next morning, I drove to the store where I bought the ticket. I signed the back of it before I held it under the ticket-checking scanner. The words "Winner, See Retailer" appeared on its tiny screen. I asked the clerk, "Does this mean I've won something?"

She checked my ticket on her side of the counter and then looked up at me, eyes wide. "You've won the jackpot!"

I won the Lucky for Life lottery! I receive $52,000 a year for the rest of my life. The winnings allowed me to go back to college and earn a bachelor's degree. Immediately afterward, I was accepted into a creative writing program at the University of Washington's graduate school. I graduated at the top of my class with a 3.98 GPA and got my MFA in Creative Writing. I've written four poetry chapbooks and last year I published my first collection of short stories.

Sometimes it still seems like a dream. I followed the instructions in my dream about the lottery, and I ended up being able to pursue my dream career!

~Kelle Grace Gaddis

16

Befriending a Superhero

I am Sailor Moon! I stand for love.
And I also stand for justice.
~Sailor Moon television series

My sixth grade English teacher had us write letters to our heroes. While my peers wrote to Nelson Mandela or Hillary Clinton, I wrote to Jennifer Cihi, an actress and singer who was popular on Nickolodeon in the early 1990s on a show called *Roundhouse*. We didn't actually mail the letters, so mine was stashed away with my other memorabilia in my parents' attic.

In that fan letter, I promised to dedicate my first book to Jennifer. As an adult, I did in fact become a published playwright, and did in fact dedicate my first book to Jennifer, but she was a mere passing thought that surfaced maybe once every five years. Then, at age thirty-one, a social media twist of fate allowed me to connect with Jennifer Cihi. I sent that first Facebook message excited to reminisce about my childhood, even if just to myself.

I didn't want to seem like a crazy, stalker fan. And so I spoke honestly. I simply said, "I want you to know that you inspired me to live the amazing life that I've led. I have written a published play, been an actress in New York, lived in South Africa for two and a half years, and now I am a teacher. Thank you." By that afternoon, I'd forgotten all about the message. But two days later, in the wee hours of the morning, my phone made the familiar "ding" that signaled a Facebook message.

Ironically, that very day, I was visiting my parents, with the arduous task of going through all my boxes in their attic. And there, right before my eyes, was that twenty-year-old school assignment. Jennifer had me mail her that fan letter, a virtual time capsule, and we exchanged a few more pleasantries via Facebook. I told her that I was teaching at a unique school in New York for kids with mental illness, when suddenly Jennifer asked if we could talk on the phone. I pretended to think it over and act a little busy. But, of course, I would want to talk to her!

After several phone calls, we shared our experiences with mental illness. We realized that we both shared a passion for being active in the larger societal discussion regarding this topic. I shared my insights as a teacher and writer, and she shared her experiences as a performer. The more I spoke with Jennifer Cihi as an adult, the more I pondered my childhood recollection of what a "hero" really is. A hero is someone who does what's right when presented with the opportunity. A hero is someone who sets herself apart to serve others, even if there is no recognition or praise.

Within months, I had traded in New York for Nashville, where Jennifer lived. Together, we began to develop programming for schools to implement support systems for kids suffering from depression, bullying, and other mental health issues. Ironically, as I grappled with the word "hero," I learned that Jennifer is actually the English singing voice of a famous television superhero, Sailor Moon. That little project she did many years back now resurged in the form of Comic Con.

Jennifer and I began traveling to many different cities in the United States, Canada, and even the island nation of Malta in Europe. She would go as Sailor Moon, and I would be invited as a writer. That fun side project helped inspire us even more in our quest to give voice to mental health issues. Together we founded, Mariposa, dedicated to providing support and education on mental illness. One highlight was when we were both selected as presenters at the Mental Health America 2016 Annual Conference in Washington, D.C. We both facilitated a breakout session on the intersection of theatre, celebrity, and mental health.

As I think back to my eleven-year-old self, writing a fan letter in vain, I cannot help but wonder if that young girl could ever imagine what a serendipitous adventure lay ahead of her. God scripted our unique story, and as many chapters are yet to be written, I know they will be filled with humble service.

~Stefanie DeLeo

17

Happily Ever After

The way to a woman's heart is through her children.
~Author Unknown

Early one morning, I awoke from a dream and found myself grinning from ear to ear. It had been eons since I felt this content.

In this vision, I saw the figure of a large, muscular man. His face was blurry, but I could distinguish that he had dark features. His warmth and affection were very comforting, and his presence was homey.

I wished this dream had lasted longer and tried to savor this blissful state.

During the following week, I was haunted by the image of this enigmatic man. I believed that this dream was more than a fantasy, perhaps a message, but trying to keep the memory alive by being overly analytical did not bring me any closer to understanding what it all meant. I even replayed this dream in my head while trying to fall asleep, hoping to encounter this mystery man again in my slumber, but I couldn't make it happen. As time passed, key moments of this dream remained strong, but the rest faded. Other matters took priority in my life, and I was no longer obsessed with figuring out what my subconscious was trying to tell me.

A year later, I was invited to view a friend's new house, which was under construction. I showed up one hot summer afternoon with my two-year-old son, Lee.

"I really like the design and layout of the home," I said as we walked around the various rooms. "It's going to be beautiful!"

The carpenters on site noticed Lee's animated face as he observed their labor, and they seemed pretty amused.

"All little boys love tools," the head of the crew said with a grin.

For some strange reason, this carpenter looked familiar. I ran through various possibilities in my mind, but I just couldn't place him. I gave him a friendly smile, reached for my son's hand, and continued to explore the house with my girlfriend.

"You're welcome to pop in anytime," my friend said to me. "I can see how much Lee loves watching the guys work."

"Yes, he does," I agreed. "I will. Thanks."

In subsequent weeks, I found myself, with Lee in tow, heading over to my friend's house, even without her presence, in order to give my little guy more access to carpenters swinging hammers and sawing boards. I sensed that as long as my son was not getting in the way, they didn't mind our presence.

Many trips later, I confessed to myself that I had an ulterior motive. Dave, the large, muscular head carpenter, was the main reason I made excuses to visit the house so often. This man was fun loving, easy to talk to, and had a great sense of humor. I was also charmed by the way he interacted with my son.

"How's my little buddy?" Dave would say to Lee as we entered the building.

He remained on his break noticeably longer, chatting with me and demonstrating "guy stuff" with various tools to my toddler. In time, a strong connection was forming between us, which I couldn't ignore. I considered inviting Dave over for dinner, but I was conflicted. *Was it the right decision to be allowing another man into our home and my young boys' lives? Would it be damaging to them if our friendship didn't work out?* I weighed the pros and cons, and then listened to my heart.

The next time I saw Dave, I struck up my nerve and asked, "Would you like to come for supper?"

"I'd love to," he answered without hesitation.

The initial time Dave spent with my family was truly unforgettable.

During that evening, the phone rang just as Lee vied for my attention. To avoid a typical two-year-old outburst, I scooped up my son and answered the call while Lee sat on my lap trying to grab the phone. After a few seconds, to my astonishment, I watched as two strong arms reached out and relieved me of my pesky little boy.

"Let's go over here," Dave said to Lee while carrying him away.

I sat there in awe, almost moved to tears by the sensitivity of this large man.

From the onset, Dave established a caring relationship with both Lee and his older brother, Nathaniel, and made an effort to spend time with my "little men." I learned early on in our friendship that Dave had two girls whom he saw every other weekend and missed terribly. His younger daughter, Cheryl, was five, the same age as Nathaniel, and Jana, his older, was eight. It was obvious that being around my children and soaking up their kid energy definitely helped him fill that void.

"Why don't you bring your girls over sometime?" I suggested to him.

"I would really like that," Dave said enthusiastically.

The next weekend, two sweet girls arrived, accompanied by their dad.

"It's great to see how well all four kids are getting along," Dave said as his face lit up.

"It sure is," I agreed with a smile.

We exchanged warm glances while watching my boys share their toys with the girls. Over the next few months, Dave visited regularly. He had many entertaining stories to tell, and conversation between us was effortless. In time, our friendship grew and developed into something more intimate. Witnessing my sons bonding with Dave added to his attractiveness and was a strong extension of our friendship.

One day, as I pondered my relationship with my new boyfriend, it struck me that Dave was the mystery man in my dream. I was thrilled by this awareness and realized that the dream was a premonition, which was why it impacted me so strongly. I instantly felt more settled and was anxious to relay my dream to this wonderful man. After the children were asleep one evening, I told Dave in great detail about this vision that had puzzled me so many months earlier. He sat quietly and listened. After a few seconds of watching him deliberate, Dave looked at me and said, "I've been in love with you for quite a while now."

"I feel the same about you," I said.

It was enough to reassure us that we were meant to be together. Twenty-one years have gone by since we revealed our love to each other. The highlight of our relationship has always been sharing the upbringing of our four children. In the past few years, both Jana and Cheryl have provided us with beautiful grandchildren, and we recently celebrated Nathaniel's wedding. Life doesn't get much better than that! I will always remember and am eternally grateful for the dream that connected me with my soul mate. Sometimes, by listening to your heartstrings, you can make your dream come true.

~Dalia Gesser

18

Daddy Can

Once you have had a wonderful dog, a life
without one is a life diminished.
~Dean Koontz

The end was nearing for Daddy. The brilliant mind, fastidious habits, acerbic wit — they'd all disappeared a few years earlier. He'd been a leader of men. Now he had trouble guiding his fork to his mouth.

Gone were the days of erect posture and immaculate grooming, well-cut suits and blinding white dress shirts. It was easier now to keep him in pajamas. He was still terribly handsome for a man of his years, but shaving that cleft chin was a chore.

He'd cursed us recently for installing a zoo in the back yard. It was "unsanitary." It was "unthinkable."

It was the great-grandchildren's inflatable toys bobbing in the pool.

I had always relied on Daddy. No matter how big the problem to be solved, my first thought was, "Daddy can." I didn't know how to let him go.

The time came when a gray hearse took him from us.

When I saw him next, he looked plastic, made up. We, as a family, do not fear death as some do; we never skirt the subject in conversation. So it was no great surprise to anyone but the undertaker when I shooed him away and reapplied Daddy's make-up myself. My father would never go out in public not looking his best. He didn't "feel" right, his skin not responding as it would have in life, but I'd expected that.

Mother had chosen his navy suit for burial because it made his eyes so very blue. It didn't matter that nobody would see those clear blue eyes again.

Arriving home from the service, my heart in shreds, I found my closest companion of thirteen years whimpering in her dog bed. The knots and lumps under her skin had reached critical mass, and she shivered with pain. *Now? It couldn't be. How could I give up my best friend today, of all days?*

My skin went clammy, and I felt faint. I lay on the floor and wrapped myself around her, murmuring soft words with a coppery taste in my mouth.

Eventually, my husband pried my arms from her and lifted her, bed and all. "I'll take her back to the vet and see if he can do anything for her. But if not…"

I told her goodbye.

Bereavement settled its weight on me. Moving through quicksand, I laid aside my black suit, now dappled with gray fur, and huddled between cold, white sheets to wait. *God, how can I bear this?* I could not judge the passage of time. I began to hear something, some mournful sound, low and guttural. The volume grew. I was alarmed by it, but the heaviness of despair held me fast, and I could not rise to investigate. It morphed into a wail, and I began to shake, as I realized the noise was coming from me.

By the time he returned, arms empty, I had quieted. "He put her on an IV drip and will keep her overnight, but he doesn't know of anything else to do. We'll see how she is in the morning. Then we'll decide."

You will decide. I cannot.

When sleep finally overtook me, it was the heavy, drugged feeling of one who doesn't care about ever waking. Daddy came to me in a dream.

He wore the navy suit he was buried in, but he'd taken off the jacket and neatly rolled up his sleeves the way he had every evening after work when I was a girl. He was holding my dog. A balm of warmth permeated me, carried by his subtle spicy scent and the light that came from everywhere.

"Don't worry, child. I've brought her back to you." His baritone voice was warming and silky, like his favorite single malt.

I had so many questions, but he was gone, and I would never see him again. The warmth of his light receded.

I squirmed back into the cocoon of my bedding. Many hours passed. I was unaware of the sun forcing its way around the edges of the drapes, trying to break in.

Then a familiar sound dragged me out of the numbness — the clicking of thick toenails on hardwood. I pushed my hair out of my face and pulled myself upright as my husband lifted her onto the bed beside me, stubby tail wagging her entire rear end, wet nose nuzzling my neck. I held her tight and stared a silent question at my husband.

"The vet said he came in early this morning to check on her and found her trying to claw her way out of the kennel. She seems fine. Tumors have shrunk. He can't explain it."

Gratitude ran down my cheeks. "Daddy can."

~Kemala Tribe

19

The Winner

The best luck of all is the luck you make for yourself.
~Douglas MacArthur

I put on my best shirt, finest jeans, and favorite cowboy hat. I want to look sharp when I win twenty thousand dollars at the casino. It probably won't happen, though, because last night I didn't dream that I won.

I've had two dreams about winning a lot of money. The first was on Christmas Eve a couple of years ago. My wife Debbie and I planned to go to the Seneca Niagara Casino in Niagara Falls, New York, on Christmas day. The night before, I dreamt that I sat down at a video slot machine — one of thousands at Seneca Niagara — and I bet $2.50. I never bet that much in real life. Fifty cents is my usual bet; a dollar is my absolute limit. But in my dream, I bet $2.50. I pushed the button, and the virtual reels spun. The next thing I knew, "X 27" came up at the bottom of the screen because I had twenty-seven matching lines. The machine said I won $500 X 27, which added up to $13,500!

When I woke up on Christmas morning, I remembered my dream and laughed. *Thirteen thousand dollars! What a present that would be! Too bad it was only a dream.* I was getting close to retirement, and after raising four kids, my savings could have used a boost.

Later that day, while driving to the casino, I told Debbie what I'd dreamt and how I specifically remembered "$500 X 27." I didn't think about it again until we arrived and saw some slot machines exactly like the one in my dream. People were busy playing on them, so I looked over someone's shoulder. Below the title, "Wicked Winnings II," was an illustration of a woman with horns. She was lying on a purple couch, and around her, cloth bags with dollar signs written on them sat in front of several fireplaces. I remembered those bulging bags of money from my dream. The way they were sitting in front of the fireplaces, they seemed to be saying a winner would have money to burn.

"That's the one I dreamed about," I said, pointing.

Debbie nodded, but she didn't take it seriously. After all, it was just a dream.

We moved on to "Prowling Panther," "Siberian Storm," and "Kingdom of the Titans." An hour and a half passed, and I forgot all about my silly dream. When we returned to where we'd started, a seat was empty at "Wicked Winnings II." Debbie walked ahead of me and sat down. She bet fifty cents and pushed the spin button. Letters, numbers and characters spun around. Witches were wild, and ravens paid the most. If one raven appeared in each column all the way across, she'd win $50. The matching lines didn't have to be straight; they could connect in any direction, even in zigzags.

Debbie squealed when the reels stopped turning. Witches and ravens lined up in twenty-seven different directions! It might have been any number, but it was 27, exactly like my dream! The screen said "$50 X 27," and with her fifty-cent wager, she won $1,350! My dream had been off by only a zero. *What were the odds of me dreaming those same numbers? Was it just a strange coincidence? If only I'd sat down first and bet $2.50!*

Debbie and I started going to the Seneca Niagara Casino every Saturday night for our "date night." It was more fun than bowling or seeing a movie. We wore our cowboy hats to help us find each other when we got separated. We always decided ahead how much we'd spend, and when it was gone we'd leave.

A few months ago, Debbie and I saw a crowd around a row of new slots. There were four of them, each called "Winner's Choice, Cleopatra." On the screen, the name "Cleopatra" covered the lower part of a woman's face like a veil. All you could see were her green eyes and the jewels on her forehead.

Everyone wanted a turn because these machines had a lot of "specials." If the Egyptian symbols lined up a certain way, a jackpot wheel popped up. You could win free spins, or you could hit one of the jackpots. The silver jackpot might be worth hundreds, while the gold one often reached thousands. The machines were linked progressives, which meant every time someone played on any of the linked machines, more money went into the jackpot until a lucky gambler won it all. My wife and I watched others play for a little while, and then walked away.

The following Friday night, I dreamt that I won the jackpot at "Winner's Choice, Cleopatra." This time when I woke up, I tried to remember every detail. Whenever I go to Seneca Niagara, I always get a cup of coffee at Tim Hortons before I start playing. Then I walk around the game floor with it while I check out the machines. But in my dream, I didn't stop for coffee. I went right to "Cleopatra."

On Saturday at the casino, I wanted to make sure I did everything the way it happened in my dream the night before. When we came to Tim Hortons, I passed by without stopping. Debbie asked, "Aren't you going to get coffee?"

"No," I said. "In my dream, I went straight to the machine. I have to do it the way my dream told me to!"

Without waiting for Debbie, I hurried to "Winner's Choice, Cleopatra." The second seat was open, and I sat down. I hadn't realized the maximum bet on this one was $3.00, much higher than my usual bet. But because my first dream was so prophetic, I played the max bet. My first two spins weren't spectacular. Then on my third, the jackpot wheel came up on the screen. I hit the spin button and held my breath.

When the wheel stopped, a light on top of the machine started flashing. "You've won the gold progressive," the screen said. "An attendant will be there soon." My heart raced when I saw the amount: $3,005! I couldn't believe it.

I waited for someone to come. A tall, muscular man approached me, wrote down my name and social security number, and then left. A few minutes later, he returned and counted cash into my open hand.

He placed a card on the machine that said, "Congratulations, Jerry! You're a jackpot winner of $3,005."

I wanted to tell my wife, but I'd lost track of her. I looked around and spotted her cowboy hat a few sections over. "Can I take this card with me?" I asked the man.

"Sure," he said.

I caught up to Debbie and showed her the sign the employee had given me. She shook her head. "You're kidding!" she said. I had the cash in my wallet to prove it.

Those were the only two dreams I've had about winning at the casino. Now, the night before we go, I always hope to have a dream. I'm waiting to see winning lottery numbers, too. If I do, you can bet I'll buy a lottery ticket!

~Jerry Penfold

Lost and Found

*Happiness is a simple game of lost and found: Lose
the things you take for granted, and you will feel great
happiness once they are found.*
~Richelle E. Goodrich, Making Wishes

I was terrified that my mom would find out that I had lost the beautiful silver flute she bought me. She had given me a big lecture about how valuable it was, and that I had to take good care of it. Now it was missing! I was only ten at the time, so it felt like a huge responsibility.

Mom was a soft-spoken woman who never yelled at me, but she would surely have docked my allowance for a year or two in order to pay for it if I couldn't find it. The worst punishment, though, would have been disappointing her and being forever regarded as an unreliable person.

As I was in the band, I would take the flute to school and bring it home in the evening twice a week. During the day when I wasn't at band practice, I would leave it in the cloakroom behind my homeroom, always in the same place. This was safe enough during school hours, but it wasn't intended as a place to leave anything overnight.

I normally remembered to collect it after school, but inevitably the day came when I forgot. Mom didn't notice that I didn't bring it home that day, and I didn't remember it until after dinner, when it was too late to go back to school. I knew I'd be in big trouble if I lost it, so the next day I went to school early to get it from the cloakroom — but it was gone!

Being afraid to tell anyone, I looked all over on my own, but it was nowhere to be found. I could hardly focus all day, and I was practically in a state of panic by the time I got home. Luckily, Mom still didn't notice either my mental state or the fact that I didn't have my flute, even though I was supposed to practice at home every day.

My prayers before bed naturally included a fervent wish to find the flute. Somehow, I fell asleep in spite of my anxiety… and then I dreamed a most amazing dream about my flute, quite unlike any other dream I had ever had.

In the dream, I saw the janitor take my flute from where I had left it and place it on the top shelf behind a pile of books, way out of my reach. He carefully put some extra books in front of it so it couldn't be seen even by a very tall person, which I certainly wasn't. It was obvious that he had hidden it deliberately, maybe to keep it safe for whoever had lost it. The dream was incredibly clear. I had a deep feeling that it was a true vision of what happened and could hardly wait until morning so I could go and see.

In the morning, I raced to school as early as possible. I got a chair and climbed up to the top shelf. My flute was exactly where I had seen the janitor put it! I was saved! I laughed and cried and collapsed in a heap; I was so relieved. My feelings of gratitude knew no bounds.

When I calmed down, I looked around and noticed that the cloakroom — and the janitor, when I saw him later that day — looked exactly the same as they had in the dream. Every detail, even the pile of books, matched up to my dream precisely. It still gives me goose bumps to think of it.

~Teri Tucker

21

The Middle Child

Sisters function as safety nets in a chaotic world
simply by being there for each other.
~Carol Saline

Soon after my twentieth birthday, I had the dream. *An angel was coming toward me, carrying a small bundle — a baby. It was a tiny, tiny newborn.* It was a pleasant dream. So why did I awaken with the sheets in tangles and my nightgown drenched?

Well, it is August, I reasoned. *And we have no air conditioning.*

It was unnerving. There were no babies in my life. I wasn't married, had no intention of having a baby in the foreseeable future, and my mother wasn't expecting. There was just my older brother and me.

A few months later, the dream returned. *The baby was in the arms of the angel, but it was reaching out its tiny hands to me as if to say, "Take me" or "Up, up." The infant had grown.*

I was intrigued. I researched the meaning of dreams. An angel can symbolize goodness. A baby can signify the desire for innocence or new beginnings. It didn't explain much to me.

After that, the dream returned about once a year. The angel looked the same — just your typical silhouette in willowy white. I had a feeling it was the baby that held more significance.

The baby kept getting older. It went through the toddler phase, and eventually she, a little girl, appeared to be five or six. By then, the angel had disappeared. The child would walk toward me, but as soon as she was within reach, I awakened.

One day, I had friends visiting. My older brother was off in another part of the room, reclining on a sofa. My friends were discussing families. One talked about her siblings, saying how nice it is to have a sister with whom you can discuss everything. I agreed.

Then she asked me, "So, it's just you and your brother?"

"No, I'm the middle child," I replied without thinking. As soon as the words came out of my mouth, I realized I had made a mistake.

My brother overheard and sprung up: "What did you say? There are only two of us. You're the *younger* child."

"Yes, I mean I am the younger of two. I don't know why I said that," I answered, laughing at myself.

That night, I wondered why I had blurted out I was the middle child. It's not like I wanted to be a middle child. But I had always wanted a sister. Brothers are fine and friends can provide a certain closeness, but not like a sister can.

Soon after, my mother offered to take me on the trip of a lifetime. We'd visit my father in Czechoslovakia, where I had been born. After a few days with him, we'd vacation in other parts of Europe.

My parents were divorced when I was very young. When I was eight, my mother brought us to live in America. At Christmas or birthdays, my father would write, but that's it. I hardly remembered him. All I remembered is that when he smiled, his eyes sparkled like Roy Rogers' eyes.

The first night in my father's tiny apartment, my dream returned, more vivid than ever.

On that visit, I got to know and love this kind, gentle and funny man as if we had never been apart. It was enlightening to have a father at last. Instead of traveling to other places, we stayed with him for almost three months.

On the day before our visit ended, while my father went to work, Mother got chatty with a neighbor. She learned that Father had remarried and had even fathered a child. When Mother questioned him about it, he denied, denied, denied.

I could not possibly understand my father's reason for denying that he had remarried and, even more, that there had been a child.

I could only imagine that the bitterness between them was so great that by refusing to accept the child, he could pretend it had never existed. I cannot excuse his behavior, but it's not my place to judge.

Supposedly, the marriage was very short-lived. The story went that the woman's only reason for marriage was to have a child. Once the baby was born, the woman went from the hospital to her parents' home, refusing to let my father see the infant. He paid child support, but that's it.

Whatever reasons he had, he would not speak about that part of his life. Maybe by denying it had ever existed, he convinced himself that it hadn't.

He never knew I knew.

I was curious about my half-sister, but I didn't try to find her. I felt it would be disloyal to my father. Imagine such a ridiculous, heartless, senseless excuse.

Twenty-seven years later, when Father passed away, I decided my loyalty to him had been misguided. I had a sister, and I wanted to know her. I reasoned that my father, being in heaven now, would no longer hold earthly grudges. He might even be thankful that, by accepting my sister, I was making amends for what he should have done. At least, that's how I rationalized.

After some research, I found her. Her name had changed due to marriage, but she did exist. I wrote her and sent her my e-mail.

Weeks went by without a word. I was about to give up when, one day as I was clearing out my computer, I had a hunch to check my spam. There it was — an e-mail from a person named Dana.

We began corresponding, bridging the distance of countries and the twenty-year age difference, through the Internet. We exchanged life stories.

Essentially, neither of us had known a father. I had a loving mother who only praised my father, often comparing me to him with pride: "You're just like your father."

Dana had a mother who only focused on the negative. Throughout her life, she was told in anger: "You're just like your father."

Last May, the dream-baby came to visit.

My husband and I were at the airport, looking at the flight board, checking for her arrival. I was on pins and needles when I felt a tap on my shoulder. I turned and gazed into Roy Rogers' sparkling eyes — or my father's eyes. It was my sister.

She stayed with us for two weeks. How I wished our father could have been there to see his daughters together in harmony, but I could feel his spirit with us.

We continue to correspond and plan on seeing each other again.

The baby in my dreams was not a figment of my imagination. She had been born right around the time I first had the dream — even in the same month. She may have been a premonition at first, but she was real.

That dream never returned. It didn't have to. I finally knew what it had meant. I had a sister after all.

~Eva Carter

22

The Power of the Mind

*There are three things we cry for in life: things
that are lost, things that are found, and
things that are magnificent.*
~Douglas Coupland

Aunt Nancy, now in her mid-eighties, has always been
that unique, creative, thoughtful aunt who took me
"good-deal shopping," hid silver coins for me to find
in the back seat of her car, and made photo books
documenting my childhood in Maine. A now-retired art teacher, she
came up with a clever way to share my grandmother's vintage charm
bracelet, which jingled with Victorian-inspired, silhouette cameos.
Nancy decided to share a cameo with each of her five nieces, so that
each of us could enjoy the memory.

I watched as cousins made their charms into necklaces and displayed them in memory boxes. However, I never received mine. Nancy
insisted that she gave it to me while on holiday in Florida, but I didn't
remember.

I moved to Atlanta for college in 1990, graduated in 1994, married in 1996, and moved into my first home in 1997. All those years,
the mystery of the cameo was a source of contention when it crept
into conversations between my aunt and me. She steadfastly insisted
that she gave it to me, and I just as resolutely avowed that I'd never

received it. This was a stalemate that would last for nearly two decades.

Then, in 2008, I had a vivid dream.

I was at the checkout in a local Walmart store. I looked down at the slender finger of the cashier and noticed her unique ring. Recognition flooded my dream mind. The ring was set with the exact bronze-backed, white-silhouetted cameo that was on the antique charm bracelet my aunt had so carefully distributed to my cousins years ago. In the dream, I remarked to the cashier how beautiful the ring was and told her about my grandmother's charm bracelet. The cashier stopped scanning my items and looked me so deeply in the eyes that it felt like her energy entered my bloodstream. She said, "This was my grandmother's charm, too. I had a friend make it into a ring after I found it in her garage."

The next morning, I told my family about the dream over breakfast and went about my day. We were packing to move and going through very old boxes in the garage. After opening and re-sealing boxes for hours, I was about to quit for the day when I opened a bin full of shoeboxes. I opened one of them, fully aware of the potential rabbit hole I was entering, and found a host of saved letters and cards. *Ah,* I thought. *This was a box that I recovered from Mom and Dad's house....*

I opened a letter from my beloved grandmother, Mildred, and read her familiar handwriting with a nostalgic smile. I opened and read a handful of greeting cards that I had saved. And then, at the bottom of this box of cards and letters, I found a large unopened yellow envelope. My name was written on it in Aunt Nancy's handwriting. I opened this envelope and carefully unwrapped the letter, which described the significance of the gift enclosed. This letter held, in its protective grasp, a tiny baggy containing a gift: the cameo!

Nancy was right — she gave me the cameo, but in a sealed envelope that I never opened. It lay in my garage for years. I have never been one to put much faith in the magical power of dreams, but I will always wonder about this dream. Did it plumb the deepest recesses of my memory? Did my subconscious mind know that Aunt Nancy had given me an envelope that I never opened, that got mixed up with all the cards and letters that I *did* open that ended up in that box? However it happened, I have new respect for the way that dreams can guide us through our lives.

~Heidi Campbell

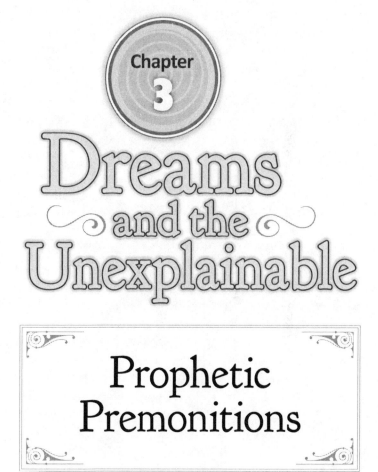

Chapter
3

Dreams and the Unexplainable

Prophetic Premonitions

A Mother's Vision

It is through science that we prove, but
through intuition that we discover.
~Henri Poincaré

One of the most exciting times of a woman's life is the day she finds out she is going to have a baby. I was no exception to this, and I was not new to this amazing miracle of life, as I had already had my son three years earlier. However, from the time I entered into my second trimester, I felt anxious, and it was different from the anxiety I had felt during my first pregnancy.

I pushed it away as I prepared for my second child, who I was certain was a girl. But the feeling persisted so much that I finally expressed this to my obstetrician, who was very quick to reassure me. After all, the ultrasounds had confirmed a perfectly healthy pregnancy, and I had no health issues that would compromise the pregnancy or the baby.

As the pregnancy progressed, I was eventually able to let go of that feeling of foreboding. I focused on our new house, decorated the nursery, and prepared my excited son, Daniel, for the arrival of his little sister.

The rest of the pregnancy went very smoothly, and I went into labor one very cold January morning almost exactly on my due date. Alexandra was born during one of the worst snowstorms that winter.

We settled into life as a family of four and all was well for about two weeks. Then, suddenly, the dreadful feeling came back. I simply could not shake it. I knew that something very serious and life threatening was going to happen to my baby.

One night, as I was nursing Allie by the dim light of the hallway outside our bedroom, I caught a glimpse of myself holding her in the mirror facing my bed. I could see myself holding her in my arms in the reflection, but she appeared to have a white gauzy sheet covering her. From the time I was a child, I had always experienced visions and premonitions, but this one alarmed me so much that I jumped out of bed to turn on all the lights. I told my husband that we had to take her to a hospital. I was certain that something was very wrong and that time was of the essence.

We took Allie to the emergency room of a local children's hospital. The staff admitted her for observation and then sent us home, assuring me that she was perfectly healthy.

I should have been relieved at that point in time, but I was not. The feeling only intensified, as did my fear that the doctors were missing something very important that could cost my daughter her life. I took Allie to the emergency room of another hospital. They ran a new panel of blood work on her and compared it to the results at the first hospital. Everything checked out as perfectly normal. Nevertheless, they agreed to admit her for twenty-four hours for observation.

The next day, they brought me her discharge papers to sign. I refused. My family tried to convince me. One of the doctors came in to speak with me and suggested they order a psychiatric consult for me. At this point they were certain that I was having a postpartum psychotic episode. I agreed, as I figured it would buy me more time in the hospital for my daughter! As we waited for the psychiatrist to come, they called on one more doctor to come and examine Allie. However, when this doctor arrived, he only wanted to speak to me, asking me questions about my pregnancy and delivery, and ultimately where this persistent feeling was coming from.

I'll never forget the moment he said to me, "You're so sure there is something wrong with your daughter that I want you to tell me what it is." In that moment, I looked at Allie and simply knew the problem was in her abdomen. We needed to do a CT scan right away. Surprisingly, this doctor listened to me and ordered the scan.

Within an hour and a half of that scan, Allie was in surgery. The scan indicated she had peritonitis, a bacterial infection and build-up of toxic fluid in the abdominal cavity that can be fatal if left untreated. She'd had no symptoms at all, and the blood work never revealed any kind of infection anywhere.

Allie had to have a portion of her colon removed during that surgery, but I knew in that moment that she was going to be all right. Almost as intensely as this foreboding feeling had taken over my entire being, it left me in that moment. And following a lengthy hospital stay and recovery, I was finally able to take my baby home and be at peace.

~Lynn Darmon

Marcela's Vision

*Where there is hope, there is faith. Where
there is faith, miracles happen.*
~Author Unknown

Foggy from the drugs, I prepared to kiss my husband, Greg, goodbye. The coma came with risks, and death was one. We'd discussed it at length. But it was my only chance at having a life worth living. I struggled through the pain to stroke his scruffy face. Covered in ulcers, I weighed a paltry eighty-five pounds. He touched me like I was made of tissue paper.

"I'll see you in five days," he said. His voice was steady, confident. But his eyes were terrified.

I nodded and pointed at him. Then I placed my hand over my heart and mouthed the words, "Right here."

Gently, Greg kissed me. I wondered if it would be my last.

"Are you ready?" Dr. Cantu asked.

I nodded again as they began the drip.

Then the world went dark.

***

For seven years, I suffered from Reflex Sympathetic Dystrophy (RSD). The hallmark symptom is excruciating, unrelenting pain that starts with an injury. Mine was a nerve tumor. At first, we were relieved to learn the tumor was benign. But strange symptoms emerged once the tumor was removed.

I constantly felt like I'd been doused in gasoline and lit on fire. My weak, spastic muscles betrayed my legs. Embarrassed by my awkward gait, I began using a cane. Eventually, my arm no longer supported my weight. I switched to a wheelchair. Neuropathic ulcers engulfed my right arm.

American doctors gave us little hope.

"She's not going to make it two more years. She'll die from infection if she doesn't kill herself first."

"Her arm needs to be amputated. The risk of sepsis is too high."

"Put her in permanent care."

We'd heard it all, but we refused to accept it.

In Germany and Mexico, comas were being induced with ketamine, an anesthetic, to reboot the brains of RSD patients. The preliminary results were promising, but the treatment was risky, experimental, and expensive.

We felt we had no other choice.

On April 12, 2007, Greg and I flew to Monterrey, Mexico, in search of a miracle.

***

I don't remember those first five days of the coma. Greg has had to fill in the blanks for me. How I struggled to free myself from the tubes that were keeping me alive. How he helped the nurses restrain me as I fought hallucinations. How my breathing tube was to be removed on day five.

And then how everything went wrong.

Greg kept friends and family apprised through web posts and was about to start his daily entry when he saw Dr. Cantu rush toward him, gesturing to a room that nobody wanted to enter.

It was the "bad news room."

I had been extubated according to schedule. But then it happened.

"Shannon's had a seizure. We had no choice but to reintubate her. We've ordered some tests to try and determine the cause."

"Will she be okay?"

Dr. Cantu weighed his words carefully. "Right now, we don't know the answers."

Back in the waiting room, Greg opened his laptop. He put his head in his hands and cried.

"*Qué pasa, amigo?*" Greg hadn't noticed the man now sitting next to him, arm draped over his shoulder. Smile lines crinkled the corners of the stranger's tired eyes.

"My wife…" Greg's chin jutted toward my room. "*Mi esposa está…* sick… *enferma?*" The man nodded, beckoning a group of people from the other side of the room.

"*Mi nombre es* Javier."

The crowd grew as Greg explained our situation in broken Spanish. But it was one woman, Marcela, who would change our perspective — and our lives — forever.

"*Puedo rezar por tu esposa?*" Marcela asked, searching for the words in English. "I… pray… for her? Tonight?" she asked.

Greg nodded, tears blurring his vision. "*Si,*" he said. "*Por favor.*"

The family went home. Greg shuffled back to my room and hit Play on the iPod. Olivia Newton-John, my favorite singer from childhood, crooned as he watched my heart rate and blood pressure rise and drop. Machines beeped and buzzed around my still body. Eventually, a nurse tapped Greg's shoulder. About ten hours had passed. He hadn't left my side.

"Mr. Stocker? You have a guest in the waiting room. You must sign her in."

As he approached Marcela, she embraced him.

"A poem," she said. "I write it. In English."

"You wrote a poem for her? Today?"

"Yes. A letter. I read to her. Also, this." Marcela pulled a small glass bottle from her purse. "The mother of my mother give this holy water to me. It was… blessed? Yes, blessed. In Rome, by the Pope. She say, 'You know, Marcela. You know when right time use this.'"

Greg nodded.

"I know," she said. "I use now."

Marcela knelt beside me, whispering into my ear. She prayed and sprinkled holy water around my body. Nearly three hours passed before she emerged from my room.

"Greg?"

"*Si.*"

"You maybe think I am... crazy...," she began, obviously reluctant to share her thoughts.

"No," Greg implored. "Please."

Marcela nodded. "God speak to me. He say Shannon be okay. She have baby girl next year."

Greg didn't want to embarrass her, but he knew better. I'd been sick for so long with this horrible disease. I hadn't had a period in over two years. He hadn't been able to hug me for months. Not to mention the fact that I was thirty-seven years old, had just been induced into a coma, and didn't appear to be waking up anytime soon.

"You 'stand me?" she asked.

Greg nodded. He understood that this sweet, wonderful woman might be just a little crazy.

But that night, I improved drastically. My vitals stabilized. It took two more days, but I finally opened my eyes.

"Blink slowly if you know who I am," Greg said.

I closed my eyes.

When I opened them, Greg was crying. Somehow, I just knew. The nightmare was over.

***

I was heartbroken to say goodbye to Marcela and her family. But by mid-May, I was home and pain-free.

As Christmas and my thirty-eighth birthday approached, Greg and I decided to try to start a family. Greg thought it would take months, but I never doubted what would happen.

My very first pregnancy test came back positive.

It was early December when we called Marcela for the first time since returning home.

"*Hola*?" The voice was young.

"Andrea? Is that you? Is your mother there?"

"Greg? Shannon? My mother just told me! She just told me you're pregnant!"

"Wait, what?"

"She just told us! Congratulations!"

Greg and I stared at each other, jaws slack. We hadn't told anyone yet.

The miracle was sinking in.

At my twenty-week appointment, we shared our story with the ultrasound technician. She promised to stay as long as it took to determine the sex of the baby. She smiled as we mentioned Monterrey.

"My family is from there," she said. "And… it's a girl!"

As the tech headed for the door, I called to her.

"Wait! I'm keeping a journal for my baby. I forgot to ask, what's your name?"

I'll never forget the warmth of her smile.

"Marcela," she said.

Marcela.

Of course.

~Shannon Stocker

Prayer of a Soldier's Son

When prayers go up, blessings come down.
~Author Unknown

J ake was supposed to be asleep, but I heard his voice through the fog of 2:00 a.m. fatigue. It sounded like he was calling for his daddy. I waited to see if he'd fall asleep again on his own. At thirty-six weeks pregnant, I didn't want to get up for *anything* if I didn't have to. Still, I realized as soon as I shifted in bed that I also needed to use the bathroom, so I might as well check on him. After all, he hadn't called for his daddy since just after Steve left for Afghanistan several months earlier.

Jake and I had moved into my parents' house to wait for his little brother to be born, due in the middle of Steve's nine-month deployment — or, as Jake and I called it, "Daddy's big, big trip." Before every meal and at bedtime, Jake bowed his head and repeated, "Daddy safe, amen," his own variation of the prayer for Steve that I'd taught him.

When I went to check on him, two-year-old Jake was standing up in his crib. In the dim blue light of night, I could peek in and see him before he saw me. He wasn't crying, as I expected. He was saying his prayer for Steve — but he'd added something new.

"Fire! Fire! Daddy, fire! Daddy safe, amen."

Jake repeated his prayer a few more times, and then lay back down and went to sleep without noticing me. I was more than a little frightened, and for a while I could only stand there, praying myself. *Why was Jake talking about a fire? I began to shake. Was Steve in danger?*

In the morning, Jake was smiling and content. He prayed for his dad before breakfast, but didn't mention the fire again. Steve and I were only able to talk on the phone every few days, so it wasn't unusual that I didn't hear from him that day or the next. I remembered that a fire on a nearby forward operating base had made headlines several weeks before, when a burn pit had tossed flaming trash into an ammunition store and exploded, causing casualties. I combed through the news looking for any new reports of fires on American bases or outposts in Afghanistan, but didn't find anything.

Two days later, my phone rang. It was Steve. He was sorry he hadn't been able to call, but things in his area had been busy. He'd been out on patrol checking up on his platoons, plus there'd been a small fire on his company outpost. It wasn't a big deal, he explained. It could have been bad because it had started when something popped out of the burn pit toward the ammunition — just like the tragic fire on the other base.

"It could have ended the same way, but don't worry," he assured me. "We were able to put it out right away, and no one was hurt."

"When was this?" I asked, even though I already knew.

"About two days ago," Steve said, and moved on. "So, how's our Jake doing?"

~Christie Chu

26

Maybe Not

*Love is a partnership of two unique people who bring
out the very best in each other, and who know that
even though they are wonderful as individuals,
they are even better together.*

~Barbara Cage

My doctor said that I was too sedentary and needed more exercise. Since walking was not doing the trick, I decided to go back to my first love: swimming. I researched the public and private pools in the area and found one that fit my work schedule: the YWCA. I was excited to get back to swimming. But my husband, for some reason, didn't feel the same. He watched me prepare my swim bag for my first swim after work and then asked me to reconsider.

"Why, sweetheart?" I asked.

"I don't know why. I just don't feel right about it."

I tend to be a bit stubborn, and as he didn't have a good reason why I shouldn't go, I saw no reason to change my plans.

I went to work with my swim bag in the trunk and dreamed of my swim. I talked excessively to my co-workers about my swim. During lunch, my husband called and tried to convince me not to go. He said, "I can't explain it, but I don't feel right about it." As for me, I didn't see a need to change my plans.

Someone got sick and had to leave work early. I ended up working an hour later. I went to my car and looked at my watch. Taking into account the traffic, parking, and time for dressing, I would have less than a half-hour to swim. I reluctantly decided to try again a different day.

I drove home and got stuck in Los Angeles traffic, which added an additional forty minutes. By this time, I was thankful that I didn't try to go to the pool.

As soon as I pulled in the garage, my husband came running out. "Oh, good, you're home!"

My husband is always glad to see me at the end of a workday, but never like this.

It turned out that the roof of the YWCA pool building had collapsed, smashing the pool and injuring several people. It was at the exact time I would have been swimming. Words cannot describe the utter shock I felt watching the news that night. Slowly, this tragedy sank in. My life had been spared.

For the longest time, I couldn't swim at an indoor pool, but now I can swim anywhere. Sometimes, we can't explain how things work. We just need to be grateful that they do.

~Janet Elizabeth Lynn

27

Lessons in Faith

When you open your mind to the impossible,
sometimes you find the truth.
~From the television show Fringe

I can pinpoint the day I decided that we are not alone, that some greater force exists, something that influences what we call fate and our experience in this world. On that day, the ubiquitous heat of steamy Lagos, Nigeria, was laced with the rank smell of open sewer. It assaulted my nostrils as I stood on the roadside wondering about what manner of destiny had brought me to such a dangerous place.

It was not uncommon to be robbed on the streets of Lagos in broad daylight, and people had informed us that the police often turned a blind eye to the mayhem to receive their cut from the thieves. In the outlying areas, we heard ominous stories of roving brigands robbing and even killing people. As a green, young expatriate businessman in Nigeria, I was always conscious of two things: the lack of personal safety and the absence of the kind of law that Americans take for granted.

Nigeria was in the midst of its first oil boom in the 1970s. The country was inundated with fiercely competing foreign businessmen like me. It was also overwhelmed by poverty. The oil wealth, much of which was siphoned off by corruption at the top, stood in stark contrast to the subsistence living of much of the population. I don't know how it is in Nigeria today, but back then the wealth imbalance was like waving red meat in front of a starving dog. Many people naturally resorted to a life of corruption and lawlessness borne of the desperation that permeated every level of society.

My father and I were on a grimy street that day trying to get out of the city. We had an important meeting to attend far in the north, but we had a problem. It was one of those days when the commercial airplanes in Nigeria did not fly for one reason or another. We hailed a private transport, a vehicle that was like an unofficial taxi for hire for long hauls. We intended to board it for the eight-hour drive to our destination.

I climbed in the car first so my father wouldn't have to crawl over the back seat to make room for me. With one foot in the door, I froze. A cold wave of fear washed over me for no apparent reason, but this feeling told me something very wrong lurked on the horizon. I turned and told my father we could not get in. We argued for a few minutes until he finally relented.

Now let me sidebar here. In those days, I lived for long stretches of time isolated from normal social interactions in a foreign land. I was skinny as a rail, my diet consisting of pineapple, papaya, and coconut to avoid the many diseases that plagued foreigners. The combination of a restrictive diet and long periods of time in meditative isolation had made me prone to frequent visions. On occasion, local "bush doctors" — wise men or psychics — would sense something about me and approach me unsolicited. In short, I was frequently dwelling in another consciousness, and apparently that attracted people with perception.

My father had seen me diagnose people's illnesses with no information to go upon. He had even periodically relied on me to make counterintuitive business decisions. So, after some words with my dad, and despite his anxiety to make the meeting, he caved because he had enough experience to realize that I wasn't crazy. Well, at least not most of the time. We didn't try another vehicle because my bad feeling extended to any trip on the road that day.

As we made our way back to our dreary hotel along the dusty, pungent, congested streets, I'm sure my father was questioning his own judgment as much as mine. Missing meetings is not good business protocol in any country.

We learned about a week later — news traveled slowly back then — that the same transport had picked up other Europeans that day, and brigands had attacked them on the road. They killed a passenger. From that time on, my father, a fairly logical man, came to appreciate the possibility of unseen things.

Despite the daily insecurity of my three years in Africa, I loved the Nigerian people. They were natural entrepreneurs and some of the brightest people I've ever met. I was always devastated by the thought that the system they were born into so often killed their potential. I came to appreciate that whatever criticisms people levy against America, and no matter how low we may start out in life, no American is ever so weighted down by the corruption and inequality that I saw in Africa.

I often wondered about the fate that brought me to Nigeria. I had a number of close calls there, and so much of my life back then seemed futile and frustrating, even hellish. I look back on this event and others like it, and I realize there was a purpose in it for me: It was how I came to the conclusion that we are not alone.

A guiding hand preserved me, of that I'm quite certain, but only years later did I realize something had led me safely in and out of Africa with a greater purpose. I used my experiences there to write the critically acclaimed *Pope Annalisa*, a book that has inspired many people. So, yes, I do believe in dreams and premonitions. More importantly, I was fortunate to touch the world from whence they arise, and for that I feel eternally blessed.

I'm no different from anyone reading these words. The same force that protected me can protect you. It's like a 24/7 radio broadcast, but life throws a lot of noise at us, so be patient. If you work at tuning that dial with a little desire, contemplation, belief, and expectation, the message will cut through the static. Please try it. You have everything to gain and nothing to lose. It will work in ways you may not even notice at first, but it will slowly take hold and alter the course of your life as it did mine. And the most wonderful thing of all? Perhaps it will allow you to help others too.

~Peter Canova

The Accident

The relationship between parents and children, but
especially between mothers and daughters,
is tremendously powerful, scarcely to be
comprehended in any rational way.
~Joyce Carol Oates

"I just want to let you know that I'm running into town to pick up a few groceries. Will talk with you when I get back home." It was not an uncommon message for Mom to leave on my recorder since she often kept me informed as to her comings and goings. So why did I feel so troubled at missing the chance to talk with her?

I grabbed the phone quickly and dialed her number, hoping to catch her before she left, but she must have hurried out the door after leaving the message.

Then I saw it in my mind as clearly as if it were happening directly in front of my eyes.

Mom made a left turn onto the main highway. She apparently hit a patch of icy pavement and slid into the guardrail on the opposite side of the road. Wham!

Mom lived just up the private gravel road from our home. My parents moved to the countryside to be closer to their five grandchildren. Sadly, Dad passed away a few years later, so we tended to keep a close eye on Mom.

Without giving it a second thought, I grabbed my purse and ran out the door. I don't know whether I thought it was a premonition and I could save Mom from the crash, or if the accident had already taken place. Regardless, she needed me, and I had to go.

It was only about a five-mile drive to the highway from our house, and I made it in record time. As I pulled up to the stop sign and looked to the left, I saw Mom's black Mercury Sable crashed into the guardrail exactly as I had seen it in my vision a few minutes earlier.

No other vehicles had stopped to help, so I must have reached her within seconds of the crash. Looking carefully both ways, I tried to remain calm so I wouldn't fall victim to the same fate. I pulled slowly out onto the highway and parked directly behind the scrunched-up vehicle.

Mom looked at me strangely when I ran up and opened her door. "How did you know what happened?" she asked, somewhat baffled. I don't think it even occurred to her that I could have simply been driving by at the same time.

Other vehicles began to stop to offer help, so I didn't have the chance to explain how I happened to be there so quickly.

Later that afternoon, after dealing with the local towing company, the auto body shop and the insurance agent, Mom and I finally got a chance to sit down and chat about the accident. When I told her about my premonition, I was shocked and somewhat disappointed that she wasn't in complete awe.

"Mom, why aren't you more excited about me knowing you were in that accident?" I inquired with a bit of attitude.

"Honey," she responded, "how do you think I always know when you need me?"

She was correct — there is an inexplicable bond between a mother and her child that transcends the toughest boundaries, and I was just beginning to grasp what she had known for years.

I felt blessed to have been privy to what had transpired that day — and so thankful that I could be there when *Mom* needed *me*.

~Connie Kaseweter Pullen

The Funeral

Don't cry because it's over. Smile because it happened.
~Dr. Seuss

One morning, I make what I think is going to be a routine call to my ninety-two-year-old mother. For the past eight months, she has been living in an adult home. She is popular with the residents and staff, who appreciate her sense of humor and consideration for others. Although she has memory issues, she generally has a good grip on reality.

"How are you doing today?" I ask.

"Not too well, I'm afraid," she says.

"What's the problem?"

"I'm supposed to be at my funeral," she says. "But I'm not ready."

"Did you say your funeral?"

"Yes. My funeral. I'm supposed to be there. I think it's next Monday. If I'm not there, or if I'm late, people will be inconvenienced. Some of them have to take time off from work or drive long distances to attend."

"But aren't you forgetting something?"

"What's that?

"You're still alive." I pause. "Aren't you?"

"Well, I woke up this morning," she says. "That's a pretty good sign." She laughs. "But when I was getting out of bed, I suddenly remembered I had to be some place, and I wasn't ready. Haven't you ever had that feeling? Then it hit me. Of course, it's my funeral."

"Look," I say. "Today is Sunday. I'll call Bonnie and see if she

can meet me at your place after lunch. Then we can sort things out."
Bonnie is my younger sister.

"I'd like that. Funerals are important," she said. "We only get one, you know."

I call my sister and tell her about my conversation with Mother.

"That's odd," Bonnie says. "It's not like her to be so out of touch with reality."

"I'm not so sure that she is," I say.

"What do you mean?"

"You know how uncanny her intuition is."

"You think she's sensing her own death? She just had a checkup, and the doctor said she's in perfect physical health for someone her age."

"Why not play along with her? We'll need to make funeral arrangements sometime anyway. Maybe it would ease her anxiety if we made them now."

"And reinforce her delusion?"

"To us, it's a delusion," I say. "But to her, it's reality."

My sister, my mother, and I meet and agree to plan the funeral. I make an appointment with Fred, one of the funeral directors of our local funeral home. The next afternoon, the three of us arrive at our appointment.

Fred is a pale, silver-haired gentleman of medium height and build. He shakes our hands and escorts us to the back of the funeral parlor. We sit at a large, round table set on a thick, red carpet just off a showroom lined with miniature display coffins and cremation urns.

"I think it is wise that you came as a family to plan Mrs. Brigham's funeral," Fred says. "I will walk you through all the necessary details so that when you leave here today, you can rest assured that everything will be taken care of."

"That would be wonderful," says Mother.

For the next hour and a half, the three of us plan every aspect of the funeral. Mother decides on a pink theme: a pink coffin with crepe interior, pink flowers, and memorial cards with a pink rose. And, of course, she wants to wear her favorite pink outfit. The funeral director says he will make all the arrangements for the burial at the cemetery, including having the family headstone professionally cleaned and the date of her passing added. He apologizes for not having a pink hearse and almost laughs.

"Is there anything else I can do for you today, Mrs. Brigham?" asks Fred.

"No. You covered everything."

"There is one more thing," I say. "This may be an unusual question, but Mother would like to know how she can be sure she will make it to the funeral on time. She has been worrying about this lately."

Fred turns to my mother and speaks directly to her. "Mrs. Brigham, when the time comes, we will send a car and bring you back here. We handle every facet of our services from this facility. Your funeral will not proceed until everything is ready, including you." I am pleased with how well Fred handles this question.

On Wednesday, I call Mother again.

"How are you doing today?" I ask.

"I feel so much better," she says. "I've invited everyone I know to my funeral."

On Thursday, I receive a call from the adult home telling me that Mother had been taken to the hospital in the night. When my sister and I visit her bedside the next morning, the nurse tells us that Mother's large intestine has ruptured, and she is in kidney failure. Death is imminent. Although Mother appears pale and weak, she has a peaceful expression. She drifts in and out of consciousness with no sign of pain or discomfort.

"Where am I?" she says.

"In the hospital," I say.

"Am I dead?"

"No. You are alive. Bonnie and I are here with you."

"Tell Fred to send the car for me," she says. "I'm ready."

~D.E. Brigham

Author's Note: The funeral was held on Monday, September 9, 2015, and Mother was on time.

Irritating Intuition

Trust yourself. You know more than you think you do.
~Benjamin Spock

The cold January wind was fighting my car as I sped down the freeway. Morning classes were over, and I had a few hours free until I needed to be back at the community college for my evening class. Rather than drive the half-hour home, just to turn around again, I was planning on spending the afternoon studying at my grandma's house nearby.

"Go home."

I actually jumped, thinking someone was in the car with me! But no, I was alone in the old Pontiac. I shrugged my shoulders and tried to shake off the creepy feeling. *I must just be hearing things,* I told myself, *like when you'd swear someone just called your name, but no one has.*

"Go home."

This time, I realized the words were coming from inside my mind. *Wow, I must have had way too much coffee or something. I'm freaking myself out.* My exit was coming up, and I slid the old car into the right-hand lane. I was about to take the ramp when…

"Go HOME!"

I swerved the car back out of the exit lane just in time.

All right, fine. Like any sane person would do, I will follow the voice in my head. I will drive a whole thirty minutes out into the country, all the way home, only to turn around and drive thirty minutes back to school. You win, oh voice of insanity.

A half-hour later, still fuming at myself, I pulled into the driveway... and found the yard on fire.

Our dogs had chewed through the extension cord for the Christmas lights, setting the dry January grass ablaze!

The fire was still small, so I jumped out of the car, hiked my long skirt up into my waistband, and grabbed a shovel. I threw some dirt on the fire and then stomped it out.

Nobody else had been home. If I hadn't heard that insistent, irritating voice on the freeway, our family home likely would have been damaged.

As it was, the only damage was a scorched lawn and melted soles on my boots.

~Jessica Ghigliotti

The Fallen Temple

Our inner teacher, our sixth sense, is our authentic self.
~Angie Karan

I was in an apartment complex, surrounded by chattering, friendly people. The place was fairly new, with crisp beige bricks that shimmered in the bright sunshine. I'd somehow crawled through a bay window in an apartment and landed outside on the lawn. The sill was only a few feet from the ground, so I wasn't harmed.

I looked up to a mountain above the apartment complex and to the ancient Roman temple that was nestled there. As I watched, the columned temple shook and collapsed straight down into the earth. It looked and sounded for all the world like a Nintendo graphic come to life — like the castle that disappeared at the end of Castlevania.

I opened my eyes and sat up. I was thirteen years old and in the eighth grade. The dream puzzled me. Nothing about it had been frightening, but I was left with a sense of foreboding.

I was gifted with a touch of premonition. Occasionally, I dreamt of conversations with friends that were later repeated, word for word, in real life. For the most part, though, my nocturnal journeys were extremely run of the mill for an adolescent, and were filled with friends, rock stars, and whichever boy I was crushing on at the time.

Some of my dreams flitted through my conscious memory like fireflies — experienced, appreciated, and then forgotten — but others lingered. The dream of the ominous fallen temple was one of the latter. I was so intrigued by it that I recorded it in my journal. For years afterward, every now and then, the collapsing temple would pop into my mind. However, neither temple nor mountain nor apartment complex ever made an appearance during my waking hours. I was inclined to believe that, like ninety-nine percent of my dreams, it was just my brain being imaginative.

In my teens and early twenties, I wandered through ancient ruins in several European countries, but I never found the fallen temple. Even the temples that were actually situated on mountains didn't match. When I lived in France, I walked an ancient Roman footpath to the top of Puy de Dôme, an extinct volcano in the Auvergne. The ruins of a Gallo-Roman temple to Mercury greeted me at the summit, but they were peaceful and safe — the polar opposite of what I'd seen in my dream.

By the time I was twenty-three and starting postgraduate classes at the University of Cape Town in South Africa, the dream was all but forgotten. Since I was not a study abroad student — I had applied to UCT independently — I was in the regular postgraduate dormitory. It resembled an apartment complex, albeit with single rooms. Devil's Peak, a pointed outcrop on the end of Table Mountain, loomed above the campus. Something about it seemed familiar to me. Since I'd never seen photos of the dorms before arriving in Cape Town, however, I couldn't figure out why.

My South African friends, Megan and Jody, spent a few days driving me around Cape Town to show me the sights. As we rounded the side of Devil's Peak on the freeway, I looked up… and my blood ran cold. The temple from my dream was nestled on the side of the mountain.

"What is that temple up there?" I asked uneasily.

Megan smiled. "Oh, that's just Rhodes Memorial." It turned out that the "temple" had nothing to do with ancient Rome. It was an early twentieth-century memorial to Cecil Rhodes, who had lived on the estate that became the University of Cape Town. The small Cape Dutch house that served as the reception and common area at my dorm had actually been part of the grounds. Rhodes had hosted Rudyard Kipling and his family there.

I suddenly realized why the dorm looked so very familiar to me:

It was the apartment complex from my dream. Everything matched: the layout of the buildings, the color of the bricks; the bay windows with black frames. And the temple was exactly where it had been in my dream, presiding over the complex from the mountainside… a mountainside called Devil's Peak, no less.

I was uneasy at this revelation, but there wasn't anything I could do about it. I wasn't about to hop on a plane and go home because of a dream I'd had eleven years earlier. Almost everything in Cape Town seemed to be an ordeal for me, though, so the trepidation I'd had about the dream's setting seemed justified. I spent the semester contending with an unprofessional, nasty course advisor and several bouts of ill-ness. Whenever I looked up at Rhodes Memorial, I blanched a little, but it didn't seem to be in any imminent danger, and neither did I.

The beginning of my second semester in late August found me curled up in bed in my dorm room, watching a video. The latest chal-lenge I'd faced had been substantial: an emergency appendectomy. I'd been excused from my classes for a week or two to recuperate, and I was doing my best to rest quietly. Winter in Cape Town was exceptionally mild, so I'd opened the windows to catch the midday breeze.

As I drifted in and out of sleep, I heard something outside my windows. Since I lived on campus, I was well accustomed to noise, but this time, I had a sudden, insistent feeling that I needed to secure my room. I hobbled over to the windows as quickly as I could, slammed them shut and locked them. Then I completely drew the heavy curtains.

A few minutes later, someone pounded harshly at my door. I didn't answer, even though they knocked several times. I wasn't expecting company; my friends knew to call before they stopped by. My door was double-locked with a deadbolt, but I still muted my television, picked up my cell phone in case I needed to call for help, and held my breath.

As the pounding on the door finally subsided, I caught a glimpse of a shadow at the windows. A man's silhouette was visible on the other side of the curtains. He lingered for a tense moment, and then moved away.

I later discovered that thieves had infiltrated the dorm complex. They'd swiped radios through open windows in other students' rooms and stolen items from the communal kitchen. I couldn't help but feel, however, that if I'd left my windows open — or answered the door — the crimes they committed that day might have been far worse than theft. In my dream, I had climbed through a window, the temple had collapsed, and I'd sensed danger.

I never spoke of it to anyone; I was too apprehensive to piece it all together until much later. For whatever reason, though, the rest of my time in Cape Town was much easier for me. Whatever peril or bad mojo had existed had run its course.

I also stopped being afraid of the Rhodes Memorial. Before I left Cape Town, and after I'd recovered from my operation enough to resume my normal activities, I trekked up Devil's Peak to visit the "temple." It couldn't tumble down on me anymore.

~Denise Reich

Burning Questions

By failing to prepare, you are preparing to fail.
~Benjamin Franklin

My mother-in-law, Catharine, is a dreamer. Not the spacey, skipping-among-the-daisies type. She's the type who dreams things, and then they happen.

So when she called one day several years ago and said she didn't want me to be alarmed, but she'd had a dream that our house burned down, I *was* alarmed. She tried to assure me that we just needed to pray and trust God, but my faith wasn't quite strong enough to withstand the rush of dread. I hung up the phone and started praying. I was determined to pray forever if I had to.

That lasted about a day.

It isn't that I didn't take her warning seriously. I knew better than to dismiss a warning dream given to Catharine. It's just that I was busy — three little kids and a part-time job busy. Oh, and a husband, a dog, and a cat.

A couple weeks after the warning I was getting dinner started while the kids ran amok. Our four-year-old, Drew, came in asking for help with his shoes. The neighbor kids were out front, and he wanted to join the fun. I left the pot I was heating on the stove and went over to help him tie his shoes, bending down in a position where I could no longer see the stove. A few seconds later, Drew shouted, "Mommy, the stove is on fire!" Leaping up, I ran around the corner and saw that the oil I'd been heating in the pot had caught fire. What happened next is an epic tale of fire-safety ignorance.

Despite my limited understanding of household fires, I did realize I couldn't put water on an oil fire. But that was the extent of my knowledge. Not knowing what I *should* do, I grabbed the handle of the pot and started spinning around, trying to decide where to deposit it. I considered the sink, but I knew water + oil + fire = bad.

I had to get that fiery pot out of the house. So I ran to the sliding glass door, scorching my hand in the process, and tossed the pot of flames onto the back patio. I know, I know. Rhodes Scholar move, right? And wouldn't you just know but the darn thing bounced and landed on the dog's bed. There was a moment of terror as I watched the flames spill out of the pot and onto the bed. *Here comes the inferno,* I thought. But the inferno never materialized. Apparently, some really smart person at the dog-bed manufacturer had chosen to make the bed out of non-flammable material. So rather than ignite like a beach bonfire, the bed simply melted, and the fire died.

I stood there shaking, holding my singed hand, feeling like a zero of a mom. Even worse, little Drew had witnessed the whole debacle. I can't remember now what he said about how I managed the situation, but knowing him, it was probably something wise like, "You should have just removed it from the heat and put a lid on it," or "Gee, Mommy, don't you know that baking soda kills oil fires?" After all, Drew was on a first-name basis with the firefighters at Station 41, where he dragged me on a weekly basis, and he surely would have handled the fire correctly.

It was only later, after I'd calmed down enough to confess to my husband Andrew my shameful near miss, that Catharine's dream came back to me. And, with it, the (also shameful) realization that I hadn't been praying about it like I said I would. I called her up.

"So, remember that dream you had about our house burning down?" I asked. "Have you been praying about that?"

"Yes, I have," she replied, calm as ever.

"Well, I think you might have saved our house." I went on to tell her about my misadventure, and how I gave that fire about 1,600 different opportunities to set our home ablaze. I told her the whole humiliating affair, feeling there was no sense in trying to hide my stupidity from the one person who'd clearly had my back.

I also readily agreed the next time Drew badgered me to visit Fire Station 41. Apparently, I needed to ask those men a few questions.

~Barbara A. Owens

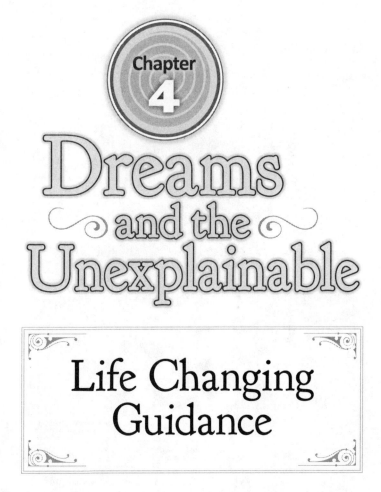

Chapter

4

Dreams and the Unexplainable

Life Changing Guidance

Waking Up

*A dream which is not interpreted is
like a letter which is not read.*
~The Talmud

I was thirty-three years old and living in Cheyenne, Wyoming. I'd spent the last four years of my life building a dream house that had proven to be more of a nightmare than a dream. My contractor, the friend of a friend, had agreed on a very good price for my house, with the understanding that I would pay for the house as it was being built. He would have lumber, concrete, shingles, appliances, and flooring delivered to my job site. And as the bills were presented for them, I would pay them — up to the limits of the agreed-upon price of my house.

After a year, every other house on my side of the block had been completed, but mine, which had been started first, was still only three-quarters finished. Something started to look fishy. Finally, one of the subcontractors told me the ugly truth. My contractor had had material for all of the other houses delivered to my site, and I had been paying not only for my house materials, but for many of the others. Then the big news came. My contractor said that although I'd paid the agreed-upon price, materials had gone up, so he was going to have to raise the price of *my* house!

At this point, I got a lawyer. I discovered that the contractor's claim was that although I'd agreed to pay a certain amount for the house to be built, there was nothing in the contract that stated I would own the house once built! To add insult to injury, he got a restraining order forbidding me from entering my own house and started installing in other houses the material I had researched and gone to great lengths to find while he put substandard material in my own. The time leading up to the court case and the eventual trial meant there was a period of almost a year when I could not enter my *own* house!

It was agony, but I finally won my case. I could not recover the money I'd lost paying for the material of other houses or sue him for legal fees without going back to court, and my attorney suggested I just finish the house and enjoy it.

I was out $12,000 in attorney's fees. In addition, when the contractor realized he would probably lose the case, he took a chainsaw to the kitchen countertop, drove deep tire tracks through my sod, splashed varnish over the walls, and dumped trails of concrete all over the floors. In addition, it was not until someone saw in the paper that my house was about to be sold for taxes that I discovered he hadn't been paying any of the property tax on the land — which, up until the time of the court judgment, he had owned!

It took approximately four more months to fix the damage he'd done, to carpet the house, install kitchen flooring, and move in. Then it took an additional two years to replace material he'd chosen with material I'd ordered, build the shoji screen drapes and a wet bar, and furnish the house.

Finally, after two years, the house was perfect — just the way I'd wanted it. And it was then that I had the dream.

I was sitting in a bar or restaurant with a man when a woman approached us from across the room. When she got to our table, she threw a drink in my face, hit me on the top of the head with the glass, and shouted "Just wake up!"

I woke up to the sound of myself screaming "Just wake up!" I was soaking wet and had a bump on my head. I realized that I had picked the glass of water off my bedside table, poured it on my own face, hit myself over the head with it, and shouted to myself to wake up!

It was a Saturday morning when this astonishing act occurred. Needless to say, I had some big thinking to do. *Just what was I supposed to wake up to?* I then did something I hadn't done for ten years. I sat down and wrote a very long story, pretty much based on my own life. When I finished it, I knew what my dream was trying to tell me.

At the end of that school year, I would have been teaching for ten years. In that time, I had taken ten thousand or more student stories, essays, and compositions home to grade, edited a teen anthology, and been sponsor of a creative writing club for students — but I had not written one thing myself. In spite of a master's degree in creative writing, I had been exhausting all of my creative energy in instructing kids to write — and living vicariously through them, while any additional time and effort had gone into planning, designing, and decorating the house.

Now I understood that I needed to create something myself. I needed to write.

At the end of the year, I put my things in storage and rented out the house. I resigned from my job, and I moved first to Oregon and then California to write. I've been writing ever since. Eventually, I sold that dream house and used the money to *live* my dream rather than live *in* it.

For two years, I stayed with a college friend in Orange County, California, going to the beach every day to write. I then moved to Los Angeles to study screenwriting and film production, and got a job with a TV production company. I became involved in a poetry workshop and gave numerous readings in the L.A. area, eventually marrying and moving to the Santa Cruz area where I made my living by art for the next fourteen years. I continued to write, give readings, and publish in a few literary journals.

Since moving to Mexico fifteen years ago, I have published a number of poems and articles in various English language print and online magazines. I've published one book in conjunction with my women's writing group and gone on to publish three of my own. Four more children's books and a book of humorous poetry await formatting, as blogging has more or less taken over my life for the past year and a half.

And this is why, ever since, when my dreams speak to me, I listen.

No longer am I going to make it necessary to hit myself over the head with a good idea — as I had to do to force myself to recognize the best idea I ever had!

~Judy Dykstra-Brown

The Aware Train

Your work is going to fill a large part of your life, and
the only way to be truly satisfied is to do what you
believe is great work. And the only way to do
great work is to love what you do.
~Steve Jobs

I was at a crossroads in my life, trying to create my next career move. I was living in Los Angeles and working freelance in television production, but I knew I was missing a sense of purpose in my life. So I started taking classes on developing my intuition and visualization practices to explore what I felt was missing. During this time, I started to have a recurring dream.

My dream was of a train, a silver streamlined train with rounded corners, a symbol of the future. The train seemed to be traveling very slowly and was so long that I couldn't see the end. I had a very strong sense that the train was coming from somewhere eternal and going somewhere eternal, like a kind of spirit train.

I would jump on the train, and inside were not the typical rows of seats and an aisle, but something that looked like a television control room with television monitors and audio boards. This was very high-tech audio equipment that appeared to be monitoring a television or radio network.

Operating the controls were visionary leaders, doctors, scientists and new thought leaders. They were all sitting in high-backed black swivel chairs, but it was what they were doing in their chairs that was the essence of the dream. They were spinning around and swiveling in these chairs like little kids, and they were laughing and giggling and having a great time. They were emitting a sense of total playful joy and having so much fun that it didn't seem like work at all. Then I would step off the train, and I always remember seeing on the side of the train the word "Aware."

One day, I awoke suddenly from this dream and said the words, "You're supposed to do it." *Do what?* I thought. *Where did those words come from? And what am I supposed to do?* Later that day, a friend called to tell me of a Los Angeles radio station that had been sold to a Korean company, and the drive-time hosts were leaving to find new jobs. This left an opening in the middle of the afternoon at the radio station.

I went in to the station and asked if I could host my own show. I started broadcasting a show interviewing some of the mentors in my life who were doing amazing things, like my acupuncturist who came from a 5,000-year-old lineage of Chinese medicine. I also interviewed my teachers from the intuition classes and doctors who were increasing longevity by eating apricot pits in the Hunza Valley. I called my radio show "Aware" because of my dream. Fifteen years later, I still broadcast "The Aware Show" to more than three million people globally per month.

I feel the significance of my train dream was to teach me to follow my dreams and listen to my intuition. The visionary leaders in the high back swivel chairs were the guests and experts I interview about how to create a life of joy, good health, and happiness. I talk about how to follow our dreams and listen to our own truth. And I invite people to stay "Aware" at the end of each show, just as my dreams invited me.

~Lisa Garr

This I Know

From the bitterness of disease man
learns the sweetness of health.
~Catalan Proverb

If we spend a third of our lives sleeping, is it possible the time is more productively spent than we imagine? I like to think so. I've heard in dreams we are able to solve problems, get in touch with our own subconscious minds, and even be more receptive to the messages of loved ones who have passed on. I'm convinced I once managed all of those in the course of a single, life-changing night.

When my mother died, I couldn't be with her at the end. That bothered me so much that I secretly asked for a sign that she knew I loved her. I told myself that if I dreamed she said the words, "I know," it would be my sign she had heard.

"I know," she said in the dream. I awoke with a start. Even though she'd said the words, it wasn't at all the dream I had envisioned. It wasn't sentimental. But then, neither was my mother. In the dream, I had just finished telling her I needed to quit smoking. Leave it to my mother to find a way to correct my behavior even after her death!

So when I woke up, I tried — unsuccessfully again — to quit. By that point, I had probably quit close to two dozen times. Usually I'd make it a couple of days. Sometimes, I made it several months. Once I even made it a year. I always started again. Life was just too stressful.

My mother always had ways of making herself heard, though.

Around that time, I had the mother of all nightmares — a marathon of mayhem that made Ebenezer Scrooge's Christmas Eve saga seem like a frolic. It felt like it lasted the better part of a year rather than one night. It was a nightmare that I had lung cancer. In the dream I had to live through every single stage.

It started with worry over a nagging cough. I went to the doctor and had some tests.

After receiving the diagnosis, I sat in my car and broke down, wondering how I would ever be able to drive home. I had to tell my children and watch them cry, knowing I'd failed them. I had to see the pity and horror on people's faces when they found out what I had brought on myself.

I struggled through each treatment — biopsies, surgeries, chemotherapy, radiation — in agonizing detail, just as if it were really happening. I watched my hair fall out in clumps and wore a wig that didn't look right.

I witnessed the agony it put my family through at the same time I went through an agony all my own. On top of it all, I had to deal with my own guilt and the mounting doctor bills.

In the end, I was forced to say goodbye to my family, my friends, and my life. I worried about what would happen to my children and pets, but it was too late. On and on and on the wretched dream went, refusing to allow me any escape. At long last, I was struggling for each breath on my deathbed.

When I finally "died," I was given the most incredible gift, a rebirth of sorts. It was a true awakening in every sense. I wasn't merely shaken and horrified. I was sobbing uncontrollably.

I woke up and staggered out of bed on wobbly legs, searched for my cigarettes as I wiped away the tears of relief. When I found them, I hurled them into the garbage, knowing without question that if I touched those things again, the nightmare would come true. For all I knew, it might still come true someday, but for the moment, I was going to do everything I possibly could to have more time.

That was more than a dozen years ago. I don't remember the exact date. I never commemorated it in any way because that was too much like quitting smoking. I wasn't quitting anything — I was starting over, choosing life. Even now, I continue to choose life every single day.

I used to tell myself I'd find "a better time" to quit smoking. I'd wait until I was less stressed. I'd wait until my life was more settled. I'd wait to get over the next hurdle first… but, of course, there are always more hurdles. Life is never settled. It is too dynamic.

Now I sometimes joke that I quit smoking, got a divorce, and went through menopause all at the same time, and they canceled each other out. I joke about it, but it's still true. I was already sleepless and crabby and sweaty and stressed, so what did a little more hurt? I decided it could only get better… and thanks to my nightmare, I always knew it could be much, much worse. I told myself I was entering this new stage of my life with a fresh start, no matter how crazily I was approaching it.

In fact, I was later surprised at just how much better things became.

The ups and downs are just the way life is. I accept and embrace that every single day. Sure, I was incredibly foolish to have started smoking in the first place, but I've worked hard to make better choices, and that feels good. Knowing I tackled a seemingly insurmountable goal gives me an amazing sense of empowerment. The dream did more for me than simply get me to quit smoking. It began a chain reaction that taught me I can change my life with one magic tool: resolve that is fierce enough to overcome my own ridiculous excuses.

My children are grown now, and I no longer have to worry about what would become of them if I died, but I still wouldn't touch a cigarette because of the (literal!) nightmare that smoking put me through. Recently, I had another dream of my mother.

She was standing in front of me, expressionless, as if waiting for something. "I quit smoking," I announced proudly, "and I feel wonderful."

This time, a slow smile spread across her face as she said, "I know."

~T'Mara Goodsell

36

Walk Backwards

Follow the light of your intuition, and keep
away from the darkness of convention.
~Michael Bassey Johnson

O h, my god, the searing pain! I could hardly get out of
my car. It felt like someone had stabbed me in the back.

The trip from St. Louis, Missouri, to Lexington,
Kentucky, takes about five hours on a normal day. But
this was no normal day! An ice storm had shut down the Midwest for
a week. I had already cancelled two appointments and could not wait
any longer to leave St. Louis and drive to Lexington.

I was terrified. Only one lane of I-64 was open because the rest of
the highway was blocked with snow and ice-covered. I saw semi-trucks
and cars in ditches, turned in all directions from losing control. My
hands gripped the steering wheel. I didn't dare use cruise control, so
I drove with one foot on the accelerator for the eight hours it took to
make the drive.

My whole being was tied up in knots. Exhausted, tense, and
afraid, I felt the muscles in my back getting tighter and tighter from
sitting so long in that awkward position.

When I finally reached my destination, I was alarmed. I could
tell that I had wrenched my back, and it was not going to relax. I had
never had that kind of pain before. I worried that if I lay down, I might
not be able to get up. I have a couple of friends who periodically have
their lower backs go out and can't move for days.

I could not afford to do that. I had already postponed my trip and had a series of appointments over the next few days in Lexington and Indianapolis. I had to be able to move and drive.

What could I do? I visited a chiropractor, who further upset me. He suggested I take muscle relaxers, return to him every day for a week, and then get adjusted every other day for another week. That was out of the question.

I had another resource to try: my dreams! I had never before incubated a dream for healing, but I had been keeping a dream journal for years and had heard tales of miraculous healings in dreams.

That night, before going to bed, I wrote in my dream journal: "Please give me a dream that tells me what I need to heal the pain in my lower back, and please let me wake up pain-free."

I was a bit skeptical that the searing pain could actually disappear overnight, but I thought if I was going to ask, I might as well ask for what I really wanted.

I went to sleep, exhausted from the drive and exhausted from the pain. The next morning, when I was in that not-quite-awake state, I heard in my mind a clear voice that said, "Walk backwards."

I wrote those words in my dream notebook: *Walk backwards!*

When I became fully awake, the first thing I did was gently stretch, and I noticed that I was, indeed, pain-free! That seemed like a miracle because I could hardly move when I went to bed!

I didn't want that good feeling to go away, so I just lay there quietly, contemplating the joy of being free of pain. Then I looked at my dream notebook and saw those words: Walk backwards.

Weird, I thought. But I figured I would try it, so I gingerly got up and walked around the room backwards.

It felt good! It seemed to adjust something by walking that way.

I had to get back in my car that morning to make the drive to Indianapolis. I dreaded it and wanted to listen to something to keep my mind off worrying about the treacherous road conditions. I didn't feel like listening to the radio, and for some unknown reason, I reached for a tape that was in my glove box. A friend had given it to me, and it had been there for months. Never before had it appealed to me, but that morning I felt the urge to pop it in the tape player.

It was an instructional lecture from a man who makes essential oils for healing purposes. He was talking about some of the countries where he travels, places that grow the plants from which he distills the oils. He described a trip to China and said that on the college campus there, the students walk backwards because it adjusts their spine!

Wow! It was a waking confirmation of the message from my dream.

Why did I feel the urge to listen to that tape that day? Hearing that message knocked me on the head, telling me that I had better pay attention to the message that came to me in my dream. Strange as it was, it worked.

Had I not heard it, I might have doubted my dream because it just seemed so weird. But twice in one day I received a wake-up call I couldn't ignore.

To this day, when I've been sitting in a car too long, I feel my lower back tighten up. So I get out at a rest stop and walk backwards. Even though the people around me might think I'm a bit strange, my dreams gave me some good advice, so I'm following it.

~Laurel Clark

37

Not My Time to Go

The heart of human excellence often begins to beat
when you discover a pursuit that absorbs you,
frees you, challenges you, or gives you a
sense of meaning, joy, or passion.
~Terry Orlick

I had not prepared myself for this news. "Unfortunately, you have breast cancer." Those words cut like a knife through the uneasy silence after I answered the phone.

I was still grieving the loss of my vivacious forty-six-year-old mother-in-law, Miss Linda, who, after a well-fought battle, passed away of the dreaded disease a year earlier. I didn't know much about breast cancer when Miss Linda told me of her diagnosis in 2003, one year after I married her only son. I remember going into research mode, the left side of my accountant brain hard at work. I discovered that the stage and size of the tumor determined survival, and when Miss Linda told me they had found it early enough to treat it, I stopped worrying. Chemotherapy after the surgery, she assured me, was more precaution than anything.

So, when her sister called me on a cold dreary winter day in January 2004, shortly after my husband Nate and I had celebrated and prayed in the New Year, I was confused by the tone of the conversation. "They rushed Linda to the hospital this morning because she was having trouble breathing. The doctor says there is fluid in her lungs." I ended the conversation quickly and called the hospital because it sounded like pneumonia to me, which, though serious, was not necessarily life-threatening. The nurse at the hospital desk patched me through to Miss Linda's room. Still somewhat out of breath, she said, "They are saying there is fluid on my lungs, and they think it's cancerous."

Later, I would learn that Miss Linda was actually diagnosed with advanced, terminal Stage 4 cancer after her first visit to the oncologist. It meant the cancer had metastasized and spread to her lungs. All of the surgery, chemotherapy, and drugs prescribed by Miss Linda's oncologist were done in hopes of extending her life because she would never be cured.

After this return trip to the hospital, my mother-in-law was advised to get her affairs in order. We were told she had ninety days to live. Miss Linda lived only half of that time. She had just gotten married months earlier and didn't even live to celebrate her first wedding anniversary. She didn't get to see her youngest daughter graduate high school, and she didn't live to meet her last three grandchildren. She made me promise that I would make sure her youngest daughter graduated from high school and went to college.

Now, here I was on an unusually warm day in May with the same diagnosis Miss Linda had received. Everything said by my surgeon after the words "breast cancer" was a blur. I heard "surgery," "mastectomy," "radiation," "staging," "chemotherapy," and "tumor size," but couldn't connect any of it. I had to call back with a friend after I had calmed down so I could figure out my next steps. I also had the difficult task of telling Nate, who was still grieving the loss of his beautiful, young mother to breast cancer. And I had to tell him the day before our third wedding anniversary.

I'm not going to lie. I thought death was certain. I only had Miss Linda's battle with breast cancer as a reference point, and it didn't look good for me. The surgeon told me that there was no way to determine how advanced the cancer was, but based on what he saw from the biopsy, it appeared to be small and at an early stage. But he still could not give me any assurances until the surgery, so I was not convinced I'd survive. Miss Linda appeared to be cured and thriving after her surgery, and then a year later, she was gone.

I told my husband about the diagnosis that night and then reassured him that I would be fine. After he fell asleep, I lay awake in the dark, wondering if I truly would be okay. After what felt like an eternity, I finally drifted off into much-needed slumber. And then Miss Linda came to me in a dream.

Dressed in all white, Sunday Best finery, Miss Linda appeared with a woman from my childhood, Miss Bea, who had passed on some time before. Miss Linda sat down in a rocking chair on her mother's porch. Her mother's house was always the gathering spot after church most Sundays for family fun and delicious Southern comfort food that one could smell miles away. I sat at Miss Linda's feet and did not move. I hung on her every word, delighted she was there. Nonstop laughter permeated the balmy spring air until dusk started to fall rapidly.

Miss Linda abruptly announced that it was time for her and Miss Bea to go. I started bawling and begged her to let me go with them, but she refused. After my incessant begging, Miss Linda finally relented, but it was clear from her body language she wasn't happy about me accompanying them on their trip home.

I told her I couldn't go dressed in what I had on and needed to go change into my "white" clothing because they were dressed in theirs. I made her promise not to leave me, but when I returned in my beautiful white gown, I saw Miss Bea and Miss Linda drifting away in the distance, the setting sun outlining Miss Linda's frame in a ray of perfect light. I started screaming in the dream, and real tears woke me up.

My chest was tight, and my eyes were wet, but I knew what that dream meant. It wasn't my time to go.

Blessedly, I survived breast cancer — not just once, but twice. I took the spirit of my mother-in-law with me through my countless treatments (radiation, chemotherapy) and my surgeries (lumpectomies, full mastectomy, reconstruction, reconstruction complications and reconstruction again). I became a breast cancer advocate and spokesperson, volunteering with Susan G. Komen. I became the face of the Race for the Cure in 2013. I also became a board member and later president of the Bridge Breast Network, an agency that provides free, life-saving medical care to uninsured and underinsured women diagnosed with breast cancer. And I started my own nonprofit called Sock It to Cancer, which provides comfort items (socks, blankets, house shoes and pillows) to women in active treatment for breast cancer.

My long-term plan for my nonprofit is to honor Miss Linda by providing scholarships to college-bound students who have lost their mothers to breast cancer. I know she would be proud that in my personal pain I found my purpose. Every time I share her story or honor her in some way, her legacy lives on. And I thank her for coming to me in that dream and reassuring me that it wasn't my time to go.

~Sheila Taylor-Clark

Drawing Inspiration from Dreamland

*A dream is a small hidden door in the deepest and
most intimate sanctum of the soul, which opens
up to that primeval cosmic night that was the
soul, long before there was the conscious ego.*
~Carl Jung

"Come on, Sir Charles, get up and get to class," *NBA Hall
of Famer Charles Barkley told me. Barkley was right.
I needed to wake up. Class was starting, and I was
still asleep. My subconscious was using the 1993
NBA MVP to motivate me.*

*"Hey, Cha-lee, what do you say you get to class, my man? Do us all a
favor, Cha-lee." Academy Award winner Christopher Walken leaned over
my bed, looking down on me as he did Snoop Doggy Dogg in the music video
for "Murder Was the Case."*

I started having these dreams a lot as I neared graduation from the
University of Kentucky. The dreams worked. I made more of an effort
to get to class on time. I found myself feeling guilty, albeit amused,
and I stopped skipping out on morning classes.

Celebrity appearances in my dreams, however, haven't stopped.
Ever since I was little, I've experienced celebrity cameos in dreams.
I've met Eddie Vedder, Fiona Apple, Kurt Cobain, Michael Jordan,
Edward Norton... the list goes on.

The cameos weren't always friendly, especially when I was little.

I used to wake up screaming in the middle of the night. I'd run to my mom and dad's bedroom and nearly fall on my face after tripping on our black Lab, Amanda.

"We grew to accept and expect it," Dad said, "even Amanda."

Every night, it was the same guy after me. It started in 1988 during the Presidential election.

"Bush is the good guy; Dukakis is the bad guy," my dad told me. I was five at the time.

My subconscious then created a monster. Despite looking more like Howdy Doody than Michael Dukakis (or, as I called him, "Dukonkis"), he was more terrifying than anything.

If Dukakis appeared in the dream, I had to close my eyes and hold my hands over my eyes. If I was unable to do so, Dukakis would capture and torture me.

But as I grew, the nightmares faded. Dukakis even apologized about ten years later, appearing in a dream looking like a beatnik professor, wearing a red turtleneck and sporting a brown ponytail.

Intrigued by my vivid and unpredictable dream world, I began researching the art of interpretation.

These dreams, often humorous, aren't just entertaining; they are insightful. Using the dream interpretation techniques created by Carl Jung, there is much I can discover about myself if I take the time to explore the meaning behind the dreams and the reason for the cameos.

According to Jung, the dream is about the dreamer, and those who appear in our dreams represent a part of us, a quality we have — perhaps even a quality we haven't been using or forgot was important to us.

For example, I met six-time NBA champion Michael Jordan in a dream, perhaps to remind myself to strive for greatness. I had the dream when I was feeling guilty for not living up to my potential.

Just as I had celebrities encouraging me to go to class, I have had celebrities encourage my passions. Johnny Cash encouraged me to write more songs. In this particular dream, my subconscious used

Cash to represent my interest and passion for writing songs based on hardships.

Some dreams are harder to explain.

In 2004, I dreamt about a high school friend named Jason dying while participating in a robbery. The details are foggy, but I remember I was supposed to have been with him. Instead, I was stuck without a ride at some seedy apartment in a bad part of Indianapolis.

Two days later, a friend from high school called and told me Jason had died the same night I had the dream. I hadn't talked to Jason in years, and I didn't know what to think of this bizarre, random premonition.

Months later, I met with Jason in a dream for lunch at a mall food court.

"I don't know why you dreamed about me that night," he said, "but I want you to know that I am all right. I'm in a better place now."

Having such premonitions inspired me to learn more about dream interpretation. I would not just interpret mine, but I'd interpret others.

At a house party in Kalamazoo, Michigan, I ended up with a line of people asking me to explore the meaning of their significant dreams. It started with a casual conversation, and it ended up going on for what felt like hours.

"I was stuck on an escalator," one girl told me, "with my ex-boyfriend."

"Are there characteristics your ex has that you see in yourself? What are they? Are any of those characteristics stalling you from moving forward?"

Around this same time, I had a dream I was going to die at twenty-five, which scared me.

In the dream, I sat by a placid river surrounded by green hills and mountains. The scenery reminded me of the Gallatin Valley in Montana.

A black woman with bright white wings walked over to me, smiling.

"Am I dead?" I asked.

"Yes," she said. "You're twenty-five."

"No, I'm only twenty-three."

"Oh, then you still have some time," she said encouragingly.

Concerned, I went to see a Jungian analyst. She told me I had nothing to worry about.

"Death in a dream represents change," she said. "Perhaps twenty-five will be a big year for you in other ways. Perhaps you will truly awaken."

There is much significance to this truth, and I have carried it with me ever since. After all, the Jungian analyst was right. At twenty-five, I moved to a small town in eastern Montana where I knew no one and started writing for a twice-weekly paper. Today, I continue to enjoy my career in journalism.

Just as Barkley and Walken motivated me to get to class in college, pop-culture characters continue to motivate, inspire or just remind me to enjoy life to the fullest, one dream at a time. Whether it's about doing what you should be doing, being yourself or finding yourself, there is much to learn from the dream world. I encourage everyone to buy a journal and keep it by the bed. The more you write down your dreams, the more you will remember them. You may be surprised what you discover.

~Charlie Denison

Dream Prep

For the night is dark and full of terrors.
~George R.R. Martin

I woke with a gasp to the sound of someone screaming. I sat up in bed and waited, trying to listen for sounds outside my bedroom, but it was difficult to hear because my heart was pounding so loudly. After a minute or two of foggy post-sleep confusion, I realized the sound must have been coming from me. I'd been dreaming.

In this dream, I was driving down the freeway, and a little red car cut me off. I slammed on my brakes and lost control of my little pickup truck. It started spinning across the busy freeway lanes like a crazy carnival ride, and I was screaming.

I had a hard time getting back to sleep that night. I was extra careful on my drive to and from work the next day, ever watchful for little red cars, but nothing out of the ordinary happened. The next night, I had another bad dream.

Again, I was driving on the freeway, but this time it wasn't a little red car. A large black pickup truck in the lane to my right started swerving and coming into my lane. I swerved to the left to avoid being hit, but I hit the barrier, and my truck turned sideways, partially blocking the lane. An oncoming car hit the back end of my truck and pinned me against the barrier. The car that hit me came to rest against the driver's side of my truck, and the passenger side was against the barrier, effectively trapping me. I was hurt terribly.

I woke up screaming again. Every night for a little more than a week, I woke from a horrific nightmare involving a crash. I was scared to drive, but I had to get to work. My vigilance while driving became heightened. I felt the need to watch every car on the road with me, just in case. I left plenty of room between my vehicle and the vehicle in front of me, especially on the freeway. But I was getting tired. I wasn't getting enough sleep.

During the last nightmare, something changed. It wasn't as if I realized I was dreaming, but instead it seemed that my hyper-vigilant driving carried over into my dream.

I was in the right lane on the freeway this time, and I saw two cars collide ahead of me. Because I was paying attention and leaving extra space, I was able to get onto the shoulder and drive around the accident.

I don't remember the rest of the dream, but for the first time in several days, I didn't wake up screaming.

Then the nightmares stopped. I wondered why I was having a recurring dream. Even though the accidents were different each time and involved different types of vehicles, it was strange to dream about car crashes over and over. Enough days passed that I stopped wondering and got lost in the details of day-to-day life.

Even so, I remained extra aware of the cars around me. I kept my phone and radio off while I was driving. I always paid attention to the amount of space in front of my truck and noticed whether there were vehicles in the lanes next to me.

And then it happened. I was driving to work on the freeway — the same freeway I drove every day and the same freeway from the nightmares. I was in the lane next to the far left lane. Ahead of me, a little red car suddenly moved to the right with no turn signal or other warning, directly in front of a semi. The red car cut off the semi, and the semi braked hard. Even though it happened so fast, everything seemed to slow down.

The semi hit the back of the little red car, and the back end of the semi started moving toward the left, toward the lane I was in. I was flying down the freeway, just like everyone else. A car behind the semi moved to the right to avoid becoming part of the accident, but ended up hitting another car.

I was strangely calm. I felt as if I'd done this exact thing before. I had to decide, in a split second, whether to brake or try to get around what was quickly becoming a tangled mass of damaged vehicles. Because I'd been paying attention to my surroundings, I knew there was no vehicle in the lane to my left. Without slowing down, I moved into the far left lane, partially onto the left shoulder, and got around the back end of the semi before it came all the way into that lane. It was close, but I got safely around the accident.

I pulled onto the shoulder, still oddly calm and somewhat surprised at myself, and called 911 to report the accident. There were several people out of their vehicles and help was on the way, so I got back on the road and went to work.

I saw the story on the news later. The accident involved eight vehicles. Luckily, everyone involved escaped with fairly minor injuries. And thanks to all those scary dreams, I managed to stay calm and avoid becoming one of the victims.

~Rachel Fort

40

Working It Out

We cannot accomplish all that we need
to do without working together.
~Bill Richardson

I have never been one to find much meaning in my dreams. In fact, my dreams are usually so chaotic and confusing that I sometimes wonder what that says about the state of my mind! I will never forget, however, two dreams that were so clear, meaningful, and helpful that they instantly healed my relationship with two co-workers at the advertising agency where I was a writer.

The first dream involved a man with whom I was always butting heads. We could never see eye to eye, and we argued about almost everything. One night, I dreamed this man and I were at it again — yelling and screaming and stomping our feet. Suddenly, another person entered the room, looked around, and said, "Oh, I'm sorry. I was looking for some adults."

When I woke up the next morning, not only was that dream still clear in my mind, but its meaning was also obvious. I was behaving like a child! My heated exchanges with this man were little more than temper tantrums I was throwing because I couldn't get my way.

After that dream, I finally began to behave like the forty-year-old professional I was.

The second dream occurred only a few months later. I had been assigned a permanent partner to work with — a lovely lady I'll call Linda. Our partnership was supposed to be ideal because we were both very much alike — perfectionists. Can you see the potential problem here?

Two perfectionists don't work well together when their ideas about perfection differ! On a personal basis, I really liked Linda because I could relate to her persnickety ways. But our professional relationship was quickly growing tense and uncomfortable.

Then, one night, I dreamed that Linda walked up to me in the lobby of our office building, and we embraced. And as we embraced, I felt genuine love for Linda. I didn't feel like I was "in love" with her exactly, but I certainly felt a very deep sense of compassion for this lady.

And guess what? When I woke up the next morning, that warm, tender feeling stayed with me. And from that point on, I was able to treat Linda with the loving kindness she deserved. Sure, we still had our differences of opinion. But after that dream, I was able to work things out with her in a way that was much more patient and respectful. My heart had opened up, and our troubled relationship was healed.

To this day, I don't know whether those dreams were something that arose from my own personal psyche or were something more "heaven-sent." All I know is how grateful I was — and still am — for the power of dreams to resolve a troubling issue in an instant.

~Steven Lane Taylor

41

Stay of Execution

Out of difficulties grow miracles.
~Jean de la Bruyère

Less than ten days before Christmas, Greta, our party planning lady dropped by my office to remind me I needed to bring a "dish to pass" for the university's computer department Christmas party on December 18th.

"You know, I'm not coming, Greta," I reminded her.

Greta's eyes grew wet. She was such a wonderful person, and I hated to upset her. She nodded and smiled. Patting my arm, she turned and left. I was the talk of my department — probably of half the university — because of my legal entanglements in divorce court over the last few years. Most people get their lives back on track in a few years, but not me!

In fact, I had been in divorce court for almost six years and would remain there for over a decade more. There were no assets. My children and I had lived in poverty as my husband never wanted to work.

At the time, my children would, by court order, spend the Christmas holidays with him. I had taken food, clothing, toys, supplies, and even buckets of water up to his isolated cabin (without plumbing) in the mountains, which they all enjoyed. He felt he should personally receive regular cash payments from me instead of getting a job because he was so wounded from the divorce. He had explained that repeatedly to the courts over the past years. If they were taking away his property (me), he needed to be compensated. How else could he live? The children were not his concern as they had always lived in poverty.

Of course, everyone who knew me, including my co-workers, knew all the intimate details of my divorce: The sheriff came, the process server came, my ex-husband came, all bringing news of hastily arranged court dates set without my knowledge. I used up all my vacation and sick days going to various courts in various counties on bogus motions.

Now, I was to start a six-month sentence at the local jail on December 18th for littering and trespassing, a direct result of the ugly battle with my ex-husband. I had "trespassed" on his property when I dropped off the children's Christmas gifts — the "littering." I had resigned my position effective the afternoon of December 18th, with no clue of a future.

The shame and humiliation were awful, but not as hard as the fact that I had been trying to finish my college degree for decades. It was very important now so I could be a good example for my children and provide for them.

My stuff was packed in storage. I had found a place to stash my car. The night of the seventeenth, I laid out my clothes for work, trying hard not to think about the next day and what I was about to experience.

About 3:00 a.m., I woke, but I thought I was dreaming. Three words were lodged in my brain: "Stay of Execution." The only time I had heard those words was on the news when someone was waiting for the electric chair or the gas chamber. But I was to learn that "stay of execution" refers to any decision that stops or undoes a court order or judgment. I didn't have an attorney, though, so those words didn't mean anything to me.

I got out of bed, dressed, and ate breakfast. I tried to write an argument as to why the court shouldn't send me to jail for six months for trespassing and littering, stressing that even if I were guilty of these charges, they were not usually offenses that resulted in jail time, plus that I needed to take care of my children and keep my job.

I stayed very level headed as I got ready for work. When I would start to slip into panic mode, the words would come back into my head: "Stay of Execution!" I didn't even know how that would work but I couldn't stop thinking about those words that had come to me in the night.

I was there when the university library opened at 7:00 a.m. I quickly found a legal book with a court form for a "Stay of Execution," typing it out at one of the computers. The words in my head — "Stay of Execution" — were coming as often as my heartbeat. I worked hard and fast, writing down my reasons why I should not go to jail on a bogus claim for something that would normally just generate a fine. Pushing the print button, I grabbed the multiple copies of the court motion and tore across campus to my office, arriving just on time.

One of my supervisors called about a computer issue. After that was resolved, I asked to leave for an early lunch to take some papers to court. "Sure," came the sad reply.

At 11:00 a.m., I walked the half mile to the courthouse. The clerk's office directed me to a judge's clerk.

"Oh, he went to lunch early," the clerk said. "But you can sit down and wait for him. I will give him your papers." The papers were rather rumpled by now.

I sat on a hard, wooden bench in a long hallway. As I looked up, a man in business clothes approached me. He was a district court judge with my wrinkled papers in his hand. I watched his mouth for words.

"I signed your Stay of Execution," he said. I wasn't dreaming those words! I had heard him say them. Apparently, he thought I misunderstood.

"I have signed your Stay of Execution papers," he said very loudly. "Good luck!"

I yelled, "Thank you!" and ran down the long hall and stairs. I ran all the way to the computer department office. Greta was greeting the party guests at the door. "What are you doing here? I thought you weren't coming." There were tears in her eyes again. She led me to a chair, took my paperwork, and went to find the boss. Someone brought me a glass of water. I was too winded to even talk.

My boss was all smiles. "Grab yourself some party food, and when you are done, come see me in my office. I have a surprise." The

Christmas party turned into a wild victory celebration for me. The boss was waiting when I arrived at his office. "You know you are a good employee, so I am going to throw out your resignation letter. We are glad you are back."

While I was taken aback with his kindness, I knew I couldn't accept his offer. "No," I told him, "I can't come back."

I went home and signed up for my final semester of college to start in January. Christmas didn't exist in the traditional sense that year for me as I spent everything I had on tuition and books.

But less than six months later, I graduated debt-free with an English degree that had taken decades to finish. Yes, I heard those words, "Stay of Execution," again in my head as I walked across the platform to receive my diploma.

Nothing, I believe, is an accident. God always has my back, even when he's filling in as my lawyer.

~Ela Oakland

Hopes and Dreams

New beginnings are often disguised as painful endings.
~Lao Tzu

I bolted upright in bed, tugging at the sweat soaked T-shirt that clung to my heaving chest. Every hair on the back of my neck stood on end. I blinked and rubbed my tear stained eyes as I frantically reached out for my husband, who was snoozing beside me.

"Are you okay?" Todd asked groggily, placing his hand on my shoulder. "You were clearly having a nightmare."

I touched my face. My cheeks were wet with tears.

"It was so strange," I mumbled. "I dreamt that I was living back in Indiana... with my parents."

Todd chuckled. "No wonder that freaked you out. I know how much you love living here."

He was right. After Todd and I graduated from college, we got married and moved south so he could pursue a doctoral degree from Florida State University. I promptly fell in love with our new life in the Sunshine State — the palm trees, eternal warmth, and blue skies. The fire ants and cockroaches I could do without, but everything else was an utter dream. I loved my job. My friends. My neighbors. My church.

That's partly why this dream had me so rattled. My trembling hand squeezed Todd's, and I said, "It wasn't just about living with Mom and Dad. I woke up with a profound sadness in my heart." I hesitated. "I don't know. It's hard to explain. Something just felt ominous."

"Well, you can relax," Todd said. "It wasn't real."

"But it seemed so real," I muttered breathlessly. "In the dream, I was lying in bed, sobbing uncontrollably."

"Well, don't worry," Todd said, as he readjusted his pillow and rolled to face the other way. "We're not going anywhere."

"You promise?" I asked. I had never been so desperate for reassurance in all my life.

"Yes, I promise," he said.

And just like that, the bizarre but vivid dream started to fade from my memory. Years passed, and I never had another one that affected me so deeply. In fact, most nights I slept like a baby and awoke feeling rested. It was the days that wore me out, especially as Todd progressed in the stressful doctoral program.

Graduate school took a toll on our marriage as Todd immersed himself in classes, study groups, dissertation work, and mega amounts of research. Thankfully, I managed to get pregnant after eight years of marriage. The pregnancy gave me something wonderful to focus on.

"I'm so excited to become a parent," I told my mom one day. "But I must admit that I'm worried Todd won't be a hands-on dad. How could he be? He's never around."

"I'm sure it'll get better when he earns his degree," Mom said. "He'll have more time for you and the baby then."

I hoped she was right. As it was now, communication between me and Todd was pretty much nonexistent. So was our joy.

Once our son was born, I was elated, but I was also sleep deprived and overwhelmed. Todd didn't have time to help take care of the baby because he was so wrapped up in post-graduate responsibilities. We rarely spent time together as a family or as a couple, so we continued to grow farther apart. On top of it all, graduate school had transformed Todd into a hypercritical person. He had been taught to overanalyze everything he touched, and that bled into his family life.

When he came home at night, he snapped at me if the house wasn't picked up or I'd folded the towels the wrong way. If I pulled too far into the garage or the yogurt was placed on the wrong shelf of the refrigerator, he let me know. As a result, every night when I heard the garage door go up, my body tensed, and my stomach knotted. *What would I get into trouble for today?* The constant turmoil in my heart was shriveling up my soul.

Every night for a solid eighteen months, I said the same prayer. "Please, Lord," I asked. "Lead me to whatever path I'm meant to be on. Help me find my way back to happiness."

I didn't know when an answer would come. All I knew was that despite being married, I felt very much alone. I took my baby to the park, gym, library, zoo, or grocery store, but Todd never joined us. People at church assumed I was a single mother. Six months later, they were right.

Todd and I divorced, and I moved in with my parents. It was a whirlwind. I spent weeks packing, moving, filing paperwork, and job hunting, all while taking care of my son. I had little time to process the many changes in my life. Then, one Friday night, I collapsed into bed, dog-tired but wide awake.

A roar of anger shot through me, and I sat up in bed, hurling pillows across the room as hard and as fast as I could. I screamed and cried — that kind of ugly, guttural, uncontrollable cry that's reserved for childbirth. In between sobs, I shouted, "I can't believe this is my life!" The harsh words echoed on the bare walls and bounced back to me like a boomerang.

I felt like a loser. I had emancipated myself from my parents in my twenties when I built a career for myself in Florida — and a nice house, to boot. Now here I was, thirty-four years old and living back home with my parents and my kid — like some sort of lame high school dropout.

Exhausted and emotionally spent, I fell back onto the mattress, now devoid of pillows, and stared blankly at the ceiling through swollen, burning eyes. Finally, my heavy eyelids fluttered shut.

In the stillness, I could hear my shallow breath and feel my steady heartbeat. Then, as if I were struck by lightning, my eyes popped open, and I clutched my chest and gasped. My heart started racing as I realized that this was my dream from three years earlier — the one that frightened me so.

It was like déjà vu with a twist. I had dreamt about this very night, and now I was living it. This was the moment I so feared, but now that I was in the thick of this reality, it wasn't so frightening. Suddenly, my panic vanished, and a sense of calm washed over me. The premonition proved that I could survive that which I feared the most and still come out on the other side.

I wasn't a loser. I was a survivor. A strong one at that.

I walked across the room to gather my pillows. I tossed them back on the bed and crawled under the covers, eager to tap into my subconscious mind. Perhaps tonight's dream would give me another glimpse into the future—a future filled with uncertainty, yes, but mostly hope.

~Christy Heitger-Ewing

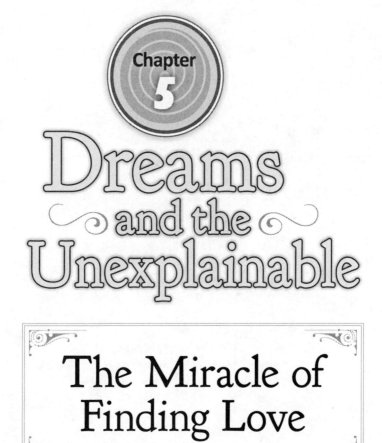

Chapter 5

Dreams and the Unexplainable

The Miracle of Finding Love

Dream Girl

You know you're in love when you can't fall asleep
because reality is finally better than your dreams.
~Author Unknown

The dreams started when I was a senior at Berkeley High School in 1974. About a month before I graduated, I fell asleep in a physics class after lunch and had the first dream:

A beautiful Asian woman was standing next to me, talking in a strange language. She was stunning — the most beautiful girl I had ever seen. She was in her early twenties, with long black hair, and piercing black eyes. She had the look of royalty. She looked at me and then disappeared, beamed out of my dream like in Star Trek. I fell out of my chair screaming, "Who are you?" She did not answer.

About a month went by, and then I started having the dream repeatedly. Always the same pattern.

Early morning, she would stand next to me talking. I would ask who she was, and she would disappear. She was the most beautiful, alluring woman I had ever seen.

I was struck speechless every time I had the dream.

I had the dream every month during the eight years I went to college and served in the Peace Corps. In fact, when I joined the Peace Corps, I had to decide whether to go to Korea or Thailand. The night before I had to submit my decision, I had the dream again and it made me sure that she was in Korea waiting for me.

After the Peace Corps, I still hadn't met my dream woman. I got a job working for the U.S. Army as an instructor and stayed in Korea. I kept having the dream, until I had the very last one: *She was standing next to me, speaking to me in Korean, but I finally understood her. She said, "Don't worry, we will be together soon."*

Why was that the last time I had the dream? Because the very next night, the girl in my dream got off the bus in front of me. She went on to the base with an acquaintance of mine, a fellow teacher, and they went to see a movie. I saw her and found the courage to speak with her. We exchanged phone numbers and agreed to meet that weekend.

The next night, she was waiting for me as I entered the Army base to teach a class. She told me she was a college senior and she had something to tell me. I signed her on to the base and left her at the library to study while I taught, and then we went out for coffee after class. She told me she was madly in love with me, and that I was the man for her. I told her not to worry as I felt the same.

That weekend, we met Saturday and Sunday and hung out all day. On Sunday night, I proposed to her. It was only three days after we had met, but for me it felt like we had met eight years ago. I had been waiting all my life for her to walk out of my dreams and into my life, and here she was.

Her mother did not want her to marry a foreigner. One day, about a month after we met, she invited me to meet her parents. I brought a bottle of Jack Daniels for her father and drank the entire bottle with him. He approved of me, but her mother still had reservations. After a Buddhist priest told her my future wife and I were a perfect astrological combination, she agreed, and we planned our wedding.

The wedding was a media sensation in South Korea. My wife explained it to me years later. At the time, I was overwhelmed just by the fact that we were getting married and I didn't fully understand how unusual this was. My wife was of the old royal clan, distant relatives to the former kings of Korea. In the clan's history, only two people had ever married foreigners: my wife, and Rhee Syngman, who was the first President of South Korea. My father, who was a former Undersecretary of Labor, came out for the wedding, which fueled even more media interest. Our marriage defied the stereotypical Korean-foreign marriage where the women married some hapless GI just to escape poverty and immigrate to the U.S. We were the first foreign/Korean couple to get married at a Korean Army base. Over 1,000 people came to the wedding, and my father was interviewed on the morning news programs.

This all happened thirty-five years ago, and I am still married to the girl in my dreams. Now, whenever we are apart, I still see her in my dreams, watching over me as I sleep.

~Jake Cosmos Aller

One Last Thing

Dreams are today's answers to tomorrow's questions.
~Edgar Cayce

When I was in high school, I was certain that I had my life figured out. I was going to graduate, go to college, and have a great career. None of my plans included marriage. I thought I would never find someone, mainly because no one had ever been interested in me. At least, that's what it seemed like. I had crushes, and had even asked a boy or two out, but I was always rejected.

This was something that I kept to myself. Nobody knew my deepest fear about my future. Then, one night in December 1997, I had a dream that changed my outlook.

I was walking aboard a Navy ship with my grandpa. He was showing me around and talking to me about my worries of being alone. He said I needed to let go of the idea that I would be alone because he knew I would have love in my life. We stopped in a room where a sailor was standing with his back toward us. All I could see of him was that he was tall and had dark hair.

"Here, sweetheart," my grandpa said. "This is the man you will marry. He will love you more than you know. Please do not worry anymore. You are going to be okay."

I woke up after that to the sound of my sister sobbing downstairs. A chill passed through me, and I knew something terrible had happened. I rushed downstairs, worried that something had happened to my sister's disabled son. I was relieved to see him lying in his crib, just fine, but I turned into the living room to see my family gathered. They all wore sad expressions. The grandfather I had just dreamt about had died.

I didn't want to believe it. I had just seen him a few days earlier. He was healthy and happy. He had just married a few months before, after a long time of being alone after my grandmother had passed away.

My dad told us that it seemed like Grandpa knew his time had come that morning. He had woken up, kissed his new wife, told her he loved her, retrieved his temple clothes from his closet, and laid them out. Then he lay back down and passed soon afterward.

I would also come to learn that I was not the only one who had dreamt of him the night before. I knew then that my dream was him saying goodbye.

Four years later, I was in a much better place. I had more confidence. I no longer worried about being alone, even though I thought marriage was a long way off. I had had a few relationships by then and knew I would find the right man when the time was right. I was preparing to attend school in California. I had also just started to speak regularly to a new guy friend on the phone. He had just re-enlisted in the Navy. Our conversations grew into a long-distance relationship.

In November 2002, I married that friend. Shortly after I did, I was telling him about how I wished he could have met my grandpa. Talking about him reminded me of the dream I had the morning he passed away. I cried, not because I was sad, but because I realized the dream was not just a goodbye. My grandpa had shown me my future husband after all.

~M.D. Krider

45

Twenty-Five Reasons Why

If ever two were one, then surely we.
~Anne Bradstreet

In 1956, after high school graduation, I found myself aboard the Michigan Empire State Express train en route to New York City. Along with a steamer trunk of clothing, I carried my Screen Actors Guild card representing fifteen years of professional childhood acting, modeling, and singing experience punctuated by hours of piano study and competitions. My parents had invested in me; the New York trip was a gift, their way of giving me wings. I wanted to make them proud. Always the obedient Catholic daughter, my pattern of daily life had been cut with my mother's scissors. I was leaving behind a childhood I had never visited.

Like many other ingénues harboring dreams of Broadway and billboards, I moved into the prestigious Barbizon Hotel for Women on East 63rd Street. The hotel's previous residents included the likes of Lauren Bacall and Grace Kelly. Excitement and possibility coursed through me as I planned my new start in Manhattan. I'd continue my training at the American Theatre Wing, go on casting calls, and seek commercial work and parts in off-Broadway plays.

What I hadn't planned on was the loneliness. Perhaps that's what drove me inside the Church of St. Vincent Ferrer one afternoon as I walked down busy Lexington Avenue. I had stopped to admire the church's magnificent architecture and suddenly remembered a prayer card I'd once found: *St. Francis, please lead me to those I seek and to those who are seeking me.*

An invisible hand seemed to push me inside the attached five-story brick priory that day. There I found Father Francis. He wore a white robe and a long rosary around his neck. He extended a warm hand. I laughed at his introduction. "Really?" I said. "Francis?" Then I told him about the prayer card.

He seemed amused. "Do you often pray to St. Francis?"

I blushed. "Only when seeking God's direction."

"Well, then." His eyes looked into mine. "God has directed you to me."

Father Francis became my spiritual advisor and friend. His church became a refuge from the chaotic city. On certain nights, I'd rush from the theater straight to St. Vincent's to watch cloistered monks chant the evening service. Amazingly, I learned that Father Francis had a theatre background. In addition to his theological wisdom, this Dominican priest knew the lure of the stage as well as its pitfalls.

One day, feeling disillusioned by the proverbial "casting couch," I told Father Francis that I was thinking of giving it all up to become a nun, something I had considered as a young teenager. "I saw an ad for the Carmelite Sisters of St. Teresa," I explained, waiting for his enthusiastic response. "I've started my application."

Father Francis chuckled. "Jocelyn, my dear, do you realize that the Carmelites take a perpetual vow of silence? You wouldn't last a day!"

Then he told me I should start dating.

Strangely, a few days later, I got a phone call from a man who introduced himself as a friend of Bill Friedberg, the jewelry store owner I had worked for before leaving Detroit. "Bill gave me your number," the stranger on the phone said. He introduced himself as Byron Krieger, also from Detroit, and in New York for the week. After a bit of small talk, Byron casually mentioned that he was an athlete — a fencer — training for his second Olympics. I was impressed. Then he asked, "Would you be interested in having lunch with me?"

I smiled, thinking about the Carmelite application still sitting on my desk. "Sure."

We arranged to meet at the theater after my morning rehearsal.

"How will I recognize you?" I asked.

"I'll be wearing a blue suit. Just look for my fencing pin on the lapel."

I didn't tell him I was nearsighted.

I stepped out of the theater the next morning wondering if Father Francis would approve of a blind date.

And then I saw him. We moved toward each other like magnets. My heart was pounding. Byron was tall and trim and exceptionally handsome, with dark hair and blue eyes.

He looked surprised as he approached me. "You're... so young!"

I guess Mr. Friedberg forgot to tell Byron that I was still a teenager. I was afraid to ask Byron's age.

He took me to lunch at the Penthouse Club overlooking Central Park. I could barely appreciate the spectacular view as I couldn't take my eyes off Byron. The minutes turned to hours, and our conversation flowed. Later, we strolled down Fifth Avenue.

He called me the next day. Would I help him shop for a wedding gift for a friend of his? Between the china and linens at Bloomingdale's, Byron's hand found mine.

The next night, we sat in box seats for the show *Damn Yankees*. By the third act, Byron's arm slid around me. I could barely breathe.

The next day, I watched him practice at the Fencers Club. Byron, decked out in a white uniform and brandishing his foil, charged down the strip toward his opponent. The strength and grace in his movements captivated me. My knight in white armor! I was in love.

Saturday night was our last evening together before he left for the Olympics in Melbourne. We danced the tango in a candlelit restaurant. After dinner, I knew it was time to ask the questions I'd been afraid to ask, and Byron seemed to avoid. I learned that he had been briefly married, was a non-religious Jew, and thirty-six years old. Three strikes.

I tried pushing this new knowledge out of my mind as Byron took me on a late-night horse and carriage ride around Central Park. He turned my face toward his and kissed me for the first time.

The next day, Byron left for Australia, and I ran to St. Vincent's. I cried to Father Francis, "What am I supposed to do?"

"Wait for Byron to come back. Then get to know him better."

"But he's Jewish!"

Father Francis grinned. "So was Jesus."

"And he's seventeen years older than me!"

"So, get him a wheelchair."

I stared at Father. "And he's divorced."

"We'll cross that bridge…"

I saw tears in Father's eyes. What was he trying to tell me? *St. Francis, please lead me to those I seek and to those who are seeking me.*

Father Francis remained my lifelong friend until his death a few years ago. And I married Byron and we both became observant Jews.

We had fifty-seven wonderful years together until Byron passed away at age ninety-five. Our union resulted in six children, sixteen grandchildren, and three great-grandchildren — twenty-five human reminders that the synchronicity of finding the prayer card and walking into the priory changed my life forever.

~Jocelyn Ruth Krieger

46

We Dreamed a Little Dream

*If two people are meant for each other, it doesn't mean
they have to be together right now or as soon
as possible, but they will... eventually.*
~Nina Ardianti

From the time I was a very little child, my dreams were vivid and real. Most of them were filled with images of playing in sunny meadows or flying over surreal places, so dreams of the more ordinary sort simply passed through my consciousness like the blur outside a train window. But there was one particular dream that felt very special, and I knew it, even though I was only about five years old.

My great-grandparents emigrated from Japan to the Hawaiian Islands at the turn of the 19th century. Four generations later, my family still held onto some Japanese cultural practices. One of them was the *furo* bath where, after washing with soap and water outside the tub, we would enter the hot water to soak. The temperature of the water is notoriously hot. In the old country, it would be heated over burning coals. The entire village would take turns soaking in a large public bath.

Although our modern day *furo* was not heated with coals, but just very hot water from the faucet, I recall being worried that the water would cook me. Boil me alive. I learned to enter very slowly, one toe at a time, as my body acclimated to the searing heat. By the time I emerged, my skin was lobster red. Cooked lobster red. But I loved it. We all loved soaking in the *furo*. It made us feel clean inside and out.

One night, I dreamed that I was sitting in an old-fashioned Japanese furo. *My great-grandmother, with her white hair pulled into a tight bun, sat nearby crocheting and looking up occasionally to be sure I was safe. Next to me was a little blond boy. He was a little older than I was, and we didn't speak to each other at all. But we were friends. That much I could tell because of the overwhelming feeling of wellbeing and happiness I felt while with this playmate.*

And when I woke up, that was all I could remember: A sweet joy. All I knew was that I wanted to spend time with my friend. But waking life compelled me to focus on growing up, and so I did.

Little did I know that thousands of miles away and across the vast Pacific blue, a little blond boy was growing up, too.

And he, too, had had a dream.

Nearly twenty years later, I was living in California and struggling to end a five-year relationship. One night, I went to bed, sad and uncertain, and prayed to God: "Please, God, help me to know what to do. If it is your will that I marry this man, I will stay with him. If not… if there is someone else for me, please let me know."

That night, I had a dream that I saw a filmy veil that hung like a curtain across the window. I saw the shadow of a figure of a man. And my heart skipped a beat. There was someone else for me.

The next day, I made a clean break. And then, like an ensign that signaled my new beginning, I got a new job, in Newport Beach in advertising. And one week into my new job a blond man walked through the door.

When our eyes locked, something tangible occurred. We both felt it. There was something so familiar about us together. So much so that the company secretary who had been sitting at the front desk came to me later to ask, "What was *that*? Something *happened*. What's going on?"

I didn't know, frankly. All I did know was that there was something remarkable and alluring about this man, and all I wanted to do was be with him. We had our first date of many that night. As time passed, we talked about everything from our families to our career goals, and then finally, our childhoods.

As I explained a bit about Japanese culture, I talked about the practice of *furo-ba*, or hot-tub baths, and how I loved them. He fell silent, and his eyes grew teary. Quietly, he recounted a dream he had had when he was just a little boy living in Texas, in an all white area where no one had ever encountered an Asian family.

He was in a large hot tub with an old Asian woman sitting in the background. Next to him sat a little girl with short black hair. She looked Japanese. And although they did not speak, he felt very happy to be with his playmate.

He said that the sweet dream replayed for three nights, and he was anxious to go to sleep each night. When the dreams stopped, he felt a terrible loss that took him a while to get over. And he was only about eight years old.

What are the odds that two little children separated by thousands of miles had the same dream about each other and then met twenty years later? But we knew it was true because, for some inexplicable reason, we couldn't bear to be apart. And so we weren't — for the next thirty-two years and counting!

Now we have grown children of our own. And sometimes we sit in a large Japanese *furo* together like we once did in a very happy dream, one that continues now even while we are awake!

~Lori Chidori Phillips

Come to Orkney

You do not find love. It finds you.
~Suzy Kassem, Rise Up and Salute the Sun

I stared hungrily at the computer screen as my achingly slow dial-up connection revealed the home page. It showed seals frolicking on the rocky beach, and seagulls wheeling in elegant spirals, ghostly against the red sandstone sea cliffs at sunset, their mournful cries mingling with ocean waves and a weeping fiddle. My heart responded as it always did to this scene — with a surge of longing pain.

"Come… to Orkney," the melodious male voice tempted in its gorgeous brogue. I ached to do just that, but for a poverty-stricken single mother with four young children, no child support and more jobs than was reasonable, such a dream was literally impossible.

That was in the year 2001. I had regressed from being a hopeful young wife into a betrayed, stunned worker drone. My children and I had run away from my abusive husband and taken refuge in an upper-story apartment in a gloriously ramshackled Victorian house where we were safe and, compared to the nightmare we'd just escaped, relatively happy. I was overworked, though, and sometimes felt sad because my children were too often left alone. But I'd survived the frightening first year as the head of my trusting little household. With the crisis past and all of us comfortable with our new way of life, I longed to have something in my life beyond the never-ending work schedule. That's when I decided to write a book.

I'd been developing my writing skills for years, hoping one day to make a living from home and not have to leave my children to go to work. The fantasy novel that I decided to write made me feel like I was weaving an enchanted web over an impoverished life. I think I hoped that the act of creation would help me to find the scattered bits of my soul. The secret dream of being able to stay home with my children gave me the impetus to press forward, but I'd have to restrict my project to the wee hours of the morning since every day was already full to overflowing. I set my alarm clock for 3:00 a.m. and began to write.

For a few weeks, I played with storylines and characters, requesting books for research from the friendly bookmobile ladies who came to our town every other Saturday. My chosen setting was one of the beautiful Orkney Islands, north of Scotland. What a thrill it gave me when I noticed that some of my obscure books had come all the way from Orkney! On rare afternoons off from work, I'd leave the kids happily playing with the neighborhood children, scoop my books into a bag, make myself a cup of tea and stroll uphill on the brick sidewalk to the old cemetery. This quiet place, with its dear, crumbling headstones laced with old-fashioned names, its tall pines and its snowball bushes, became my outdoor office whenever I could manage the time. I would sit on a stone ledge in the sunshine and scribble notes on my yellow legal pad in the lovely twilight — or *grimmelings*, as I'd learned that such a time is called in Orkney. Time went on, and I began to heal. I was happier than I had been in a long time.

I ran out of source material before I ran out of questions, so I decided to contact the library in Kirkwall, Orkney, which I'd discovered had wonderful archived materials — old photos, letters, even audio recordings. It seemed presumptuous for a pretender like me to bother professionals with my silly questions. But when I finally took the chance, the Orkney librarians responded to my requests just as generously as had my dear bookmobile ladies. After tracking down archived materials and even interviewing elderly residents on my behalf, they gave me one more gift: Someone forwarded my request for information to a man named Tom Muir, an Orkney native, historian and storyteller.

To my delight, Tom also turned out to be the author of a collection of Orkney folk tales that I'd already read with much delight.

Tom and I e-mailed back and forth a few times, and I began to feel strangely attached to him, though I knew little about him — not even whether or not he was married. Finally, not wanting to use any more of his valuable time with my endless questions, I thanked him and left him alone. Did I only imagine the sensation of feeling bereft?

Many years passed. My children grew, and life became saner, but I never lost the almost supernatural yearning I'd developed for Orkney during those happy days of researching my story. I had simply fallen in love with the place — its odd and humorous words, quaint customs and lovely people. The brief contact I'd had with some of the residents had only added to that affection.

Over the years, I would periodically torture myself by returning to the beautiful website of the man with the melodious voice who first tempted me to "come… to Orkney." I would daydream about traveling there one day, as unlikely as that seemed, since I was poor and had never traveled anywhere. As much as it almost physically hurt, I couldn't keep myself from testing the strange connection I felt with the place. It was as if Orkney was my true home, though I'd never been anywhere near it. And sometimes — just out of curiosity, of course — I would Google that nice storyteller, Tom Muir, and see what he was up to.

More time passed. I was less poor and had just graduated from college. My kids were all grown, and the temporary work I was doing would allow for a couple of weeks away. I knew it was a turning point in my life, and probably my only chance to have a bit of a long-delayed adventure before I got tied down by work again. With some trepidation, I began planning an extremely low-cost trip to Orkney. Then one night, in a fit of bravery, I sent Tom Muir a Facebook friend request. I knew he'd never remember me all these years later, but I hoped we might meet for a cup of coffee some afternoon anyway. To my shock, he did remember me and… well, the rest of the story sounds like one of Tom's folk tales, but it's absolutely true. The connection we'd both felt years earlier, but never spoken of, was still there between us and as strong as ever. It grew stronger, in fact, until at last it grew strong enough to draw me across the ocean to become his wife.

I live in Orkney now, and it does feel like my long-lost home, just as I'd expected. Tom and I still can't believe that a long-ago research correspondence and a hopeful friend request could lead us both to such joy. Life is so much better than I ever thought it could be.

And the man with the melodious voice? He's my husband's cousin, Sigurd.

~Rhonda Muir

48

Man of My Dreams

In dreams and in love, there are no impossibilities.
~Janos Arany

When I first got to college, I tried to be someone I wasn't. I'd never dated in high school, and the only guys who had expressed interest in me were hoping for an easy hook-up (which I angrily declined). The conclusion I drew was that there must have been something wrong with me personally. I was, you see, a pretty huge nerd. (I still am, in fact.) Any free time I had that didn't involve reading fantasy novels was absorbed by playing videogames. But boys don't like nerdy girls, right?

So I ignored my personality, my actual wants and desires, and became what I thought a college girl should be like. And it did get me dates. With losers. I finally turned to my last resort: online dating.

On my profile, I started to be a little more honest with myself. I listed some of the books I liked, said I was hoping to find someone who could make me laugh, and even admitted to being a "nerd" (though I said this with the hopes of sounding like a flirty and fun nerd as opposed to the type of nerd who literally spent the last sixteen hours playing *World of Warcraft*).

A few weeks passed, and I had gotten a date or two (with losers), when I got a message from "SilverMan." It said simply: "If you're looking for a nerd who can make you laugh, I'd appreciate it if you gave me a shot," followed by his phone number.

I looked at his picture and recognized him from my psychology class. I'd noticed him the first day of lectures, in fact. He'd come in a little after me and was kind of hard to miss.

He was tall and lean, wearing blue jeans and a nice, button-down shirt. His eyes were so piercing he could probably see through brick walls, and they were accented nicely by his high cheekbones, regal nose, and just exactly the right amount of facial hair. If you had asked me about him at any other stage of my life, I probably would have swooned. But there was just something about him, and I never could pinpoint what, that just seemed a little nerdy. Maybe it was his attentiveness in class and willingness to ask questions. Maybe it was because he frequently printed extra copies of his notes to share with others in the class. There was just something about him that made me categorize him as a nerd.

And college girls don't like nerds, right?

I read his message over twice, ignoring the strange tingling excitement running through my chest. "Oh, great," I said aloud to my empty apartment, "it's that nerd from my psychology class." I promptly deleted my account.

That night, I had a dream about him:

I was in our usual psychology classroom. Class had either just gotten out or had not yet started. Faceless students milled around making conversation I didn't try to hear. "SilverMan" stood beside me, smiling. He said something that made me laugh. I felt warm and comfortable. Accepted. It felt like being a toddler after playing in a bath with a soft towel wrapped around me in a hug. We chatted about nothings and flirted shamelessly. Toward the end of the dream, I remember taking his hand.

I woke blearily to the sound of my alarm, the dream still vivid in my mind. My heart felt like it had tripped down a flight of stairs.

"Huh," I said, blinking at the sunlight that had forced its way through my thin blinds.

Try as I might to ignore it, the dream clung to my conscious mind. Its implications were obvious, but I spent almost half the day trying to talk myself out of it.

"This doesn't happen in real life," I insisted quietly as I finished my make-up.

Tromping down the stairs, I muttered, "I'm not going to have a dream about him, then fall madly in love with him and get married and live happily ever after."

"That sounds like the premise of a bad romance novel," I told myself after breakfast.

"Besides," I thought while walking to class, "my account's been deleted. I probably won't have access to his number anymore anyway."

I studiously avoided him in psychology and rushed home after my classes were finished.

By dinnertime, I'd exhausted all my excuses and still couldn't get the dream out of my head.

"Fine!" I said at last, prying open my laptop. "If his number is still there, I'll send him a text. I could use the dating experience anyway. But it probably won't even be there anymore."

I got online and reactivated my account. Most of my messages had been erased. Only three were still in my inbox. One of which was from SilverMan. So I sent him a text.

We'll be celebrating our seven-year wedding anniversary this December.

~Mary T. Whipple

49

It Begins with an "H"

Pay attention to the feelings, hunches, and intuitions
that flood your life each day. If you do, you will
see that premonitions are not rare, but a
natural part of our lives.
~Larry Dossey, The Power of Premonitions

I was a widow with thirteen children. Seven of them still lived at home. It had been five years since my husband died, and I was still overwhelmed. I certainly did not want to be without a companion for the rest of my life.

One evening, I took a walk alone where I could pray. "Please, Lord, don't you have someone in mind for me?"

I was shocked when a voice immediately answered. "Yes, his name starts with an 'H,' but it's a name that is not too common to you."

For the next six months, I paid attention. *Who did I know whose name began with an "H"?* While having coffee with my friends or just anywhere, I began to doodle on napkins and receipts. I wrote Hank, Henry, Hubert, Hy, Herbert, Hilton, Hans, Heinrich, and Howard. Those names weren't too common to me, but worse yet, I knew no one by those names. As the months passed, I became impatient. *Whose name starts with an "H," and when will I meet him?*

I knew for sure that I had heard right. It was something that I could hold onto because I knew that it would eventually happen.

Four months later, my friend Jenny called. "Irene, I have an extra plane ticket to England. My son can't make it. Will you go with me?

We can stay at my mother's so it won't cost you a dime. You'll just need a little money for souvenirs."

Going to England was an answer to prayer. I'd visited there eleven years earlier. The fog, darkness, old buildings and castles intrigued me. At that time, I told my girls that I would return to England and stay a month so I could really enjoy all England had to offer. Now, that wish was coming true.

Jenny's only sibling, David, met us at Heathrow Airport. He was a tall, blond chap who was in the military. He and Jenny were overjoyed to see one another.

It seemed we dined with old friends and acquaintances almost every night the first week. I had the opportunity to enjoy Indian cuisine, as well as many other fancy restaurants. But my recurring pangs of loneliness made me question what I was doing there. One lovely evening, while in a ritzy café, soft strains of romantic music were playing. Immediately, I recognized the piano pieces played by Richard Clayderman. I could barely contain myself as I listened to song after song during our meal. My heart was bursting with memories that I had shared with my late husband. We had played that very same music on many occasions.

"Irene looks tired," David said, motioning to the waiter. "Let's be going. I guess she's not used to the time change."

I laughed. I felt partied out. All I wanted was to go back to Jenny's mother's house and fall asleep.

Finally, in bed, I surprised myself when the floodgates of my heart broke forth. I sobbed so loudly that I hoped Jenny and her mother wouldn't hear me in the adjacent room. I'd always been strong, hiding my own fears and disappointments. I didn't know exactly why I was weeping uncontrollably, but I knew that I needed to share my life with someone. I lay in bed, praying through my tears that God would comfort me. "Lord," I prayed, "I want a companion, someone I can walk this path with, someone who really cares for me." The last words I recollect before falling to sleep were, "Lord, I thought about everyone I know, and there is no one whose name starts with an 'H.'"

My dream was shocking, yet clear as a bell.

An old friend I had known for more than thirty years, someone with whom I hadn't connected for quite some time, appeared. He had the biggest smile on his face. "You haven't thought of me," he said.

On that note, I awoke with a light peeking through the bedroom curtains. A joy I hadn't experienced for a long while surged through me. I knew that my dream was my answer. Not only was this man a gentleman, patient, kind, and giving, but he was available. And, the best part was, his name began with an "H."

"Hector Spencer," I said, as warm fuzzies accompanied me all morning. I repeated his name over and over in my mind.

All the while, Jenny and her mother commented, "You sure look happy today." I kept my dream to myself, tucked in my heart. I could hardly wait until my vacation was completed.

Upon my arrival back to the United States, home never looked so good. Every day, I would think about Hector and wonder what he was doing. I knew he lived in St. George, Utah, but I had absolutely no clue when or how we'd meet. Three days later, a dear friend, Rhonita, invited me to lunch. I felt we had not seen each other often enough, and it was a delight to spend the afternoon with her. No sooner had we seated ourselves at the table in Denny's when she presented me with a book. I read the title, *How to Fall Out of Love.*

"I brought this book for you, hoping you will read it. Maybe you will be able to move on with your life. You need to find someone to share your life with."

I laughed. "I don't need this book. I already know who I'm going to marry."

She looked shocked. "How can we be this close, yet you haven't shared this with me?"

"I just found out myself," I laughed, hoping she wouldn't think I was crazy.

"Who is it?"

"Sorry, I can't tell you because he doesn't even know yet."

We both cracked up.

"You're so funny," Rhonita exclaimed. "If he doesn't know about it, how do you think it will ever happen?"

After swearing her to secrecy, I cautiously revealed to her my earlier premonition about the "H" and my dream.

"Wow, you sure seem certain about this, don't you?" Skeptical, she asked, "Who is he?"

"All I will say is that we both know him."

"Don't do this to me," she said. "We're friends! If you can't share with me, then who can you share it with?"

"I understand, really I do, but it's not right. I would absolutely die if he ever heard about this. It would ruin me, for sure."

"When will you know?" she ventured.

"The problem is," I confessed, "I don't know how we'll ever meet. He lives so far away."

"Well, I may be able to help you if you'll tell me your secret. Please, Irene, I promise I will not tell a soul!"

Desperate as I was, and knowing I could believe her, I shared my anticipated destiny. "It's Hector Spencer."

"Oh my, I can see you guys together. Honestly, I can. Did you hear that Hector's youngest daughter, Amanda, won Miss Pre-Teen Utah?"

"No, when did you hear about that?" I asked.

"I heard about it last week. In fact," she advised, "I think this is a perfect time for you to call and congratulate him. Maybe something will come of it."

I called directory assistance that evening. Extremely nervous and not wanting to sound too forward, I dialed his number.

"Hello?" answered the familiar voice. "This is Hector Spencer speaking."

For the first time in my life, I was absolutely at a loss for words.

"Hello?" he repeated.

"Oh... hi... uh... this is Irene." I grasped for words, hoping to make sense. "I heard about your daughter Mandy being crowned. Congratulations!"

Hector was very cordial. In fact, I felt his excitement in just sharing memories of old times together. Before I realized it, we had caught up on one another's lives, not realizing forty-five minutes had passed.

"Are you going to be in San Diego long?" he asked.

I told him that I was visiting my daughter indefinitely.

"Every now and again, I travel there for business. Would you care to go to lunch sometime?"

The rest is history. We were happily married twenty-five years. I feel comforted knowing that God gave me something to hold onto in my loneliness — a hint, the letter "H," to help me make my way to Hector.

~Irene Spencer

Crossing an Ocean to Find Brian

We determine our destiny by the actions we take today.
~Catherine Pulsifer

The voice cut through my drowsy state, jarring me so much that I sat straight up in bed, blinking hard against the bedroom light. I had lain down to rest while I waited for my boyfriend to pick me up. I worked as an au pair and English teacher for three lovely children in Athens, Greece, and I was tired after a long day.

As I waited for him, I pondered the message I had heard and realized a high-pitched buzzing noise in my ears had preceded the voice that had spoken to me. I wracked my brain trying to think if I knew a Brian. It was a common name. Didn't I know someone? But I didn't. And, more than that, I was particularly struck by its deliberate tone. It was an order. *I had to go home — leave Greece, and travel all the way back to Boston, Massachusetts — to find a man named Brian.* But why?

I didn't have any answers.

A sense of urgency began to grow within me. What if I missed the window of opportunity? Should I break my commitment to the Greek family? It had been a big decision to move abroad in the first place; it was just after 9/11, and the world was on edge. At twenty-two years old, I was eager for adventure but recognized the risks of an American girl traveling abroad alone. In the end, I decided to pursue my dream, much to the chagrin of my family. What would everyone think of me now if I arrived home months earlier than planned?

Over the next two weeks, my decision was made for me. My Greek boyfriend proposed marriage, which I turned down; this resulted in our break-up. The Greek family decided to go to their summer house weeks earlier than planned, which meant my services wouldn't be needed anymore.

In June 2002, I returned to Boston. I found a job as an editorial assistant and commuted daily via the city bus. The voice and its message, though still on my mind, were eventually pushed back as I became preoccupied with work.

Until September. As I waited to get off the bus for home one day, I glanced out the window and saw a tiny black kitten running up the sidewalk in the same direction as the bus. Immediately, I thought, *Oh, my God, that cat is going to get hit by a car!*

The bus pulled over for my stop, and I jumped off. The cat was in front of me, just watching me. Then it turned and started running. It looked back at me, saw I was trying to catch it, and ran faster until it turned down an alley that opened into a parking lot for a liquor store, a bank and a bar called Costello's. The cat approached a cement parking barrier and hopped onto it. It sat and waited patiently for me. Even more bizarre, it now calmly let me pick it up.

I called my mother from my cell phone to ask for a ride to the nearby animal hospital. Once there, I handed the black cat over to the attendant, who promised it would be adopted immediately; kittens always were.

When Monday came, I called the hospital to check up on the cat. One attendant, who claimed to be the one working the day I brought the cat in, swore he didn't remember the kitten. Another attendant said it had probably been adopted right away before paperwork could be filed. No one could give me a solid answer on its whereabouts, which was both odd and frustrating to me.

During this time, I visited the employment section of the hospital's website. I was surprised to discover that they were hiring veterinary technicians for their emergency department. The best part? Experience wasn't necessary because they were a training hospital.

Before I moved to Greece, I'd volunteered at a no-kill shelter in Boston. While in Greece, I'd volunteered and assisted in life-saving procedures for the stray cats in Athens. So when I saw the job posting, I immediately felt it was the job for me. I applied and received a phone call to come in for an interview the next day.

I was instructed to come into the hospital from the employee entrance, which opened into a long, dimly lit corridor. Doors to the medical wards lined the hallway. One door suddenly opened at the very end. A man in emerald green hospital scrubs stepped out. He leaned against the wall and glanced down the hallway at me. I was easily eighty feet away, not close enough to discern physical characteristics, but as soon as we saw one another, a bolt of electricity shot through my body. My immediate thought was, *Whoever he is, he's going to make this an interesting place to work!*

I had my interview and the head of the department offered me the job on the spot. On my first day of work, she took me into the emergency room to meet my trainer. It was the man I saw the day of my interview.

We became good friends and colleagues. Since we worked the 3:00 p.m. to midnight shift, several of us would blow off the night's emotional stressors by hanging out at a local bar after work. One particular night in April 2003, we all decided to leave through the bar's back entrance. Feeling empowered after I heard about his recent split from his girlfriend, I turned to him and quietly asked if I could kiss him. He said yes.

Shortly after that night, a realization struck me like a bolt of lightning, literally taking my breath away as all of the pieces fell into place, one after the other. His name was Brian. And not only had a mysterious voice instructed me to "go home and find Brian," but the strange black cat that helped lead me to him had waited for me on a cement parking barrier in the parking lot of *this* bar — Costello's. By leaving through the rear entrance of the bar, Brian and I had shared our first kiss where it had all started.

It blew my mind. Whoever spoke to me that night in Athens —

whether it was a guardian angel, my deceased father, or perhaps even God — he or she knew how important it was for me to find Brian.

We've been happily married now for eleven years and have an amazing four-year-old son named Joseph.

At our wedding in October 2005, my father-in-law told our story to a packed reception of family and friends. At the very end, he presented a gift to us, the happy newlyweds: an adorable, stuffed black kitten.

~Kathryn Merz

51

Matchmaker Owls

*Love is our true destiny. We do not find the meaning of
life by ourselves alone — we find it with another.*
~Thomas Merton, Love and Living

The owl spread its fluffy white wings against a luminous sky and stared straight at me with amber eyes. I stood in front of the watercolor painting, completely captivated. The scene had a dreamlike quality that was mesmerizing. I'd never seen an owl in real life, yet I felt a very strong connection to this magnificent being. I wondered why it was calling to me so powerfully.

Eventually, I tore myself away and enjoyed the rest of the art show, but I returned several times for a closer look. The owl's effect on me was magical and magnetic, but the cost was more than I'd ever dreamt of spending on a painting. Though I earned a reasonable living as a garden designer, the owl was a luxury way beyond my budget. I told myself to be sensible, and yet I couldn't bear to leave him behind. It was hard to understand why I was so smitten.

I tracked down the artist, a young woman with dark, soulful eyes.

"I've fallen in love with your owl, but I'm not sure if I can find the money," I said. "Would you hold it for me for one week? I'm hoping to get payment for a design I've done by then."

"Sure. No one has shown interest yet. Here's my card. Give me a call either way," she said.

I went home, my mind swirling between hope and anxiety.

Rummaging through my desk the next morning, preparing to pay bills, I found a postdated check. It was for one dollar less than the cost of the watercolor! Surely this was a sign that it was meant to be — the owl would be mine to enjoy every day at home. I called the artist and arranged to pick up the painting after I cashed the check.

I hung it right over my bed. Every morning when I woke, I'd gaze at the shimmering white owl and fill my soul with his beauty. I opened my arms as wide as his wings were spread, imagining my heart expanding along with his. I'd learned in yoga class that opening the heart chakra would heal past hurts and bring love into my life. The owl showed me how to practice this every morning.

My heart opened a little more each day, and I began to picture the love I longed for coming my way. But my imagination didn't match up with reality. Years after a painful divorce, I was still single. I missed sharing the joys and sorrows of my life. Each morning as I woke up alone, and each evening as I drifted off to sleep alone, I yearned for a loving companion.

Sometimes, I felt hopeless at the thought of remaining single forever. I saw a bleak future stretching out ahead of me. Sure, I had meaningful work and wonderful friends, but an important part of life was missing.

One evening, I called a good friend for relief.

She listened sympathetically, and then asked, "Would you consider seeing a psychic? I can recommend someone I talk to when I feel stuck. He's very helpful."

"I guess it couldn't hurt," I said. "Anything to give me a ray of hope. And if he says there's no love in my future, at least I can stop dreaming of the impossible!"

In his white shirt and tailored slacks, Don looked like an accountant, but his deck of tarot cards was as mysterious as the trance he entered after closing his eyes. I waited impatiently for him to come back to life. My heart thumped with anxiety as the minutes ticked by ever so slowly. Finally, he opened his eyes, picked one card, and held it up. Jagged bolts of lightning ran through the image.

"You will meet a man who will take you on a roller coaster ride.

It will be a very emotional relationship," he said.

"Really? I'm not much for thrills," I said. "This sounds scary!"

"Don't worry; you're strong enough to handle it."

"When will I meet him?"

"Some time in the next six months."

Hmm. So now I had the watercolor of the owl to help me open my heart chakra, and the psychic's promise that a man was coming into my life soon.

When I met Tom at a friend's potluck dinner, I didn't guess he was the one. A short, bald man with sparkling blue eyes and a warm smile, he was nothing like the tall, dark type I had always been attracted to. Still, after a friendly chat, we exchanged business cards. His had his barbershop quartet logo on it, and mine had a magnolia flower. I went to hear him sing in a local production of *The Music Man*, and he came to hear me read from my new book, *Garden Retreats*, at a local bookstore. He invited me to *Carmen* at the opera, and I took him for a stroll through the Chinese Gardens.

Little by little, we learned about each other's very different yet interesting worlds. He visited my garden, and we sat and talked for hours, which melted away like minutes.

"Tell me about your hopes and dreams," he said, and then listened attentively. This was completely new for me; usually, I was the one who asked the questions and listened.

One evening, Tom invited me to stop by his house on our way to dinner at a nearby restaurant. The contemporary house was spacious and welcoming, with framed art on the walls. And there, right over his bed, was a photograph of an owl with its wings spread.

"Oh, my God. I can't believe you have an owl over your bed! I have a painting of an owl over mine!"

"I've always loved owls," Tom said. He showed me a collection of owl sculptures that stood on his dresser.

"This is amazing," I said. And I thought to myself, *It's almost as if we were destined to meet, with our owls connecting us.*

True to the psychic's prediction, our relationship is very emotional, with lots of exciting highs and tumultuous conflicts that at times rock us to the core. But our love is strong enough to hold us together even when storms blow through. After all, our mysterious and wise owls showed us we belonged together.

~Barbara Blossom Ashmun

52

My Big, Burly Guy

Hope… is the companion of power, and the mother
of success; for who so hopes has within
him the gift of miracles.
~Samuel Smiles

Saving every dime to support my ten-year-old daughter, Milan, was my goal even as I was receiving eviction notices stapled to the door of our small, one-bedroom apartment. I worked at Milan's private Catholic girls' school so I could get a hefty discount on her tuition, but it meant taking a huge pay cut from the public-school teaching job I had given up in order to send her there.

I could never foresee that, within the first two years of her attending this prestigious school, her father and I would divorce. I had instantly become a single mom, and I had been doing everything in my power to keep her at the school she loved so dearly. Dealing with the emotional strain of divorce was now coupled with the financial burden of rarely receiving child support. I decided I would have to leave Miami, the city I was born in, to move five hours north to Jacksonville to live near my sister. It was much cheaper there, plus I could be near family.

One night, I had the most vivid dream of sitting at Scotty's Landing, the waterfront restaurant my daughter and I frequently visited. It was our usual spot every Sunday evening after spending a long day at the beach. She and I were sitting at a table, listening to the live reggae band, and at a nearby table sat a man who gently smiled at us. He had broad shoulders, light hair and eyes, and a big physique.

The next morning, I called my sister and told her about this "big, burly guy" dream I experienced, and she suggested this could be a premonition of meeting a man in her city. We laughed it off, and I told her to keep her eyes open for him. A week later, I had the exact same dream and called my sister once more.

"It has to be a sign," she told me, so I started thinking seriously about this possible premonition. And as I prayed each night for God to answer my prayers, I secretly wished this dream was his sign that I would find happiness again.

Two weeks later, I was invited to a wedding as the date of the best man, Gerry. We had gone out a few times in the past, but decided we would make better friends than a couple. Since we ended on good terms, I didn't hesitate to accept his invitation. Not knowing anyone at the wedding, I sat alone watching my date at the altar. I couldn't help but feel bittersweet when I watched the loving couple say their vows to each other. But I smiled politely throughout the ceremony and finally made my way to the reception.

Gerry led us to our assigned table and introduced me to everyone. There were three couples and a man named Mike, who had come without a date. Since Gerry was away from the table doing best man duties, I sat alone once again. The three couples at our table seemed friendly and engaging, but I couldn't stop staring at Mike. He had a great smile and was very handsome. We talked all night, and I was intrigued by him, finding myself feeling a little jealous as he danced with other women as I danced with Gerry.

I decided I would pursue him, something I'd never done before, because there was this pull toward him that I couldn't explain. I got up enough courage to ask him more personal questions like his last name and where he worked. He was a firefighter and obviously Irish, with his red hair and green eyes. As I admired his broad shoulders and husky physique, I guessed he was around 6'2". I left the reception giddy as a schoolgirl even though I didn't know if I was going to see him again. That night, I called my sister and told her I had met my "big, burly guy." At first, she squealed with delight, but then hesitated and asked, "Does this mean you're not moving up here?"

The next couple of days, I thought about how I was going to meet him again. I didn't want to look like a stalker showing up at his fire station, so I decided to look him up in the phone book. I couldn't believe that in a city with over four million people, Mike lived within two miles of me. Mustering up the courage I had left, I called him… but his voicemail came on. Nervously, I stuttered, "Hi, Mike? This is Angie from the wedding a few days ago. I was calling because I thought that maybe you and I could go get some coffee some time and talk. So call me if you're interested… bye!" My fingers were crossed that he'd be interested enough to call me back.

The next morning, my phone rang, and it was him! "Angie," he said softly, "it's Mike. I have something to ask you. Aren't you with Gerry?" When I explained our history, he asked if I liked sushi.

"That's my favorite food," I practically yelled back.

"Then it looks like we have a date," he concluded.

Our first date was magical. We talked for hours while we ate sushi and drank sake. I couldn't stop staring at his handsome face and I felt a strong connection with him. His calm demeanor and gentle smile were mesmerizing. Then I nearly fell out of my chair when I learned he used to work at Scotty's Landing as a bartender — the restaurant in my dream! A wave of peace came over me afterward, as if I knew he was God's answer to me. "Give love a chance again," God must have been saying. "Here he is."

I listened to my gut and continued to date him. Eventually, he met Milan, and they hit it off. We've been together for twelve years now. I can literally say that Mike is the man of my dreams. My big, burly firefighter rescued me, although he swears that I rescued him.

~Angelene Gorman

Chapter 6

Dreams
and the
Unexplainable

Dreams that Saved Lives

Highway to Heaven

Forewarn'd, forearm'd.
~Benjamin Franklin

My husband never listened to me while we were together. So when I woke up from a dream that warned of his death after we separated, I was even more sure that he wouldn't listen to me then. He was actually on his way out of town for a weekend road trip with his new girlfriend and her motorcycle club. They had started dating three weeks before, just one week after we separated.

He'll think I'm just trying to ruin his trip, I thought. *I don't want him to think I care or that I'm jealous he's going away with someone else.* So I went back to sleep and right back into the same vivid dream.

I've had lifelike dreams before, but this one was different. In this dream, everything is bright, clear, and large, like sitting in the front seat of a movie theater, but I'm in the movie. It not only feels real, but it looks real.

I'm facing east down California State Route 98, the desert highway that runs along the Mexican border. It's a sunny, warm November afternoon. The wind isn't too bad, just a cool, soft breeze — perfect riding weather. The colors are piercing. Plants are resurrecting. Summer is gone, and greenery is beginning to overtake the brown hillside.

The road is empty, desolate, as if everyone is gone or still on their way. It's a happy, peaceful place. It's how I imagine heaven.

Abruptly, I jump into another dream. At least, I think it's another dream, like someone changed the channel or hit fast-forward to the next scene. The joy and peace are gone. I'm filled with anger, grief, and regret. I'm in a stuffy, musty room. It's my husband's bedroom where I used to sleep, too.

I'm standing next to the bed we picked out together. He's dead, and I'm cleaning out his mahogany drawers. I find a card to me in his nightstand. It's blank. He never got to fill it out. I'll never know what he was going to write. Maybe he missed me. Maybe he still loved me. Maybe he was sorry and wanted me back. I hold it and try to imagine the words he might have written.

Then my thoughts are interrupted. A blond, older woman walks in behind me. It's her. I turn around in shock as I realize she has a key to our home. He had already given her a key, I think. So soon?! But their relationship is a discussion for another day I can see in the future. I yell and plead with her to tell me, "What happened? What happened?"

I woke up from that dream screaming. I knew then that I had to do something. I tried calling my husband, but his phone was off. It was always off when he slept. I told myself, *Well, I tried,* and went back to sleep. And right back into the same dream. I couldn't escape the nightmare. I've never been able to get back into the same dream when I wanted to, so when I couldn't get out of this one, I knew I had to listen. I woke myself up and tried calling all three of my husband's numbers — his personal cell, business cell, and his home office phone. I texted him, as well.

7:09 a.m.: "Call me!"

No response.

7:16 a.m.: "It's important."

No response.

7:21 a.m.: "Don't go on the ride."

No response.

7:24 a.m.: "Something bad is gonna happen!"

No response.

At that point, my embarrassment was gone and determination had taken over. I called my husband's home office phone repeatedly, hoping the ringer would eventually wake him. It did. He read the texts and called me back. He wasn't angry that I woke him. I told him about my dream. It wasn't just a bad feeling I had. I told him matter-of-factly that there was going to be an accident on that road trip, and he would die in it if he went. I rambled on and on and, surprisingly, he didn't interrupt. My husband never let me speak my mind, so I thought he had fallen back to sleep.

"Are you there?" I said, exasperated.

"I'm here," he said calmly. I expected that I'd have to plead with him, but I didn't. He got quiet again and then said, "What am I supposed to tell her? She's been looking forward to this trip."

"Tell her the truth!" I said.

"I can't tell her that," he said. "She's going to be mad that I didn't go because you said not to."

"You have to tell her," I said. "You have to cancel the trip."

"Okay, okay," he said. "I'll tell her."

I was finally able to sleep.

The next day, I was driving down the coast back to San Diego from Los Angeles when my husband called my cell phone.

"You saved my life," he told me.

"What?"

"You saved my life," he repeated. "You were right. Oh, my God, I can't believe it. You were right."

My husband told me he had just gotten off the phone with a friend of his girlfriend. She and four others had been airlifted to the hospital in critical condition. A car drove into their motorcycle pack while they were riding down Highway 98. Five others were killed instantly, including the person riding behind my husband's girlfriend — the position where he would've been riding. He was excited, happy to be alive, and kept saying, "I can't believe it; you knew this was going to happen. You knew. You saved my life. You saved my life!" Then he started to cry for his girlfriend, and I actually felt sorry for him. He never told her about my dream. He told her he couldn't go because of work.

"She's going to die," he said.

"No, she's not," I interrupted, emotionless and unconvinced.

"How can you say that?" he yelled. "She was hit by a car! Going sixty miles per hour! She was thrown one hundred feet! Her brain's bleeding! Her vertebrae are broken! Her aortic valve was torn! They had to remove her spleen!" He went on and on.

Part of me was mad that he was crying to me about another woman. And then he had the nerve to ask me to pray for her. I could've let him go on suffering, but I took the high road.

"I know she's not going to die because, in my dream, she didn't," I said, without a doubt. "One day, I will run into her, and I will confront her."

"Really?" he said, joyfully. "Thank you, thank you!"

"Don't thank me," I told him. "Thank God. He's the one who warned you. I just relayed the message."

My husband's girlfriend did live. After weeks in the hospital, she got out in a full body brace. And after months of physical therapy, she was walking and riding again. They don't talk anymore and neither do we, but he e-mailed me on the anniversary of the accident to thank me for saving his life.

~Adrienne A. Aguirre

54

Save Me, Mummy!

Our life is composed greatly from dreams, from the
unconscious, and they must be brought into connection
with action. They must be woven together.
~Anaïs Nin

I woke up drenched with sweat. It was the fourth time the dream had come to haunt me since I got married, and I couldn't understand why.

It always started the same way, with me stepping out onto the balcony of our duplex to see a little boy waving to me from across the street. He wore a T-shirt with a superhero logo on it and a pair of matching long pants. I waved back, and he said something I couldn't hear before leaping off the curb to run toward me. As he did, an out-of-control truck barreled down the road in his direction. I tried to scream in warning, but no sound came — only a muffled hiss left my throat as I watched the child fly toward me from the impact. I ran to kneel beside him. As he lay there, he looked at me helplessly and whispered, "Save me, Mummy. Only you can save me." His eyes closed, and he was gone.

My husband, Don, stirred beside me. "Are you okay?" he asked. "You were moaning."

"I had a nightmare," I whispered. "It seemed so real."

"Do you want to talk about it?" he asked, rolling over to face me.

"No, I'll be fine," I assured him. "Go back to sleep."

He did, but I remained wide-awake. I waited until his breathing evened, and then slowly crept out of bed and into the kitchen. It was 6:00 a.m., and I had to be up in an hour anyway, so I put on some coffee.

As it brewed, I thought about what had awoken me. The first time it happened, I immediately consulted the dream book that I kept on my night table, but it only gave me an ambiguous interpretation of the different images I was able to remember.

It made no sense. I was twenty-one, married a year, and we had no children. Nor were we planning to become parents any time soon, if at all. We liked kids, but we were happy the way we were — free to go where we wanted at a moment's notice. We enjoyed other people's children, but were in no hurry to have our own. Maybe we'd change our minds one day, but right then there was no reason for anyone to call me "Mummy" — let alone an apparition that came to me in my sleep.

That little boy invaded my dreams several more times over the next few years, always wearing identical clothes. Nothing ever changed — including that horrific accident. Every time I woke up from it, I was equally puzzled and disturbed, but for some inexplicable reason I kept it to myself, perhaps in the hope that it might end differently one day or stop altogether.

Eventually, like most couples, my husband and I matured. We settled down and began thinking about our future instead of living every day as if it was our last. At the age of twenty-seven, I found myself yearning for a baby. Luckily, Don felt the same way, and about a year later, David completed our little family.

I enjoyed every second of motherhood, marveling at how I could have ever thought my life was complete without a child. I reveled in all my son's stages, from being helpless and reliant on me for everything, to his first steps and the independence that milestone brought with it. As he began to explore his surroundings, I found myself seeing the world with fresh eyes from a toddler's perspective. My husband, a very hands-on father, savored his role in David's life every bit as much as I did mine.

Time passed quickly. I'd all but forgotten that terrible dream because it hadn't recurred since the night before I gave birth. However, when David turned six, he began to eerily resemble the child who invaded my sleep and called out to me all those years ago. My unease returned, heightening even more when my son became obsessed with the same famous superhero whose logo appeared on the clothing the youngster wore in the nightmare.

I tried to convince myself that it was all in my head — that not only did all children have fantasy idols they admired, but that my clouded memory of that little boy and David had simply mingled together in my mind to become one. I still had never told my husband what caused me to wake up so frightened, disturbed and disoriented all those times, and it seemed silly to bring it up now. Instead, I buried my worries and chalked off my fears to being overprotective, but they continued to niggle at me.

One spring day, when David was seven, he asked us to take him shopping so he could spend some money he'd saved up. Since one of us needed to stay home for a delivery we were expecting, Don opted to take him and make it a boys' day out — even agreeing to take the bus, something our son loved to do.

"Call me an hour before you get home," I asked my husband. "I'll start dinner so you won't have to wait too long to eat." He agreed.

At about 5:30, he called, announcing they were on their way. Forty-five minutes later, while everything simmered on the stove, I decided to take my book outside onto the balcony to read while I waited. To my surprise, when I stepped out, I spotted them on the other side of the street, walking toward the house.

Immediately, I noticed David's new sneakers. They were impossible to miss, their pristine whiteness a glaring contrast against the new black trousers he'd obviously insisted on wearing home. I grinned as I watched him stop and remove his jacket to hand to his dad, no doubt so he could show me the full effect of the outfit he'd bought with his money.

When he turned around, I gasped in horror. The front of the shirt and pants sported the same insignia I'd seen so many times, right before the little boy in the dream ran toward me! A strong sense of déjà vu coursed through my body, causing every nerve to tingle, while all movement around me decelerated into slow motion.

I watched my son's face brighten in a huge smile when he spotted me. His hand raised in that familiar wave, and my heart tripled its beat.

"Look, Mummy! I have new shoes!" he announced. "Look how fast I can run!"

Before Don could react or stop him, David sped in my direction, jumping off the curb and right into the street.

This time, my scream was shrill enough to shatter glass. Without thinking, I jumped off the balcony and sprinted toward him. Halfway across the street, I managed to grab my son and propel the two of us to the sidewalk he'd come from. As we landed on the hard concrete, I heard the deafening blare of a truck horn behind us. My long hair whipped against my face and into my eyes from the hot gust of air coming from the vehicle as it whipped past us, slamming into the sidewalk I'd left seconds earlier. The sickening crunch of metal filled our ears as the truck collided with our neighbor's metal fence, coming to a smoky standstill in their yard.

Dazed, I checked my son for injuries. Other than a scraped arm, he was fine. So was I. My husband helped us up, his face pale with shock. The truck driver, also unhurt, ran over to see if we were okay.

"Mummy — you saved me!" David exclaimed, his eyes wide.

"Yes," I whispered back. "This time, I did."

The nightmare was over, and it finally had a happy ending.

~Marya Morin

55

Sailing into Danger

Never apologize for trusting your intuition. Your brain
can play tricks, your heart can be blind, but
your gut is always right.
~Rachel Wolchin

My sailing knowledge was limited to an occasional trip around a park pond in a pedal boat. In spite of this, my friend Peter, an experienced sailor, insisted I was an ideal candidate for his crew. We would be relocating his boat to Florida from Ballantyne's Cove, Nova Scotia.

With visions of Christmas in the sun, I happily signed on for the trip. The crew would consist of Peter, me, and two others.

We spent almost a week preparing the boat. Then, when we saw a break in the unpredictable fall weather, we set sail for the south. Unfortunately, the other crewmen decided to bail at the last minute so it was just the two of us. The good news was that we had lots of surplus food supplies, meaning we would not have to make many port calls to restock.

We quickly blew our way through the Canso Causeway, aided not only by the strong winds but a lack of boat traffic. As we traversed the south coast of Nova Scotia, we faced our first bout of bad weather. That night, we stayed at sea as heavy winds and short daylight hours made it impossible to make a safe harbour.

During these first few days, we faced numerous trials. On one occasion, we got lost in a river system while seeking shelter from a storm. Then, as the weather improved, we ran aground trying to make our way back out to sea.

I was beginning to find my sea legs, and my ever-present nausea was diminishing. I came to admire how Peter dealt efficiently with our various problems despite crew limitations. We both had to take multiple shifts at the helm, and there just didn't seem to be enough time for sleep.

Finally, we made our weary way into Halifax Harbour. In the cabin, on our first day in Halifax, we discussed the next stage of the trip. The plan was to leave the coast of Nova Scotia and head due south. Peter's intention was to gain the U.S. inland waterway as soon as possible. This system of channels would afford us protection from the worst of the Atlantic weather. Looking at the forecast, we saw an imminent clearing period that might give us enough time to make the open water crossing safely.

Moored alongside us was a boat of similar size piloted by a lone sailor. Listening to his tales and adventures left us feeling like neophytes. He had sailed extensively and now spent his time following the seasons with his boat. Over dinner that evening, we found that he was also heading south. He planned to stay away from the coast and make his first landfall around South Carolina. His boat was impressive, equipped with the latest navigational and safety equipment.

We exchanged contact details and arranged to meet up in Florida. We were all leaving the next morning.

Around midnight, however, I woke in a cold sweat. Each time I closed my eyes and tried to sleep, I relived that same dream. *I saw our boat being swamped by a huge wave. With me at the helm and Peter below decks, the boat was tossed on its side like a child's bath toy.*

I turned on my nightlight and tried to read, but found I couldn't concentrate. I kept reliving the same scenario.

First thing in the morning I told Peter about my premonition. I told him that it had such a powerful impact on me, I would not be continuing the trip.

He was incredulous. "How could you possibly give up on the strength of a bad dream?" he demanded. "You were so enthusiastic last night."

"I'm sure that if you'd had the same premonition, you would not be sailing today," I responded.

He peppered me with attempts to guilt me into changing my mind. "How will you get back home from Halifax?" We had left the camper with his cousin in Ballantyne's Cove. "Hadn't you told friends and family that you would be spending the winter in Florida?"

He was exasperated, and who could blame him? He had a lot riding on this trip. It soon dawned on him, however, that no matter how strong his argument might be, my mind was made up. I would not be sailing.

I offered to stay with him until we could find a replacement crew. "We could canvas the various sailing clubs in the area," I said. "Surely we can find someone interested in making the trip." After weighing everything, Peter decided the best action would be to winterize the boat and for us to head home. I think he'd come to realize that my premonition also included him and his boat. The next day, despite a positive forecast, the weather changed from mildly unsettled to very stormy. Seemingly, this is typical of hurricane season in the Atlantic. Peter now seemed more at peace with our decision.

The strengthening storm made it difficult for us to move the boat to its winter resting place, but we managed. The next day, while preparing the boat, we were met by a helpful club member. He complimented us on abandoning our trip, as the storm was now set to be full strength for at least a week. The following day, he brought us the news that the sailor we had befriended in Halifax had been lost at sea. Despite his experience and communication equipment, his boat had simply disappeared. An automatically activated emergency beacon had been detected, but nothing else. It seemed he didn't even have time to contact the Coast Guard. The general consensus was that his boat had been swamped by a huge wave, giving him no time to react.

The possibility that our trip might have ended the same way was not lost on us. Peter never actually said as much, but I know that he was secretly glad I had taken the stand I took.

We stayed in Halifax long enough to attend a memorial service for our lost friend. Peter attended the service dressed in his naval white uniform in a show of respect and solidarity with the sailor. We both gave thanks for a premonition that was realistic and powerful enough to have re-charted the course of our lives.

~James A. Gemmell

56

Rescue from Across the Rainbow Bridge

*If there is a heaven, it's certain our animals are to be
there. Their lives become so interwoven with our
own, it would take more than an
archangel to detangle them.*
~Pam Brown

S hortly after my cat Molly died in June 2010, I started having
two seemingly different health issues. My left leg developed
a weird kind of ache, and I started to have some problems
breathing. My doctor said we all start having joint problems
at a certain age, and the problem with my leg was probably some
arthritis starting in. As to the breathing problem, she assured me it
was probably just a combination of allergies and grief over Molly's
death.

After all, Molly had spent almost every day of her twenty-two
years with me. Anyone who knew me knew it was going to take me
a long, long time to accept her passing. She was such an amazing
little cat. She was so stoic in dealing with anything that came her
way — new cats in our household, her developing kidney disease,
new relationships in my life. She was a quiet, little sentinel who was
by my side no matter what.

That June, after a cortisone shot was administered in my leg and
I was given an inhaler for the breathing difficulty, I went home. But

the inhaler didn't help much and my breathing problem got worse.

Three months later, on a Friday in September, my left ankle suddenly swelled up, and for the life of me I couldn't figure out how I'd sprained it. I mean, seriously… how could I twist my ankle and not know it?

The next day my ankle hurt a little more, and my breathing had become even more difficult. But hey! Fall allergies, right? To deal with the pain in my ankle, I started icing and taking aspirin. I figured I'd call my doctor sometime the following week if the pain didn't stop.

On Sunday, though, I had a very troubling dream about Molly. In life, her back right leg was a bit lame due to arthritis and age, but it didn't stop her from getting where she wanted to go. In this dream, though, her back *left* leg was lame. She kept falling down every time she tried to stand. And every time she fell over, she'd look at me with such sadness in her eyes. It broke my heart in the dream and even more so when I woke. Wasn't she supposed to be restored to perfect health in heaven?

The dream stayed with me. Every detail of it, including the look in her eyes when she fell, unable to stand on her left leg, cast a pall over the day.

As for me, as the day wore on my left leg hurt more and more. No amount of ice or aspirin alleviated the pain. As the day drew to a close, my breathing became even more difficult. And as I looked down at my very swollen leg, I began to cry for what Molly had gone through in the dream. Some people might say, "It was just a dream." But for me, as I looked at my leg, I knew it was more than a dream. The reality of the fact that in life it was her right leg that was slightly lame, but in the dream it was her left leg — the same leg that was giving me so much pain — hit me. I felt that my little cat, who had always looked out for me, was trying to tell me something.

I grabbed my purse and headed to the hospital. Within minutes of walking into the emergency room, I was on oxygen. The ER doctor took one look at my leg and told me I had a deep vein thrombosis, and he suspected a pulmonary embolism. He immediately ordered a CT scan of my lungs and an ultrasound of my leg to confirm his diagnosis. Just before I was wheeled out for the tests, he started me on blood thinners and assured me I'd be fine. I was never so confused or frightened.

A short time later, after the tests were done, we had confirmation. He told me it was a miracle I was still alive — I should have been gone weeks before. He paused a moment before asking me what made me decide that I needed to come to the hospital when I did. After all, I'd walked around with these issues for about three months.

He smiled in understanding when I told him about a little black cat named Molly, who reached across the Rainbow Bridge to save my life.

~Regina Schneider

No Reason Required

Trust your instinct to the end, though
you can render no reason.
~Ralph Waldo Emerson

Bright car lights showed ahead. I worried that my roommate's date was driving too fast for the Oklahoma roller-coaster hills. The moonless night accentuated the unease I felt. "Shouldn't you slow down?" I asked from the back seat.

My date's face never came into focus, and I didn't recognize his voice when he said, "He's a good driver. You don't have to worry."

Like magic, the oncoming car lights disappeared. Time slowed to a crawl as the events of the next few seconds flashed like photographs before my eyes. We were enveloped in black. An eerie glow from the dashboard lights illuminated my date's face. "Look out!" my roommate yelled. In nearly the same instant, I saw the horror in my companion's eyes before I heard the screech of tires and felt my body slam forward.

Someone screaming woke me. I realized it was me as I bolted upright in bed, disoriented. My breathing slowed as I took in my surroundings. The red numbers on my alarm clock lighted my desk where my hoodie I'd worn the night before hung on the chair. A slight snoring sound came from across the small room as my roommate slept peacefully in her bed.

That wasn't the first time I'd had that nightmare. It had pulled me out of a sound sleep two times in the past five days. I didn't know what triggered it. At first, I thought it was something I ate, but after the second time I decided it must have been a movie, TV program, or story in the news. I wasn't concerned, but wished the dream would go away.

I reached to turn off my alarm seconds before it was scheduled to sound. As I gathered up my towel and soap and headed out the door, I heard my roomie's alarm. Friday classes would start in two hours, and another week of the school year would be over.

As I went through my day, I thought about college. It was supposed to be the place to prepare for a career, meet your future husband, and embark on a new life. That had not been true for either of us. Classes, studying, and weekends playing cards with other girls in the dorm had become our routine. We joked that Mr. Wonderful must have gone to one of the other state universities. Perhaps tonight would be different. Our cafeteria joined our building and the male dorm. We'd been talking to a couple of guys who regularly sat at the table next to our normal table. They seemed really nice. When they'd asked if we'd like to go with them to the campus movie, we'd said yes.

My last class finished at 4:00. I walked back to the dorm and went with my roommate to eat. The guys were already there.

"You go sit by John. I'll get the chair by Mike," my roommate whispered. We'd previously decided who we wanted to be with and didn't want the guys to choose otherwise. I don't think they were disappointed in our plan.

"Are you ladies about ready to go?" asked Mike as we finished up our meal.

"Sure. We'll just go up and get our stuff," I said as Marilyn and I left for our room. On the way, we talked about whether to take our purses and a little money or just go. As broke college kids, neither one of us had extra cash. We decided if the group decided to go anywhere other than to the movies, the guys could pay. We brushed our teeth and hair and went to meet our dates in the dorm lobby.

We'd all laughed with the audience at the crazy antics, and everyone was in a really good mood as we left the theater. We'd met Sandy, a girl from our floor, and her date, Paul. They'd joined us outside. The fall days were getting shorter. Even though the movie started early, it was dark on the walk back to the dorm. I was thankful for the occasional campus lamppost. The moon and stars were obscured by the clouds.

John took my hand as we walked. The evening was turning out nicely.

"How would you guys like to drive to Pawnee and catch the end of the rodeo?" asked Mike.

John squeezed my hand. "I think you'd enjoy watching. It's very entertaining. Right, Mike?"

"Yeah, it sure is," Mike agreed. "The cowboys around here are really good. Several have already qualified for the national finals in Tulsa this year."

"We'd love to," Sandy exclaimed. "I've never been to a rodeo. Paul's been telling me we should go."

Alarm bells were going off in my brain. My chest felt constricted, and my heart rate suddenly doubled. All the liquid in my mouth disappeared, and I could hardly get the words out. "I don't want to go."

Everyone stopped walking and turned to look at me. I felt miserable. The idea of a night at the rodeo sounded like a lot of fun, but panic consumed me. "We could play cards in the lobby or rent a movie to watch in the lounge," I managed to blurt out.

"What's wrong with you? You look like you're scared to death." My roommate reached to put her hand on my upper arm.

"I just don't want to go. I don't want you guys to go either. It's just a feeling I've got. Let's stay on campus."

John shrugged his shoulders and dropped my hand. "Maybe you're coming down with the flu or something. A good night's sleep might do you good. We could go on, and maybe you'll feel like doing something tomorrow."

I could hear his disappointment, but the sensation I felt was too strong. "Yeah, maybe tomorrow. Please stay here with me," I pleaded to Marilyn.

As any true friend and roommate would, she agreed to stay, but I knew she wasn't happy as we watched everybody walk to Mike's car, and we went up to our room.

She and I played cards that evening. The dream didn't wake me. The knocking at our door by a fellow floormate did.

"Did you guys hear? Sandy, her date, and two guys from Parker dorm were in a horrible accident last night. Their car hit a train. They were all killed instantly."

~Rita Durrett

Dr. Dream

Faith is like radar that sees through the fog.
~Corrie ten Boom

I talk a big game. I say I believe in miracles. I was raised in a home where we attended church on Sunday, read daily from the Bible, and prayed before every meal. I knew that God appeared in a burning bush and parted the Red Sea. I knew he cast out evil spirits and caused blind men to see. I knew that he raised Lazarus from the dead and walked on water. I knew he spoke to Joseph of Egypt through dreams.

I knew all these things, but did I really believe them? When it came down to recognizing a miracle in my own life, I wasn't as faithful as I thought I was.

At the age of thirty-one, I was living a life full of love and happiness. I was the mother of three boys, the wife of a loving husband, and a health advocate and fitness instructor. Our family ate kale and played soccer. We enjoyed long walks and watching movies. Life was everything I thought it could be. It seemed nothing could interrupt our perfect world.

Yet, I could never be perfectly happy. I always felt it unfair that life could be so wonderful, that I could be surrounded by so much joy when there was so much sadness happening to those around me. Foreboding and dread entered my thoughts as I wondered when my turn would come. My mama always told me that adversity makes you strong. So, I lived my days and enjoyed my moments, waiting for the unknown bad thing to happen to me or my family.

My turn came one Monday morning as I woke up to find my left arm swollen and purple. An ER visit led to a CT scan that showed a tumor growing in my chest, a clot in my neck, and clots in both of my lungs. The world stopped spinning as we journeyed into the unfamiliar realm of biopsies, blood tests, and oncology. Weeks passed, and we continued to hope and pray. We prayed, and prayed, and prayed.

Then the real test came. Two weeks after our ER visit, at 4:00 a.m., my husband Jon sat up, wide awake, with the words "T-cell lymphoblastic lymphoma" imprinted on his brain. He quietly slipped out of bed and went downstairs, sure he'd not be able to go back to sleep. The clarity of this dream ensured it wouldn't be forgotten or ignored.

"Lymphoblastic" wasn't ever mentioned in our recent weeks of cancer talk. For all he knew, it wasn't even a medical term.

The day went on, and he continued to ponder what he'd experienced, hesitant to tell me, knowing I'd be skeptical. He waited for the right moment and approached me with the words, "I have to tell you something. I had this dream..." He proceeded to explain how clearly he'd seen and heard the words "T-cell lymphoblastic lymphoma." He explained that his research that morning revealed that "lymphoblastic" is a rare form of lymphoma or leukemia.

I was surprised and remained skeptical, but supportive. I told him there wasn't much we could do with this new information. "It's not like we can go and tell the doctor you had this dream that told you I had T-cell lymphoblastic lymphoma." We continued to wait for an official diagnosis.

The diagnosis finally came: T-cell non-Hodgkin lymphoma. Finally, a diagnosis. That was good enough for me. *These doctors are smart,* I thought. *They deal with cancer every day!* But my husband wasn't so easily convinced. No prodding or whining on my part was enough to make him dismiss what he'd heard.

Despite my persistent request that we just trust the doctor, my husband insisted on getting a second opinion. I was emotionally and physically drained from the first cancer diagnosis. I didn't want to start all over again and go through the irritation of more doctors and tests. Jon was unrelenting. He made an appointment with a lymphoma expert at Georgetown, and I accompanied him, dragging my feet the whole way.

More questions, more tests, more waiting. While we awaited the second set of results, I chose to go ahead and begin chemo for non-Hodgkin lymphoma. I would be given four drugs that would be administered every three weeks over five months. I cut my hair, had a port-a-cath placed and got ready to dive into my life as a chemo patient.

The drugs from chemo began circulating in my veins and breaking me down. My hair began to thin, and I was getting increasingly fatigued. Nausea became my constant companion, and I was slowly adjusting to my new normal.

Then we got the call. The further testing on my biopsy sample revealed that what I had was not T-cell non-Hodgkin lymphoma, but acute T-cell lymphoblastic lymphoma. *Son of a gun. My husband was right.* My treatment was changed from four to six rounds of chemo administered over five months to two or three years of aggressive chemotherapy administered almost daily.

T-cell lymphoblastic lymphoma accounts for about one percent of all lymphomas. Lucky me. After receiving the final diagnosis, my doctor sat down with us to discuss the new procedures. And we had questions. Lots of questions. Like, why didn't we get this right the first time? And what would have happened if they'd continued to treat me for a cancer I didn't have? He told us that if we'd proceeded with the treatment for my first diagnosis, it most likely would have put me into remission. However, lymphoblastic lymphoma is aggressive, and the chances for relapse are high. Chances are, the cancer would have come back much stronger and harder to fight.

Having this aggressive cancer and more aggressive treatment meant fighting cancer became my whole world. Every day, I went to my doctor's office for shots and infusions in the chemo lounge, and then curled up at home vomiting in a trashcan. Friends and family were constantly in and out, cleaning, bringing meals, and taking my children, each carrying their own load of my burden.

But I was at peace. The Lord had reminded us, through a dream, that he is all knowing. Because my husband listened, my life was potentially saved.

I'm now cancer-free and adjusting to post-chemo life. My battle with cancer broke every part of me. I cried, prayed, endured, and suffered until I thought I couldn't do it anymore. But in my darkest hour, I knew I wasn't alone. We have emerged on the other side bruised, grateful and strong.

Here's hoping Jon's next dream involves a cruise ship....

~Emily Rusch

59

The Small White Car

The most beautiful thing we can
experience is the mysterious.
~Albert Einstein

I really dislike driving. It's not that I'm afraid to drive or that I'm a bad driver. In fact, in all the years since I've obtained my driver's license, I've only had one small fender bender (the other guy's fault, I might add). It's just that when it comes to car travel, I don't have much patience for the speeders, tailgaters, or people who refuse to signal.

I don't much like traffic, either, and I try to avoid it at all costs. So much so, that when I had to choose between two jobs, I opted for a lower paying position ten minutes from home. Through the side streets I would go, grinning as I passed the parkway entrance with cars lined up for a block, their drivers desperately trying to merge in rush-hour traffic.

But all that changed one day when my husband and I found it necessary to relocate to a new apartment quickly. Though we tried as best we could to stay in our current neighborhood, no suitable apartments were available on such short notice. We expanded our borders. Still nothing. We expanded our borders a little more and then a little more until, ultimately, we were searching at the edge of the next county.

Finally, though, we found a charming apartment in a friendly area. There was only one drawback — the commute. No more pleasant side streets for me. Now my twice daily driving routine entailed negotiating a busy highway directly through a section dubbed "blood alley" due to the many serious accidents that routinely occurred there. However, I was a cautious driver who did her best to keep away from dangerous situations. So despite my longer, more complicated route, I felt fairly confident that I could get to and from my destination safely each workday.

That was, until I had a terrible dream early one Monday morning.

In it, I sat behind my steering wheel as I eased onto the parkway's entrance ramp. I checked over my shoulder for oncoming traffic, then accelerated into the merge when, seemingly out of nowhere, a white compact car lost control and slammed right into the driver's side of my car.

In my dream, I heard the screech of the tires and the crunch of the metal, and I felt the jolt of the impact so distinctly that I actually woke up on the opposite side of my bed.

As much as I tried, I was unable to fall back asleep. So, I got out of bed and puttered around my apartment until it was time to leave for work. Though I kept reminding myself this was only a dream, the unnerving scene continued to play in my head. As I pulled my car from the curb that day, I breathed a prayer for my protection on the road.

I continued that prayer as I eased onto the parkway ramp and again as I looked over my shoulder to check for oncoming traffic. Then, just as I was about to merge, I saw it — a small white car driving uneventfully in the middle lane. In that moment, I hit the brakes. And, in the next moment, the small white car hit a pothole, careened across two lanes of traffic, and came to rest directly in front of my stopped vehicle.

I arrived at work that morning a few minutes late, pale and shaken. My co-worker took one look at me. "Are you okay?"

"I'm fine," I answered gratefully. "But you'll never believe the dream I had."

~Monica A. Andermann

60

"N" Is for Nightmare

You have to ask a lot of questions and listen to people,
but eventually, you have to go by your own instincts.
~Kirk Kerkorian

The nightmare came right after I'd noticed I had a new skin blemish. *In the dream, a former college roommate and I were sitting on her front porch steps, enjoying a warm summer evening. We both had on shorts, and our legs were lazily stretched out in front of us. "I don't mean to alarm you," my friend said, "but you have something on your leg that you need to have a doctor look at." When I looked down, there were two, four-inch-long mushrooms sprouting from my ankle.*

I awoke with a gasp. Definitely one for the dream log! I'd started writing down dreams because I'd found that dreams would sometimes alert me to what was important. Besides, they can be weirdly entertaining.

That was in late March 2009. Two tiny dots that formed a crooked figure eight had recently appeared on that spot on my leg. The nightmare caused me to look more carefully at them. They didn't protrude in any way, but they were darker than my ordinary freckles and they looked strange. I'd never been terribly concerned about any of my skin blemishes before, but when I learned that a local hospital was having a free skin check, I made an appointment. I have to admit, I felt a little nervous. I was convinced this nightmare was a warning.

Because the little dots were on my ankle, the young doctor looked at them right there at the check-in station. She pronounced them "nothing" in under a second.

This seemed so anticlimactic that I felt I couldn't just leave. "Are you sure?" I asked. "Do you mind looking again?"

She refused to humor me. "Really," she said. "It's nothing."

"Isn't it weird that there are two of them together, though? And the color is funny. And they just appeared and are getting bigger."

She carefully explained, in a tone meant specifically for people who overreact, that new skin discolorations such as mine can appear "even as we age" and they are nothing. "It's okay. Really."

I wanted to believe her, but I just didn't. I was in my late forties and had already had enough age spots to know these didn't look like any of them. It slipped out. "But… I had a nightmare."

"Oh," she said. "A nightmare — well!" The smirk on her face said it all. I shuffled away, feeling foolish but still worried.

From then on, whenever I saw a doctor, I proffered the leg and asked about the two little blotches that had slowly been spreading toward each other.

"That's what we called in medical school a 'nothing,'" one doctor said.

A year later, my new family practitioner pronounced the spot nothing to worry about. It was always a relief to keep hearing it wasn't serious — until the little blob caught my eye and I felt the familiar uneasiness. Crazy or not, the mushroom-nightmare was always in the back of my mind, and I didn't like the way this thing kept changing. The two little dots had by now grown into one crooked one, and it just looked wrong.

When I developed a mild allergic reaction, I was almost glad to have an excuse to see another dermatologist. By this time, the thing I'd dubbed "The Nightmare Spot" was about the size of a large grape seed. This doctor said The Nightmare Spot could be biopsied at a later date. He didn't seem to be in a hurry because he said the border looked even as opposed to the blurry, irregular border characteristic of some types of skin cancer. It was a comment one of the other doctors had made.

Clear border or not, I suddenly realized how badly I wanted it gone, and I had begun feeling an inexplicable sense of urgency. Since this doctor was hard to schedule, I looked for another dermatologist who could get me in as quickly as possible. It had now been almost a full four years since I had the nightmare.

A short time later, in March 2013, I had an appointment with a new dermatologist. I extended my leg as usual and recited my speech.

"Yes," she said. "I believe you have a Stage I melanoma."

The word came out in a whoosh. "Melanoma?" I felt as if I'd been punched. I hadn't realized until that moment that I'd assumed I had a basal cell carcinoma, which runs in my family. Though still a form of cancer, small basal cell carcinomas generally aren't thought of as being an immediate threat because they don't readily spread. But melanoma? The deadliest form of skin cancer there is?

"Stage I," she repeated. She did the biopsy minutes later,. and within days, the diagnosis was confirmed.

I'll never know at what point The Nightmare Spot became cancerous or whether it was all along. I do know that, of the "ABCDE" warning signs of melanoma (which stand for asymmetry, border, color, diameter and evolving), the blotch on my leg had the uneven color characteristic of melanoma and was already evolving slightly by the time I saw that first doctor doing the skin checks.

The experience taught me that we understand our bodies better than our doctors do. I should have taken better charge of my own health by doing more research on my own. I should have told my doctor I needed a biopsy rather than continuing to ask. And I never should have allowed anyone to make me feel foolish for listening to what my intuition was telling me was important.

For me, melanoma has a sixth warning sign: "N" for nightmare. I feel so very lucky because the one thing I did do right was pay attention to my dream. Without it, I never would have been driven toward pursuing second, third, fourth and fifth opinions. Without that nightmare, I wouldn't still be alive.

~T'Mara Goodsell

61

The Thank-You

"Thank you" is the best prayer that anyone could say.
~Alice Walker

The cars were packed and ready to hit the road, a mini motorcade of two. My brother Douglas and I, ages nine and eight respectively, sat in the front seat of our old blue Cadillac next to my father, who was behind the wheel. My mother Laurie was driving the second car, a shiny green Buick my parents had picked up at the car rental place the day before. The driver's seat was the only spot other than the floor that wasn't piled high with our belongings. Even my mother likened it to the Beverly Hillbillies' overstuffed jalopy; that's how jam-packed it was.

"You look like Granny Clampett, Mom," Douglas and I both said, each trying to outshout the other. But with her high cheekbones and almond-shaped eyes, our mother bore a closer resemblance to Audrey Hepburn.

Every June, it was the same routine as my family left town to spend summer at the beach. My mother claimed she knew the way, but insisted on following behind us anyhow. "Just in case," she'd say, making us laugh. Her poor sense of direction was a family joke we never got tired of.

It was 1963. My grandfather, Julius, had been killed in a car accident six months earlier. All of us missed him, but my mother had been devastated. She was an only child, and she continued to feel his absence like an open wound. Sometimes, her eyes were red-rimmed from crying.

The night before we left for the beach, my mother had an unusual dream, unlike any she'd ever experienced. In it, she was driving a car while her father sat beside her in the passenger seat. According to what she told me later, he was facing forward, but his eyes were closed. The sight of his familiar profile held her gaze like a magnet as she stared at the hawk-like nose, the graying hair, and the smile lines etched into his left cheek.

Breaking the silence, Julius said, "Always be certain you can see out of the rear right side of the car."

When my mother tried to respond, she found she couldn't speak or even move. It was as if her mouth was sealed shut and her hands glued to the steering wheel. There was nothing she could do but stare mutely at her father as he repeated, "Laurie, make sure you can see out of the rear right side of the car."

Abruptly, she awakened. Trembling, she turned toward my sleeping father, grabbed his shoulder, and started talking rapidly, her voice shaking as she described the vivid dream.

"It's your grief talking," my father mumbled once she'd finished. He didn't believe in visions or spirits. "It's just a dream; you can't take it seriously." Not unkindly, he added, "Go to sleep."

She didn't think she could, not while the dream kept replaying in her head. Eventually, her eyes did close, and she drifted off. When the alarm clock jolted her awake several hours later, she jumped out of bed, thinking only of the long drive ahead. In the hectic glare of daylight, she never once thought of the dream.

By 10:00 a.m., both cars were breezing along the highway in the fast lane. Leaving the city had been the hard part. In order to keep other cars from getting between hers and the Cadillac, my mother drove as aggressively as a New York City cabdriver. Once that was over, she felt the tension leave her shoulders, and she reached out to turn on the radio.

She was humming along with the music when the dream came rushing back to her. Fear and adrenaline shot through her body as her father's words lodged in her brain. She didn't need to swivel her head around to know that the rear right window, as well as the one on the passenger side, was blocked, making it impossible to see what was happening behind her on the right side.

Holding the steering wheel with her left hand, she kept her eyes fixed on the road, and her foot pressed down on the gas pedal. Swinging her right arm over the seat back, she reached for the tightly packed mountain in the rear of the car, but it was too far away. Again and again, she stretched out her arm as her right hand clawed at the air. A burning pain had started in her shoulder. Ignoring it, she forced her body higher in the seat to gain leverage before arching her back and propelling her arm into a deeper sweeping motion. That's when her frantic fingers grasped the sleeve of a jacket and, with one desperate tug, sent an avalanche of boxes, toys, and bags tumbling to the floor. The flash of sunlight shooting through a porthole-sized opening in the rear right window was good enough for her. She sighed with relief and pulled back her arm.

Moments later, as the car started wobbling like a vibrating drill, my mother leaned forward to glance through the window. She expected the road to be unpaved and gravelly. Instead, it looked perfectly level, even as the jerking and swaying intensified. Up ahead, the Cadillac was driving smoothly while the Buick had become a bucking bronco.

She gripped the wheel tightly but she was barely managing to stay in her lane. Unable to see if a car was directly next to her on the right, she increased pressure on the gas and sped ahead. Then, clicking on the right turn indicator, her eyes and head began shooting backward and forward, continually checking and rechecking the limited view through the rear right window as she maneuvered across lanes of fast moving traffic.

She didn't realize she'd been holding her breath until she careened onto the far right shoulder of the road and skidded to a stop. Exhaling loudly, she put the gearshift in Park and removed the key from the ignition. Grabbing her purse, she pushed open the door and ran to a clump of trees fifteen feet away. From there, she inspected the car's exterior.

By the time, my father had doubled back with his two dumbstruck passengers to join my mother, she was leaning against the Buick and smiling. I remember thinking how cool and glamorous she looked in her oversized sunglasses, even as my father rushed from the car and grabbed her in a desperate hug, nearly sending the glasses flying from her face. He kept his arm around her as the two of them walked toward the passenger side of the Cadillac.

Douglas and I stared in disbelief at the mangled lump of shriveled black rubber encircling the silver rim. It was all that remained of the rear right tire.

Soon, we were back on the highway, heading toward the first exit and the nearest gas station. Unlike my brother, I wasn't asking about tire jacks or tow trucks, although I did have a question. All four of us were crammed into the front seat. Douglas was by the window, while I sat squished between him and my mother. Tilting my head upward, I whispered in her ear, "Mom, why did Dad say, 'Thank you, Julius'?"

~Hanna Kelly

62

Knowing When to Say No

Good instincts usually tell you what to do long before
your head has figured it out.
~Michael Burke

Moving from a small rural town to a larger city to start a new business was hard on our children. They had to leave all their friends and begin all over again. Our older daughter, Jodi, was outgoing and made new friends easily. Our eight-year-old son had plenty of children in the neighborhood his own age. Thirteen-year-old Cindy, however, was at a more awkward age and it was harder for her to make new friends.

We were happy that Cindy had finally found a small group of girls who had common interests and seemed to be respectable young ladies. The father of one friend, BJ, owned a construction business, and since our business was similar, we allowed Cindy a little more freedom to hang out with this group of girls, even though they were older than her, at ages fifteen and sixteen.

One Sunday afternoon, BJ and two other girls from their little group drove up to our home in an open-top Jeep with roll bars. It was a warm spring day, and we had enlisted our children to help with yard work with the promise of going to Dairy Queen afterward. All of us were sweaty and dirty from doing our annual spring cleanup.

BJ had recently turned sixteen and was excited to have passed her driver's license exam. Her parents gave their permission for her to pick up some friends. They wanted Cindy to join them and make it a foursome for the afternoon. We could see Cindy was envious of their carefree attitude, as these girls came from wealthier and more privileged families.

My husband was about to give Cindy permission to go with her friends when I stopped him. I had an uneasy feeling and I couldn't really explain it, but I insisted. "We need Cindy to help finish with our yard cleanup. Maybe next time she can join you," I said to them.

Of course, Cindy was not happy with my decision, but I felt I had no choice.

After we completed our yard work, all five of us piled into our Ram Charger and made a trip to Dairy Queen.

After we picked up our treats at the drive-through, we heard sirens. Then fire trucks and police cars sped by. Being a former volunteer firefighter and EMT, my husband wanted to see what was going on. Since we were just out for a ride, he decided to follow the fire trucks and police cars.

The fire trucks and police cars stopped on a steep curve in the road on the outskirts of town. As we drove by, we stretched our necks and noticed a vehicle rollover. I had to do a double take as I turned and looked at the same vehicle that had been in our front yard a few hours earlier. We said a prayer for the girls involved. We heard the ambulance siren coming behind us, so we drove on out of their way.

It was then I remembered the dream I had the previous night and I realized why I had objected so strongly to Cindy joining her friends.

In my dream I was walking and floating on clouds. I felt exhilarated as I floated along peacefully. Then I saw my father, who had passed away nine months earlier. He was standing in the clouds by a gate, and I saw Cindy float by me and go toward him. He turned and started to go through the gate, and motioned for her to follow. I tried to run after her to stop her from going through the gate with him, but my feet would not allow me to move. I stretched out my arms, and called for Cindy to come back and not go through the gate.

I woke up from that dream very upset and hadn't been able to go back to sleep, but like many people, I pushed the dream aside and went on with my day. I was so grateful that at least I didn't push away the feeling of dread that dream had instilled in me.

We found out that evening that Cindy's friend BJ was thrown from the vehicle and died at the scene. She was not wearing a seat belt. The other girls sustained injuries but were still alive and were treated by the paramedics on the scene.

Cindy has since become one of the finest police officers in her city's police department and has received several commendations for her contributions to the department. She has taken many defensive-driving courses and has taught defensive driving to both of her own children.

~Judith Rost

Chapter

7

Dreams and the Unexplainable

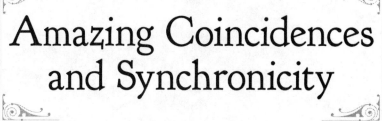

Amazing Coincidences and Synchronicity

63

A Close Encounter

There is no greater romance in life than
this adventure in realization.
~Meher Baba

The sights and odors that filled the streets of Ahmednagar, India on a Friday afternoon were dizzying; the streets seemed labyrinthine, the signage rarely in English. I had been in India for several weeks, visiting the tomb of Meher Baba, but this was my first venture into town, accompanying friends who wanted to do some shopping. With a real fear of getting lost should I wander off, I started humming the theme song from the Indiana Jones movies. It was one way of reassuring myself that all would turn out well in the last reel of my current adventure.

I only had three more days left in India before I would begin my journey back to California. Perhaps it was humming that tune that gave rise to my growing obsession but, for whatever reason, I could not stop thinking about sharing my Indian experience with Steven Spielberg. Having worked on a Lucasfilm production, I assumed I could figure out a way to get a letter to him. On the other hand, I worried I would come off as some sort of weirdo. No matter. The obsession gripped me firmly for the following three days.

Over the weekend, I would travel by bus from the Meher Pilgrim Center, where I was staying near the tomb, to Baba's former residence, around fifteen miles away. It was there that I had recently hiked up a large hill known as Seclusion Hill, so named because Meher Baba had spent time in seclusion atop it many years before. It reminded me of the Devil's Tower formation in the film, *Close Encounters of the Third Kind*. While not geologically similar, they both proved to be odd formations to which people from all over the world were inwardly drawn. During my bus rides, I would attempt to snap photos of the hill. People who became aware of my bizarre obsession would offer me their seats in order to get a better angle. My obsession was becoming increasingly public.

On my last day on the high desert, I awoke early in the dark in order to participate in the ritual cleaning of Meher Baba's tomb. This involved using a small sponge to wipe down the marble slab into which are inscribed the words, "I have come not to teach, but to awaken." These morning cleanings were supervised by a petite Indian woman named Mansari. When I'd finished wiping down the marble, she instructed me to surrender the sponge and to put my cupped hands together to receive the water she poured into them. I then scrubbed the wooden threshold to the tomb with my bare hand, a threshold that Easterners routinely knelt to kiss on their way in and out of the tomb.

Before heading out on my return journey later in the day, I went to Mansari's humble abode near the tomb to say goodbye. Holding out my right hand, I explained, "After the blessing that my hand received this morning, if it someday reaches out to grab an Oscar, it will mean nothing by comparison." She silently nodded her head in agreement.

My return home was to start with a night in Poona on my way to Bombay, but that plan was scuttled when my traveling companions, Marshall and Rozie, suggested I look into joining them on their evening flight to Bombay. I decided that made sense, and I figured I could take the shuttle bus from the airport to the Centaur Hotel when I arrived. It never occurred to me that there might not be an available room on a Monday night in such a huge hotel, but sure enough they were full. They wouldn't let me sleep in the lobby, so I would have to go out into the dark night and find another hotel.

I walked through the lobby with my head down, preparing to leave. And then, as I approached the door, and looked up, I could not believe my eyes. In walked Steven Spielberg. With him were all the producers of the Indiana Jones movies. One of them, Frank Marshall, and I locked eyes like gunslingers on a dusty western street and in unison proclaimed, "What the f@*k are you doing here?" After some mutual explanation, Frank introduced me to Steven, and I shook his hand... with the same unwashed hand that had just cleaned the tomb.

I learned that they were just passing through on their way to the airport after having scouted locations for *Indiana Jones and the Temple of Doom*. Their "people" leaned on the hotel and procured me a room. Then they invited me to join them for dinner. I ran upstairs and changed my dusty desert drought attire, splashed some water on myself, and ran back down to the lobby.

By the time I got there, the entire entourage had moved on except for one person: Steven Spielberg. As Steven and I walked to the French restaurant, I started out by asking him what he knew about India.

"The only thing I know is that it's nine hours from London," he replied.

I proceeded to fill him in about my obsession and the film I had shot for his benefit that was still in my camera. I would eventually send him the pictures along with a copy of Meher Baba's speech to the Hollywood establishment gathered at a reception in his honor thrown by Mary Pickford and Douglas Fairbanks Jr. in 1932 at their Pickfair estate. In it, Baba addressed the profound spiritual responsibility of the motion picture industry in influencing people's lives, not through grandiose religious tales, but rather through simple stories of selfless service and sacrifice played out in everyday circumstances.

Three days after my nervous humming of the Indiana Jones theme on the dusty streets of Ahmednagar, I found myself in the middle of pre-production discussions regarding the next Indiana Jones movie.

About eight hours after making that dismissive remark to Mansari about grabbing an Oscar, I was seated amongst the most successful producers in the history of Hollywood at that time, dining on Chicken Grimaldi and drinking fine French Chardonnay while sharing Meher Baba's message of cinematic healing.

It kind of makes me wonder what I should hum next.

~Brian Narelle

64

Attraction in Action

Everything you want is out there waiting for you to ask. Everything you want also wants you. But you have to take action to get it.
~Jack Canfield

While flying from my home in Australia to Los Angeles, my mind was focused on seeing my friend, Kelly. She and her husband would be filming me in their studio for a video series related to my work at HappinessHQ.

I was so happy to be taking my children, Claudia (thirteen) and Andrew (ten), with me. Claudia was excited to experience the Hollywood she'd seen in the movies; however, Andrew was consumed with thoughts of P-Rod.

No, my son isn't an aeronautics engineer. P-Rod is a person — an idol of his — also known as Paul Rodriguez, the hottest name in professional skateboarding at the time. From age seven, Andrew has loved skateboarding more than most people like breathing. He has been obsessed with it… and talked about P-Rod nonstop.

So it was no surprise that as we were wheeling our bags at the airport, Andrew looked up from his suitcase that dwarfed him in size and asked, "Do you think I will meet P-Rod in LA?"

I had to be very thoughtful with my response. This was one of those parenting moments that I knew would somehow either become a positive thing that would propel him forward, or else go completely the other way. On one hand, I wanted to encourage him in everything I had already taught him about the law of attraction. And yet I also wanted to ensure that he wasn't setting himself up for disappointment.

I finally responded, "Los Angeles is a very big city, with millions of people, but if you set the intention and then don't get attached to the outcome, anything is possible." Having heard this recipe for manifesting so many times before, he replied, "Yeah, yeah… I do know to let go of attachment, Mum!"

When we arrived in Los Angeles, the cab driver, for some unknown reason, dropped us off at a mall right in front of the Zumiez skateboarding store. Andrew was jubilant, and it quickly got better. Upon chatting with the storekeeper, we learned that P-Rod shopped there, and the owner had P-Rod's mother's number in his phone! Andrew was officially only two degrees of separation from his idol, and with that news alone, he could have happily flown back to Australia!

When we met up with my friend Kelly over dinner a week later, she asked the kids what they liked to do, and what they most liked about being in Los Angeles. As you might imagine, it didn't take long for P-Rod to come up.

"I want to meet P-Rod," Andrew told her.

Kelly responded quizzically, "What's a P-Rod?"

Within a few moments, Andrew excitedly told Kelly about how P-Rod was the best skateboarder and how much he admired him. He even pulled up a photo of him on the Internet to show to Kelly.

Kelly said, "Well, you never know… strange things happen in Los Angeles."

The next day had been set aside to film at Kelly's studio. As it was way out in the San Fernando Valley, we had made plans weeks before for the kids to be doing other things, meaning they would come nowhere near the studio. However, a strange, last-minute glitch meant that they had to be dropped at the studio near the end of the day.

When they arrived, Kelly said offhandedly to Andrew, "Too bad you didn't bring your skateboard" since there was so much space outside in the parking lot. Just as she said that, her husband Dana happened to be walking past and asked, "Who likes skateboarding?"

He explained that when they had first moved in, they had used the Wi-Fi of their neighbor. "It was called 'Rod Skate' or something," he said casually.

This was complete news to Kelly, and her eyes widened almost as much as Andrew's. As for me, I felt the hairs stand up on the back of my neck.

"It wasn't Paul Rodriguez, was it?" Andrew asked in a stunned tone.

Kelly said, "That would be far-fetched. I seriously doubt it… but Dana, you'd better check on that immediately!"

Before Dana could do anything, Andrew had darted outside on a mission. He soon ran back, announcing ecstatically, "It's P-Rod's skate park! It's P-Rod's… I recognize it!"

Having spent dozens of hours studying P-Rod videos on YouTube, Andrew had instantly recognized the equipment behind the studio.

With mouths agape, we all followed Andrew back outside to check things out.

A small group of skaters was standing around, and I asked if they were expecting P-Rod to show up that evening.

"Dunno, man" was the dismissive reply.

Then, right on cue, about sixty seconds later, a white Jaguar pulled in from the street, driving in what felt like slow motion. Although still in semi-disbelief, I whipped out my phone and began videotaping what was happening.

The car stopped right in front of us, the door opened, and out stepped P-Rod! Were we dreaming?

Kelly didn't waste a second before calling out, "Excuse me, Paul, see this little boy here? His name is Andrew… and he's come all the way from Australia. He's your number-one fan!"

At that, P-Rod walked right up to Andrew, shook his hand, and began a conversation with him. If Andrew's smile had been any bigger, the top of his head might have flipped off.

Just before putting his arm around Andrew for photos, P-Rod kindly asked Andrew if he'd like him to sign anything. Andrew just happened to have a black Sharpie on him, which he'd been carrying throughout his trip "just in case." He asked for signatures on his P-Rod brand shoes, shirt, and hat.

After some time, as P-Rod was walking away into his skate park, I told him how his name had been a household word for us for several years, and how Andrew had asked as he left Australia if he might meet him while in Los Angeles. P-Rod replied matter-of-factly, "Oh, well, he attracted it!"

The funny thing is, as a Law of Attraction coach, I help people attract miraculous things into their lives all the time. So why was I surprised by P-Rod's comment? Perhaps because I was still somehow reeling at how things had unfolded for Andrew that evening.

As we drove home, Kelly said, "So, Andrew, now do you believe anything is possible?" Andrew hesitated for a moment before saying, "Um, yes… but I already knew nothing was impossible."

And therein lies the key.

It turned out that my son was my best example in terms of using the formula to manifest a dream… a miracle. He was clear and focused, passionate (okay, slightly obsessed), and grateful at the same time. He wasn't overwhelmed or grasping at what he wanted to bring into his life. He kept it simple, and magnetized P-Rod out of the millions of people in LA… seemingly out of the blue. Andrew didn't have to hunt down the celebrity — the celebrity came to him!

Three years later, with the signed hat still hanging on his bedroom wall, along with the permanent marker that P-Rod had used, what happened that day is a permanent memory for our whole family that will certainly never wash away.

Every time we tell the story, the reaction of amazement is always the same, and our own goose bumps never fail to reappear.

And even the greatest skeptics come around to accepting that nothing's impossible!

~Amanda Lee

65

Our Dinner Partner

It's a small world, but we all run in big circles.
~Sasha Azevedo

A cruise to Alaska was an item on our bucket list, so my wife Janet and I were excited as we boarded the Celebrity Infinity. We got settled in our cabin, explored the ship, and then met the other people at our assigned dinner table. We were seated with a family of three from Georgia and a couple from Tennessee.

We were all over forty, but we didn't find some common ground to discuss until the third night when I mentioned that my mother was from the Philippines and that my older sister was born there. In 1948, my parents and eleven-month-old sister had sailed on American President Lines for San Francisco.

Hanna, the blue-eyed woman from Tennessee, set down her fork, and with her slight southern accent, announced she was born in the Philippines, too. Her parents were Czech and her father had worked for a Czech shoe manufacturing company in Manila until the Japanese invasion in December 1941. Her parents stayed in the Philippines through the war and Hanna was born there in 1942. But her father died after that and her mother was forced by the Japanese to leave the Philippines.

Two-year-old Hanna was left in the care of friends in Manila until her immigration paperwork was straightened out. Finally, in 1948, she was put aboard a ship for San Francisco to be met by her new stepfather.

"The name of the ship was *General M.C. Meigs* of the American President Lines," she said. "Is that the ship your family came on?"

It sounded familiar, but all my genealogy records were back in California. I also didn't know the exact date my family sailed, but it was etched in Hanna's soul since she was put on board alone as a six-year-old. "August 24, 1948," she said. I told her I would look it up when I returned to California. After the war, there were so many ships ferrying returning vets and families across the Pacific that I was positive Hanna and my family were just specks in the flood of people. I wrote down all her information and let this strange encounter rest. At the remaining dinners, we all talked of other things and parted as new friends.

At home, I found a copy of the passenger manifest. The ship *was* the *USS General M.C. Meigs*. I gasped and set down the paper when I saw that the ship sailed on August 24, 1948. On the manifest, the names of my father, mother, and eleven-month-old sister were listed. Directly above my father's name was that of Hanna. She was listed as Czech. I wasn't listed, but I knew I had been along for the ride, "in the oven."

I sent an e-mail to Hanna to let her know this exciting discovery, but I knew she and her husband were flying to the Czech Republic right after the cruise to visit relatives.

When Hanna returned from her travels about a month later, she e-mailed me to say I would be receiving something in the mail that I was not going to believe.

When a large manila envelope arrived from Tennessee, I quickly tore it open. Inside were several clippings from 1948 newspapers all over the United States. Each told the story of Hanna's solo trip across the ocean from Manila as a six-year-old. She was a bona fide celebrity.

Clipped to the newspaper articles was a color photocopy of the ship's farewell dinner menu. She'd attached a note instructing me to look at the back. I flipped over the menu and found a note in my mother's handwriting to Hanna:

My dearest darling Hanna,
Jeanette Carolyn and I can never forget how well you have been during
the trip. We love you so much and hope you'll grow up to be a fine lady.
Love and kisses always —
Mrs. F. B. Zeilinger & Baby Jean
David City, Nebraska

My wife and I had, in fact, been seated at a table with a woman who was at a table with my parents more than a half-century before.

We've since become friends, but still haven't figured out the cosmic significance of this meeting. Why was it important I meet Hanna at a dinner table aboard a passenger ship exactly like she met my parents so very long ago? Had we not met, I would never have known of this chapter in her or my family's life.

To this day, I still choke up at the wonder of our small world.

~Will Zeilinger

66

Destined to Detour

Sometimes I think things happen for a reason... And
I think if we're meant to run into each other
again, fate will make it happen.
~Lauren Blakely

Growing up in Florida was amazing, but not as amazing as my best friend, Denise. We were two kids trying to get through life, apparently in the hardest way possible. From puberty through high school, then marriage, babies, and divorce, we had a lot in common — likes, dislikes, dreams and fears, dark secrets, silly stuff, and lots of memories, both good and bad. We shared everything with each other for twenty years.

When my parents divorced, I moved to Texas, creating a thousand-mile gap between us. This was before Skype, cell phones, and Facebook, but landline phones connected her heart to mine. When phone calls and letters weren't enough, I managed vacation visits, even if just for a long weekend. Our visits were filled with hugs and laughter, but always ended in tears. The saddest part of a short visit to see a long-distance friend is the leaving part. I left a lot. We cried a lot. We were such passionate friends. Connected at the heart, I couldn't have loved her more if we had shared the same DNA.

Sadly, a drunk driver changed everything. My lifelong friend lost her husband and children in that flaming inferno. She was thrown from their car with third-degree burns over eighty percent of her body. I wasn't allowed to visit her in the burn unit, but I stayed in touch with her father, Joe, for long distance updates. Denise struggled to live for five grueling months until her heart simply stopped. She was thirty-two.

I never got to say "goodbye" and was unable to attend her funeral. I had no closure, and my heart grieved, not just for her, but also for her parents.

Even though Joe and I promised to stay in touch, we eventually got busy with living and lost contact with one another.

Five years later, I moved back to Florida. Driving on Interstate 10, I passed an exit sign outside Tallahassee that pointed toward Monticello. I wondered if Joe still lived there, but since I no longer had his address or phone number, I decided to drive on to my new home.

A few miles beyond that exit, my car engine literally stopped. It was as if someone had reached into the car and turned the key. I pumped the gas, but nothing happened. I struggled with the dead power steering to ease the car onto the shoulder and sat there wondering what to do next. When I turned the key, I was surprised to hear the engine start again. However, when I tried to give it gas, it just lurched and chugged. It ran in fits and starts on the shoulder until it finally picked up speed and I felt safe enough to pull back into traffic.

Was it coincidence that it stopped at the first sign of Monticello only to start again after it was obvious I wanted to go home more than I wanted to find Joe? I could only wonder.

It wasn't long before the car repeated this performance. It had over 68,000 miles on it, but nothing like this had ever happened before. Again, I pulled onto the shoulder of the highway and stopped. I could see another sign in the distance, but couldn't read it. When I turned the key, it started like the last time, but continued to balk when I gave it more gas. I drove on the shoulder and finally saw that the next exit went to the main highway into Monticello. I thought about exiting, but then the engine roared to life again and I decided to take my chances on the highway. I still had a long trip ahead of me.

I passed several more exits without event and ended up in rural Florida, a luscious land of hills, forest, and overgrown vegetation. It was as beautiful as I remembered. Suddenly, my car pulled its dying act again. I decided if it would just start one more time, even if it ran perfectly, I would take whatever exit came next, find a station, and buy some gas treatment. I hoped the problem was only bad gas.

I prayed there was another exit soon. There was, but it was desolate. There was a crusty, old, rundown station on the opposite side of the Interstate, but first I had to get there. This time, there was no hesitation, but rather a sense of urgency. The car chugged down the exit ramp, and it tried to die again at the stop sign. I made a rolling stop past the stop sign, turned left onto the two-lane country road and headed over the overpass. At the top of that overpass, my car finally died. Thanks to gravity, I managed to coast down the other side. The car rolled slowly into the station and came to a soft stop at the first gas pump with absolutely no momentum remaining. The decision to stop had been made for me.

I stormed inside, frantically scanning the sparse shelves for some gas treatment when an elderly gentleman with a large, bushy moustache approached. He said with a slow drawl, "Can I help you find something, young lady?"

My heart nearly stopped. I didn't really recognize the man, but I could never forget that voice. "I'm l-looking for some gas treatment. D-do you have any?" My heart was in my throat. Everything felt surreal, and I still wasn't certain, until…

He answered with a grin, "Well, let's just have a looky-see."

In that very instant, I knew for a fact I had found Denise's father Joe, years later and miles away in the middle of nowhere. "Looky-see" was a term I had heard him use many times when I was growing up.

We hugged a long while, caught up in the moment. Neither of us wanted to let go. I told him I was moving back to Florida and relayed the events that had led me to this place at this exact time. He didn't seem surprised.

Joe grinned and said, "Well, you certainly are one lucky lady. This is my brother's station. He called and asked me to watch the place so he could go to the post office. A little bit earlier or later, I wouldn't be here." He winked, and the twinkle in his eye told me he didn't believe in coincidence any more than I did.

That car never acted like that again. An unseen force far greater than just bad gas orchestrated my reunion with Joe at that specific time and place.

~Ferna Lary Mills

67

Just Press Play

*Memory is a glorious grab bag of the past from which
one can at leisure pluck bittersweet experiences of
times gone by and relive them.*
~Hal Boyle

I awoke at 5:00 a.m. and instinctively turned on my phone to
see the scroll of missed calls, messages, and texts. Sadly, I saw
that my beloved ninety-two-year-old grandmother, Margaret
Amelia Sullivan, had passed away. In her sleep, at home, in the
still of the night, she had floated peacefully to heaven — the way we
all wish to slip from this world into the next.

While my family and I were hunkered down in a puppy pile
of tears, hugs, "I love yous," and our favorite stories about Granny,
my husband received a phone call from the owner of the recording/
production studio we'd been renting for the past five years saying
that the studio had been sold. We had two days to move out. We had
known we would soon be moving, but we thought we had months to
do it gracefully and gradually. But now, the clock was ticking, and we
had forty-eight hours to move our belongings.

The last place on earth I wanted to be was at our 24,000-square-
foot studio on the other side of town, away from my family. My heart
was so heavy with emotion that I was not in the mindset to sort out
our mountains of business files and boxes.

With tears, sniffs, and a lot of pouting, I dutifully accompanied my husband to our studio.

As we were sorting, sandwiched between my teary thoughts of missing my grandma, I vaguely remembered dragging my husband, Dana, with me years before to visit my grandma to film her telling some of her stories. It was just after she'd suffered a broken hip, and I knew that her time on this earth with us was limited.

My husband turned on the camera, and Granny lit up like a Christmas tree, eyes sparkling and smile radiant. With her gray hair done in her classic style and wearing a lavender sweatshirt, she animatedly shared stories about sneaking out her bedroom window as a teenager to hop on a train to meet the man who would be my grandpa. She reminisced about raising five children alone while my grandpa was at war in the Navy, surviving fire, floods, storms, and keeping her highly energetic kids safe while having as much fun as possible.

I didn't dare ask Dana where those tapes might be. I knew it would be met with a sigh and an eye roll at the impossibility of finding them. My husband is an incredibly talented music producer, videographer, and editor, among many other gifts. But one of his talents is *not* in the domain of organization. There were hundreds of boxes of MiniDV tapes he had filmed over the past seventeen years since we'd been together... all of which needed to be moved.

And because all my heart wanted to do was get back to my family, I was in the spirit of "let's get rid of everything!"

Dana was contemplating agreeing with me about just torching the whole mess when, out of the blue, he stuck his hand into a random box. Like a grab bag, he pulled out two random tapes, and then he yelled across the cavernous studio, "Kelly, you'll never guess the names of the two tapes I just found!"

I responded with a despondent blank stare and shrugged shoulders.

"Granny 1 and Granny 2!"

Those were the only two tapes he'd pulled out of boxes of hundreds! New tears streamed from my eyes... tears of gratitude... tears of awe… tears that only take place when something truly miraculous and unexplainable happens.

If we didn't have to move that weekend—the day after my grandma passed away—we never would have been at the studio sorting through boxes.

Of all the boxes of tapes, how was it possible that Dana was led to the exact box that contained those exact tapes?

Did my granny orchestrate this? Was it God? An angel?

Whoever or whatever it was, it felt like the reassurance that my family and I needed that Granny was well situated in heaven, and soon we would be at peace, too.

To add the icing on top of this unexplainable miracle, I found someone who had the rare technology to transfer nine-year-old tapes to a digital format just in time to share the video of my sparkling-eyed grandma at the reception after her funeral for my whole family to enjoy.

These tapes are treasures, soul gold that we are all so grateful to have… and all my family and extended family will always treasure.

Now, when I miss Granny and just want to see her again, to hear her voice and laughter, all I have to do is press Play.

~Kelly Sullivan Walden

68

Yellow No. 2

And in today already walks tomorrow.
~Samuel Taylor Coleridge

It was my first day of college and I was walking alone across campus toward the college bookstore, one of many students headed in the same direction. I was told it would be crowded, and I would probably have to wait in line, so I was in a hurry. I was in a hurry a lot in those days. On the greens near the pathway I was on, students were tossing footballs and flinging Frisbees. The air was filled with the shouts and laughter of young men and women greeting each other, alive with first-day excitement.

Bellbottoms and miniskirts were in fashion, along with long hair and oversized afros for men and women. The air was warm and breezy, smelling faintly of a nearby freeway and the more promising aroma of marijuana. Everyone seemed excited and expectant and filled with purpose. We were in college. We had dreams. The future was ours.

I was within a hundred yards of the bookstore when I saw a yellow pencil lying on the ground under a shrub. I intended to study engineering in those early days and had purchased several mechanical pencils that didn't need sharpening. The one on the ground was made of wood. It was out of my way, and I was in a hurry. I should have paid it no mind, but without much thought and for no good reason, I made a small detour and picked it up. It was a plain yellow No. 2 wood pencil, never even sharpened, waiting there to be spotted and picked up by some passerby. In hindsight, perhaps it was waiting just for me.

The few steps out of my way lasted no more than ten seconds, but those ten seconds changed the direction of my life. I can trace every major life event thereafter — including meeting my wife ten years later, the conception of my children and the selection of my eventual profession — to that fortuitous little detour.

There was no sudden epiphany, no gleeful cheer of discovery, nothing to distinguish that small and seemingly insignificant moment from any other. In fact, I gave no thought to that pencil until more than fifty years later when, on another warm September afternoon, I drove by the old campus. For no good reason, other than to satisfy a taste for nostalgia, I decided to stop by for a walk down Memory Lane.

I didn't expect to remember much after fifty years. I thought that everything would look different — that the many miles I had traveled since then would make the campus look old and insignificant — but I was wrong. As I started to wander around, memories came flooding back. They were filled mostly with people — friends I had not kept in touch with, the few girls I had dated, the professor who had awakened my curiosity about history and politics, the English professor who helped me appreciate literature.

Fifty years later, the students were still throwing footballs and flinging Frisbees, and now kicking soccer balls as well. Their clothes and hairstyles were different, but they were still laughing, shouting and making the same joyful noises. They had their own dreams now, and the future belonged to them.

I wanted a souvenir to take home with me, maybe a sweatshirt or a coffee cup or something for my grandkids. Maybe some three-ring binders with the school's Brahma Bull mascot on the cover or some pencils bearing the college name. And so, once again, I started off for the bookstore. I'm not sure how memories get triggered. Maybe it was being on campus again on a warm September afternoon or maybe it was walking to the bookstore or thinking about buying some pencils. But there it was: The memory of that brand-new, never-been-used, yellow No. 2 floated up into my consciousness like I had just found it.

And with the memory of the pencil, I remembered the rest of the walk to the bookstore: students filing into line as I approached; the sweet girl who ended up in line just ahead of me; bits and pieces of our conversation; my telling her that I was looking for a job; her advice that I check the administration office where job offers were posted on a bulletin board. Had it not been for that pencil and the ten seconds or so it took to pick it up, I would have lined up behind someone else, and that conversation would never have taken place.

At the administration office, they were just about to pin up a 3x5 card with a part-time job offer on it: a shoe clerk at a local shopping mall. The woman who was about to pin it up handed it to me. I applied that very afternoon and reported for work the next day.

It took me another fifty years to realize that with that part-time job, the trajectory of my life was changed. The store manager and his family became my best friends, and when he left for another job with an insurance company, I followed. It was there that I was employed as a claims adjuster, met my wife, and developed an interest in the law that led to me becoming a lawyer.

I picked up that yellow No. 2 in September of 1964 when I was twenty-one years old and just out of the Navy. Kennedy was dead less than a year, and Johnson and Goldwater were battling for the soul of the country. The Vietnam conflict was escalating into a ten-year war that would mire the country in pain and nearly split it at the seams. But on that late summer day in 1964, the music of the Beatles was floating in the air, and The Drifters were making love "Under the Boardwalk." The heavy and somber protest songs of the 1960s and 70s had not yet been written, and the suffering that was to come was on no one's mind. My path through life, which until that day had been headed in a different direction, was altered by just a few seconds, but just enough to change everything.

~Andrew Garcia

69

All the Buzz

*Serendipity is the faculty of finding things we
did not know we were looking for.*
~Glauco Ortolano

A weekend visit to Las Vegas at age twenty-one turned into a forty-seven-year career in the casino industry. During those years, one of my favorite benefits was meeting many famous people, some of whom happily befriended me, a guy from a small Italian section of Queens, New York. I was spending time with astronauts, golf pros, major league baseball players, superstars of the entertainment industry, and even a few U.S. Presidents! Some people, depending on their opinion of what makes a miracle, might call it a miracle of sorts, but that's not what this story is about.

This is about the youngest of my three sons, who was seven years old and was deeply affected by my divorce from his mother. My sons and I had moved from Las Vegas to Atlantic City, and they had to start in a new school. My youngest was rather quiet and sensitive, and it was not an easy transition for him.

One day, his teacher was talking about Apollo 11, Neil Armstrong and Buzz Aldrin, the first men to land on the moon, and she asked if anyone had any questions. Robert immediately raised his hand and proudly announced, "Astronaut Buzz Aldrin used to come to my house for dinner." The teacher said that was very nice and went on with the questions.

After school, Robert was confronted by a group of his classmates. They sneered at him, called him a liar and said that he should go back to Las Vegas. He came home in tears and could not be comforted. He looked up at me through his tears and asked, "Why, Dad? I told the truth, and they all hate me."

I felt helpless, but I gave him the best answer I could: "It takes time for a new kid to fit in. Try and forget about it, and I promise everything will be fine."

Robert pleaded with me to take him out of that school. He said he never wanted to go back. After quite a bit of cajoling, I convinced him to give it a try.

The next morning, I went to work, and Robert bravely went to school. A few minutes after I arrived in my office, the phone rang, and I was shocked to hear Buzz Aldrin on the line. He said he was in New Jersey visiting his father and thought he would stop in Atlantic City to get together for lunch. My mind was spinning, but I managed to ask him if he wouldn't mind setting aside an hour for me after lunch. He said, "Sure, what's up?" I was too busy mulling over a plan so I just answered, "I'll tell you during lunch."

I told Buzz the entire story about Robert, and he rubbed his hands together in anticipation. "What do you want to do?"

I commandeered our fanciest limo, and we drove to Robert's school.

We went to the principal's office, and I introduced her to Mr. Aldrin. I explained the situation and asked if she would allow us to walk into Robert's classroom. She gathered herself together, after the initial shock of the meeting, and gladly walked us to the classroom door. As we opened the door, Buzz took me by the arm and said, "Leave this to me."

He walked in ahead of us and announced, "I'm Astronaut Buzz Aldrin, and I'm here to visit with my old buddy, Robert." I was lucky enough to spot Robert as soon as we entered and was able to see his reaction from the very beginning. I will always see that image as clear as if it happened a minute ago. Buzz rushed to Robert at his desk, gave him a huge hug and said, "How are you, old buddy? Sorry it's been so long since my last visit, but I promise to be around more often."

Of course, I looked at the faces of the other kids, and they were all looking at each other with the same dumbfounded expression. I felt so blessed to be able to do this for my son. I didn't know how to thank Buzz for making it possible. How do you manage something like that properly? All I can say is, until today, I never stopped trying. Robert was thrilled, and he went from being teased to being the school hero.

I've never gotten over the miracle — the amazing coincidence — of Buzz Aldrin calling me and visiting the day after Robert was teased for claiming he knew him. A few years ago, we lost Robert to brain cancer. He was thirty-five years old. The memory of his victorious moment still helps to ease the pain.

~Ralph S. Delligatti

70

Miss Milli and Me

It's good to have plans and dreams, but don't be
surprised if God brings you somewhere else.
~Anne F. Beiler

I had taken a day off from work to go to a doctor's appointment, only to have the appointment canceled by his office the night before. The next morning, I tried to make lemons out of lemonade by inviting a friend to lunch, only to have her become ill with a "headache" a half-hour before we were to meet.

I flopped on the sofa contemplating my next move. Days off from work were precious, and I hated the thought of wasting one. *Well*, I thought, *I'll catch up on my grocery shopping so that this day is not a complete bust.* I reached for the stack of supermarket flyers that were delivered to my door weekly. They all advertised the same old, same old: farm fresh, best selection, lowest prices. Then something caught my eye.

A new market had opened several towns away from mine. Sure, it was a haul, but the photos of the newly renovated space made it look spectacular. And the prices! They really *were* low. There was one more reason why I was so keen on shopping at this market, too. It was in Milli's old neighborhood.

Miss Milli was that special adult in my childhood — the one who stood out for making a difference. She was my childhood Sunday school teacher, and whether she knew it or not, she guided me through some tough childhood years and helped to shape me into the adult I later became.

She was a true eccentric through and through — an artist, teacher and gallery owner with a flair for the avant-garde. She was everything I aspired to be: boisterous, enthusiastic, creative and joyful — a sharp contrast to the quiet, little girl who sat in her Sunday school class for one hour each week.

I didn't always have much to be happy about at home during those days. Though my family was kind and loving, and I had many of the creature comforts a child could hope for, my mom and brother both experienced chronic illness that had me confused and afraid much of the time. I never spoke about it in Sunday school, and Miss Milli never asked. She just supported me in the best way she knew how. When she included me in a barbecue with her own children at her home, took me for an impromptu afternoon walk in the park, or spent a few hours giving me painting lessons in her studio, I forgot about the family illness that sometimes overwhelmed me. Afterwards, I came home refreshed and joyful. Just like Miss Milli.

I was tempted to drive past her house, knock on her door even. "Surprise! It's me! Your Sunday school student from forty years ago!" *No, that would be weird,* I thought as I pushed my cart through the supermarket's brand-new aisles. Even though we had kept in touch until I was well into my twenties, Miss Milli probably wouldn't remember me now. Maybe Miss Milli didn't even live in this community anymore.

I went back and forth like this in my mind for several minutes. *Oh, well,* I decided, losing my nerve, *I'll make one more stop at the produce area for that forgotten head of lettuce, and then I'll just go home.* And as fate would have it, there stood Miss Milli, between the onions and the potatoes.

I recognized her immediately. The curve of her shoulders and the unusual curl of her hair gave it away. Excited, I went over to her and introduced myself. Oh, yes, she said, she remembered me, even though I didn't look quite the same. And then the memories flooded back: the bright Sunday mornings in Sunday school, the church trip she planned for the five girls in our class, the painting lessons, the park and the barbecues. All of it remembered, nothing forgotten.

Then I hugged her and spoke from the heart. "Those were some tough times for me," I admitted. "The way you cared made a big difference."

She became teary. "I had no idea."

That day, Miss Milli and I exchanged phone numbers. By the next week, I was back at her house painting alongside her in her studio. Sometimes, we visited a museum together, and other times we simply shared lunch at my home or hers, two old friends breaking bread. We had a bond and closeness that defied time and age. For two more precious years, until Miss Milli passed away, still vibrant at the age of eight-six, we shared a wonderful friendship.

How many times have I griped over a change in plans? I always want to think I know what's best for me, and when my plans don't work out, I become frustrated. But the universe is wiser than me, and on a day fraught with disappointments, the powers that be landed me in just the right place at the right time to continue a special friendship that had started forty years prior. The universe had worked its magic again.

~Monica A. Andermann

71

Johnny Came Home

I seldom end up where I wanted to go, but
almost always end up where I need to be.
~Douglas Adams

y friend Amy appeared worn out and unkempt. Then I saw her shaking hands and her red, grim face. I did not invite her to come in.

I'd recently taken in her sixteen-year-old because he felt he was no longer welcome in her home.

Amy's voice quivered with rage. "Why did you let Johnny move in?"

"He's welcome in my home."

"You had no business taking him in."

"He had no place to go."

She made a move as though to blast past me into my home. I stood my ground. Her eyes narrowed to slits. I could practically smell her anger. "I want him to leave."

"He's staying here, Amy. He has no place to go."

My son Brian and her son Johnny had been friends since they were five years old. Their birthdays are one week apart, and both have genius-level IQs and identical interests. They were so close they were like brothers.

Johnny had not done well after Amy married Mark and had more children with her new husband. He didn't feel like he fit in their household, and he turned into a resentful and angry young man. Although I couldn't defend his outburst of rage that led to him taking a baseball bat to the windshield of Amy's car, neither could I let him go homeless.

Anyway, it wasn't that she'd come to take him home. She just didn't want him to be in mine.

"Go home, Amy."

She made another attempt to come in. I blocked her with my shoulder and glared at her. "Go home," I repeated. "You aren't coming in."

It was a tense moment between old friends.

Johnny stayed, but he didn't behave well. I'd bought the boys bunk beds, and Johnny, in the top bunk, pounded the ceiling with his feet after we were all asleep. He roamed the neighborhood at night, sometimes talking Brian into going with him. He taunted my daughter Moriah to tears. He needed more structure and discipline than I could manage. Together, we found a non-military group home with rules he felt he could live with. It didn't last long and, after that, he vanished. What could I do? He wasn't mine, and apparently, he decided to make it on his own.

Four years passed. Brian mourned for Johnny sometimes, wondering if Johnny was dead or alive, free or imprisoned. Johnny was braided into so many of Brian's childhood memories that Brian couldn't reminisce without thinking about his friend. Brian graduated and moved out on his own. I got promoted to a position as a database administrator with the privilege to work remotely from home. All it took was an extra phone line and I could stay in my pajamas all day if I wanted.

The only downside to working from home was the telemarketing calls. Solicitations. Requests for donations or to join a cause. As soon as I heard their chirpy greetings, saying my name like we were old friends, I told them, "No," and asked that they take my name off their calling lists. Until one special call.

"Leslie, you've been chosen for a free Florida vacation. Three days, two nights, all expenses paid. All you have to do is answer three questions."

I caught my breath, and my eyes widened. I stopped listening to the words and heard only the voice. I whispered, "Johnny?"

"Pardon me?"

"Johnny? Is your name Johnny?" I felt silly. What were the odds? Astronomical, to the point of miraculous.

His spiel interrupted, he stopped talking.

My eyes tearing up, I asked a third time.

His response? "Who is this?"

"It's Leslie."

As the wonder infused both our hearts, we vocally high-fived and gushed for a moment. What were the odds of his computer autodialing my number? Or, instead of Johnny, it could have been a co-worker who called me. I told him that most times I let the unknown calls go to voicemail. I asked him, "Where are you?"

"In Chicago. I met an older woman online and moved in with her."

As my mind registered the words "older woman" and "online," my instincts tingled. "How much older?"

"Fourteen years." He paused. I heard his mouth crackle a little and knew he'd plastered on that big smile he used when telling me something sure to get a reaction. "I'm a stepdad."

Ambivalence flooded me. I was happy that he was safe, but what was an extremely intelligent nineteen-year-old doing working as a phone solicitor five states away from home, raising someone else's children? *Don't go there,* I decided. *Keep the conversation focused on him.* "We miss you."

His tone shifted down like a car struggling to get uphill. "No one calls me 'Johnny' anymore. It's John."

I filed that away.

He said, "I'm on a timer so I have to go. I've got your phone number."

His tone puzzled me. We experienced a miracle together. A true, honest-to-God miracle. Didn't he miss us? God opened the door, and I sensed that unless I said the right thing, and quickly, Johnny was about to close it. Then insight struck. He'd put years and miles between himself and his family of birth. Well, Johnny might have put his past behind him, but I wasn't about to let us stay there. I went for the big gun. "Brian misses you."

He said without hesitation, "I miss him, too."

I wanted to ask him for his phone number, but instinct told me not to. "Call me back. Promise?"

I heard him swallow hard. "I promise."

It took him a while, and we waited anxiously, but his call finally came. His first visit was a momentous event. He wavered for a couple years about permanently returning to Florida, but eventually he left the older woman and came home. He fell in love with a woman, this time one eleven years younger than himself. He prefers employment that involves physical labor with a self-understanding that jobs that make him "think" also engage emotions he believes he cannot always control.

He calls me "Mom." Out of respect for my old girlfriend, I insist on "Second Mom." I still call him Johnny; out of respect for me, he doesn't insist on "John." In the end, it doesn't matter what we call each other. What matters is that, thanks to divine intervention, what was lost has been found, and the son of my heart is home.

~Leslie Dunn

An Accidental Discovery

I have always believed, and I still believe, that
whatever good or bad fortune may come our
way, we can always give it meaning and
transform it into something of value.
~Hermann Hesse, Siddhartha

On a blustery afternoon in February, I decided to leave a few hours early to pick up my three-year-old daughter from her dad's house. The trip was forty-five minutes each way, and I didn't want to risk the weather getting any worse.

The roads were slick, and the visibility wasn't great, but we were toasty in the car, listening to music and chatting about her weekend. When we reached the edge of our little village, I began to feel a bit tired. We were only about six miles from home, though.

The next thing I remember was the horrific sound of screeching metal and bursting glass. There was an explosion of screams and confusion. And the smell of burning.

Before I knew what was happening, I was being yanked out of my seatbelt. "Your child. You need to get her out. The car could catch on fire. Get her out now. You need to move now!" I was fumbling with the handle in shock. When I finally got the door open and saw my daughter's red face twisted up in terror, I snapped into reality enough to get her out of her car seat and hold her close.

"I'm okay, Mommy, I'm okay," she repeated through sobs, her body tense, and her knuckles digging into my sweat-soaked shirt.

We were ushered into a van, along with the woman and her six-year-old son who had been in the vehicle we hit. I trembled uncontrollably as we waited for an ambulance. When the officers and EMTs arrived, they flooded me with questions — none of which I could answer. I didn't know what had happened. Did I fall asleep? I had been tired. Did I slip on black ice? The roads were slick. "I don't know" seemed to be the only thing I could muster.

According to the police, the collision was so severe that nobody should have survived, let alone walked away.

The EMTs explained that the entire front passenger side of my car was gone. Since my daughter was in the back on that same side, she was closest to the point of impact, yet she was completely unharmed. She didn't even have a scratch. On the other hand, I was pretty bruised, but opted to be driven home rather than go to the ER. We'd been through enough.

About a week later, ready to get back on the road, I scheduled a rental car service to pick us up at home. I brought my daughter's car seat out into the sunlight to examine it for cracks or any other signs of damage. I tipped it over, lifted the cushions, and went over every inch. It looked fine, so I decided to continue using it until I could get a new one.

The rental car company was late at this point, so I made a quick call reminding them about my pickup. I wandered down the driveway a bit, and when the call ended, I headed back up to where my daughter was standing next to her car seat.

She had something clenched tightly in her fist. "What do you have?" I asked. She opened her palm, revealing a smooth, polished stone. When I looked closer, I realized it had a large cross etched in black in the middle of its surface.

"Where'd you get that?" I asked.

She pointed her chubby, little toddler finger to the car seat and said, "Right there in my seat."

I was perplexed. I had just examined this seat minutes before—surely I would have seen a stone that was larger than a golf ball. Why didn't it fall out when I turned over the seat?

So again I asked, "Seriously, honey. Where'd you get that?"

And in her small voice, she explained, "God gave it to me so I won't ever be scared in the car. And it will protect us if we get in another accident."

We hugged for a long time, giggling about how lucky we were to get a rock from God. We took it with us in the rental car that day. And when we got our new car, we made a spot for it right up front under the dashboard controls.

In the meantime, I couldn't stop thinking about the family we'd hit. I found the woman's name in my accident report paperwork and hunted down her address. I wrote her and her family a card, expressing my confusion over what had happened, my gratitude for their lives, and my strong belief that our paths had crossed for a reason. I hesitated before tossing it into the mailbox, but sent it just the same.

A year later, while perusing my Facebook newsfeed, I stumbled on a story that caught my attention. The article was about a young woman who was diagnosed with lung cancer after a car accident sent her to the hospital. The article said that she was driving her son home from his ski lesson at a nearby mountain and she decided to take a different route than usual because of the snow. Then her car was hit by a white SUV driving straight at her in her lane.

I blinked back burning tears as I realized that white SUV was my car. I gulped and continued to read.

The boy had a concussion and a broken arm, and the mother agreed to have a scan because she felt some whiplash. What happened next was a shock. The scan revealed that the woman, who had never smoked a day in her life, had a mass on her lung—stage IIIa lung cancer. She was only forty years old and had no symptoms. She would not have started treatment at that stage if it weren't for the accident. She shared the card I had sent to her with the reporters covering the story, including this section:

I believe that everything happens for a purpose. I've yet to find out why our paths had to literally cross the way they did, but I am confident that it will be made obvious in time.

~Ashley Previte

Chapter 8

Dreams and the Unexplainable

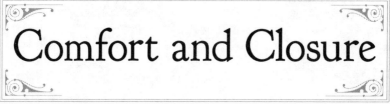

Comfort and Closure

73

Three Questions

Grief is the price we pay for love.
~Queen Elizabeth II

The church is full because he was well-loved, and because his death is so shocking, so unexpected. My husband was only thirty-three.

I sit in the front row, an arm wrapped protectively around our four-year-old son. There's a photo of my husband on our sailboat. David is grinning, tanned, handsome, full of life.

It seems so surreal. Just a few months ago, we were on our yacht with Mel Gibson and Goldie Hawn, shooting a scene for the movie *Bird on a Wire*.

Just a few weeks ago, my husband and I were planning the finishing touches on our dream home. It seemed that everything we touched turned to gold. We had started two successful businesses and had more prosperity than we had ever imagined. Even better, we had a healthy, adorable son. Life was great, and I'd never been happier.

But then, just a few days ago, my husband suddenly died. My attempts to revive him failed. The paramedics' attempts to revive him failed. David was dead.

My whole world turned upside down. I didn't know if I'd ever be able to put the pieces of my life back together again. I didn't really care if I lived or died—except for our son. For his sake, I knew I must soldier on.

The funeral service came to a conclusion, and people lined up to comfort me. "You're young. You'll find another husband," said one. I was outraged. I didn't want another husband!

"You'll get over it," another person said. "It just takes time."

Two years passed. I wasn't "over it." The foundation of my life had been swept away. I struggled to heal my grief. I tried therapy. I tried working out as if I were training for the Olympics. I tried attending church. I read dozens of self-help books. I poured myself into my work, and my first movie was produced. While I had moments of happiness, I lived in the bitter shadow of his death. I felt like a victim. I was robbed of my soul mate, and my son was robbed of his father.

Nothing helped until, on the second anniversary of David's death, I had a dream. In this dream, my husband asked me three questions, and these questions changed my life.

In my dream, I meet my dead husband at the airport. We sit across from each other, and I unleash my fury. "How could you die beside me? How could you rip out my heart? How could you abandon me?"

I pound my fist on the cold, hard, cheap table, heedless of the faceless passersby, all heading purposefully somewhere else. My fury spent, my voice quavers as I confront him with his ultimate betrayal, "How could you leave our son without his father?"

Silently, compassionately, my husband listens to the outpourings of my raging heart. He does not take the baited hook, nor does he reach out to comfort me with his warm, strong hands. He reaches out to me the only way he can — in this dream.

"If you had it to do all over again, would you still marry me?" he asks.

I think for a moment, flooded with happy memories. Love shared, boats sailed, dreams achieved — together. I'd take my time with him, though it be short. "Yes, I'd still marry you," I answer, a soft smile tugging at my lips.

"If you had it to do all over again, would you still have our son?"

This time, the answer is quicker. I wouldn't give up our son for the world! He is the light of my life, my joy, my blessing. "Absolutely!" I reply without hesitation.

"Given those two answers, would you want to know that I would die young?"

I gasp. His question hangs in the air for a long moment. Would I choose to taint our joy with dread? I look into my heart, and after a long moment, discover the answer. "No."

Peaceful acceptance washes over my rage and sorrow. I did not choose my fate. And yet — given a choice — I would choose it. Bitterness evaporates. I'm filled with gratitude for the time and love we shared.

Emily Brontë wrote in *Wuthering Heights*, "I've dreamt in my life dreams that have stayed with me ever after, and changed my ideas; they've gone through and through me, like wine through water, and altered the colour of my mind."

This dream was like that. It altered the color of my mind. It changed the trajectory of my life. I stopped wasting energy resisting reality. Gratitude replaced grief. Empowered by my new perspective, problems melted away. Opportunities sprouted in their place.

Seemingly out of nowhere, I became part of the living once again (and I needed to because I had a son to raise!). I landed a job that allowed me to provide for my little family of two.

People began to marvel at the new spring in my step and the sparkle that was back in my eyes… and asked me what caused the dramatic shift.

I happily shared my dream with them, and before I knew it, I was sharing the dream with groups and in front of audiences.

I was encouraged to write about my experience in *From Heartbreak to Happiness*, which led to me founding the Grief Coach Academy in order to help others recover from loss more quickly than I had. Sharing this dream seemed to spontaneously shift people from misery to peaceful acceptance.

I'm profoundly grateful for the three powerful questions that miraculously reframed and released my grief, instantly replacing it with gratitude. I'm grateful every day that sharing this dream with others frequently works the same kind of miracle so they can return to living fully and achieving their dreams.

~Aurora Winter

74

Dreaming in Thai

If you change the way you look at things,
the things you look at change.
~Dr. Wayne Dyer

My mother passed away in March of that year. Because I had lost my father when I was only eleven, my mother and I were exceptionally close. She was both my mother and my father, my comfort and my security. Although she had been declining for several years, the loss was very hard.

Five months later, I received a "Dear John" letter from my older sister: *Now that we don't have Mom to keep us together, I don't want to see you anymore. Goodbye.*

Wow. That was out of left field. I had always believed that once my mother passed, my sister and I would be close. Even though we had never enjoyed an easy relationship, I hoped that without all the worry about our mom's health, we might have a chance to enjoy each other in a more relaxed way. Now that was not to be.

The next year, my husband's startup folded. What had been his dream ran out of funding. Suddenly, there was no paycheck coming in!

I was reeling. I'd lost security on all levels: my mother, my only sibling, and our income. I would wake with heart palpitations in the middle of the night. During the day, I was depressed and very tense. I started to worry about my husband and daughter's safety and welfare. I couldn't bear the thought of losing my other two family members.

Over the next year, our circumstances slowly improved. My husband was offered a very good job in Los Angeles. Soon after, I started a new business that lifted my spirits. And I had the good fortune to win an international writing competition for my short stories. Things were looking up, but I still felt precarious, like I was on a tightrope. At any moment, it could all be lost.

Fast-forward two years. Even though our outer circumstances were on an upswing, and I was feeling slightly more peaceful, I was still anxious. I was always waiting for the other shoe to drop. I realized that after my dad was taken from me, I stopped trusting the universe. When someone we love disappears, what's to keep that from happening again?

My husband thought a trip to Thailand would be a good distraction and help me return to my old self — the happy-go-lucky Joan who trusted the universe. One of the things that attracted me to Thailand was that Buddhism is the main religion there. For more than twenty years, I had practiced meditation and worked hard to embrace being alive to the present moment.

Our trip to Thailand turned out to be great for me. I was truly beginning to feel moments of happiness.

The last stop of the trip was New Year's Eve in Chiang Mai where the holiday is celebrated with the Loy Krathong festival and the lighting of rice paper lanterns. Also on the special night, ordinarily locked inner chambers of the temples, called *chedis*, are opened to display sacred relics. Signs posted around Chiang Mai announced that monks would chant until past midnight.

On New Year's Eve, we hit the streets right after sunset to gather with the throngs lighting lanterns. The idea was to "say a wish" with every lantern launch.

I rallied all my energy to set my intention, praying that on this special night a miracle would be possible: *Keep my family safe and healthy, and please help me find peace and learn to trust life again.*

We lit a half-dozen lanterns that joined hundreds of others to fill the sky with a warm, orange glow.

We wound through the crowded streets, ending up at the temple where the monks were chanting in the new year. When we arrived, a gentleman wound a piece of white yarn around the crowns of our heads. The yarn connected us to the large congregation. At midnight, fireworks and sparklers were set ablaze, and a monk struck a large brass gong with a huge mallet.

That night, I had this dream:

My husband Adam wanted to meet a man I knew who was a guru. I was hesitant to make the introduction because I'd heard that the man had lost his son in a motorcycle accident. I was afraid that the man might be a sad person. Adam pressed. Finally, the man appeared. He said: "I don't know why everyone makes such a big deal about death. Life. Death. All the same."

I woke up on New Year's Day in Chiang Mai feeling that I had received an important Buddhist lesson. Even after one's worst nightmare — losing a child, as the man/guru in the dream had — life still goes on.

This dream and its message (and maybe with a little help from those floating lanterns) filled me with an inexplicable peace. Of course, I want the very best for my family — and always will — but I no longer feel like I'm on that high wire, holding my breath. My anxiety has been replaced with a deep sense of trust. And every time I notice a hint of that anxiety tiptoeing back, I remember the guru from my dream and his acceptance that life and death are part of our reality.

~Joan Gelfand

75

And This Is for Renee

One way to get the most out of life is
to look upon it as an adventure.
~William Feather

I was sitting at my desk when I got the call informing me that Renee had died. *No,* I remember thinking. *It's a mistake, or a prank, or an outright ugly lie.*

The company made the official announcement and scheduled a grief counselor. I distracted myself by running reports no one would ever read, but it didn't work. Memories of my beautiful friend filled my thoughts. The next night, I had my first dream about her.

I didn't realize it was a dream at first. We were relaxing at a table overlooking the beach and the ocean. I should have guessed it was a dream because the beach was empty, and the ocean was bluer than I've ever seen it in real life. The sun was shining, but not too hot. The breeze was refreshing, but not too chilly or windy.

I have no idea if we were at a restaurant or someone's home. It was just Renee and me sitting at an umbrella table on a balcony overlooking this perfectly tranquil setting. We were both drinking vibrant colored tropical drinks — the kind Renee could be seen holding up in dozens of photos on her social media channels. Strange, since I don't drink.

We were having a lively conversation. I have no idea now what we could have been talking about, but in the dream we were really connecting. It was one of those "Oh, I know! Me, too!" conversations where you're not only learning more about the other person, but about yourself as well.

Then, suddenly, Renee turned to me and said, "I have no fear of death."
Even in the dream, it was a striking statement.
I remember replying, "That's great, Renee."
She smiled her big smile and said, "I know exactly where I'm going."
After that, I only remember us laughing, like we were young and silly.

I woke up then, a little disoriented, thinking I would have to call Renee and tell her she'd been in my dream. As I got out of bed, I thought, *Weird. I think I had a different dream that Renee died. I won't tell her about that one.* By the time I made it into the office, I realized the truth: Renee had died. She really was gone.

Over the next week, details trickled in. She'd died of something extremely rare, and I knew it was also incredibly painful. She'd been texting and e-mailing even while at the hospital, trying to make sure everyone else was okay. Then suddenly, she stopped communicating, and some of her team went to the hospital to check on her, but she was already gone.

Renee was one of those people whom everyone liked. Her way of being herself was effortless and unforced. She didn't try to make everyone like her; everyone just did. She laughed all the time at whatever she thought was funny. She was so open and engaging, so accepting of everyone. Her parties were legendary. She loved music, especially dance and house music. Many couples met at one of Renee's parties. She brought together so many new friends through her love of dogs, music, and people.

Her sister held her memorial at a beautiful banquet room in the mountains high above the city. I debated over and over if I should go. *I don't need to go to prove my love for her,* I argued with myself. The truth was that I didn't want to cry in front of my co-workers. I was afraid that if I started crying, I wouldn't be able to stop.

I put on a black dress and heels and trekked up the mountain. I was upset because we'd always planned to go to the Sunday brunch they held at this place — outdoors, overlooking the city, an easy champagne brunch. It sounded wonderful, but our plans never came together. She'd started attending services at a church near her home and really liked it. She told me how she really respected the pastor and felt so accepted and supported there. I was happy for her, but didn't feel that I could ever find such a place.

At the memorial, everyone talked about how they met Renee at a party or at a club and how she'd introduced them to so many new friends. Then they played the song that her friend had written for her. He was a deejay and songwriter, and in his grief he wrote a song to express his sadness at her sudden passing. "Make some good and pass it on…" It so perfectly described Renee. Then the lyric came, "…And this is for Renee…" and several people broke down in tears. I bit my lip hard and ignored the sobbing girl next to me until I knew that I could hold it together and not cry. I vowed to never go to the Sunday brunch there as I would never get to go with Renee.

That night I had the second dream. I found myself in a massive lounge. The place was as big as a football stadium. It makes no sense at all, but in dreamtime it seemed perfectly normal. Huge chandeliers cast soft light all around. The place was filled with people chatting over the sounds of music and clinking glasses.

I stood with Renee in a little group. I was talking with a woman whom I thought I knew, but couldn't quite place. Again, we were really connecting, and then suddenly I realized she was my father's mother. My grandmother had been dead since the 1970s, and I'd never known her as a younger woman, but here she was talking with me. I looked over at Renee, who was talking with someone else, and she smiled at me in her comforting way.

I turned back to the woman and said, "I think you're my father's mother."

She replied, "Well, of course I am, my dear."

I glanced around the room and realized that everyone around me was dead. In a panic, I pulled Renee away from her conversation and said, "Renee, everyone here is dead!"

Renee laughed and said, "Yeah, girl!"

We both glanced around the room again, and then she smiled and said, "And it's all okay."

That's the last I saw of my friend. She was dressed beautifully in a sleek cocktail gown. Her hair was done up so fashionably, with some kind of crystals sprinkled in. Her eyes were bright, her skin was glowing, and her toothy grin was dazzling.

Now her picture hangs above my desk, and that song plays in my head. Make some good and pass it on. I miss her so much, and I hold onto what she last said to me in that dream: *It's all okay.*

As I move through my days, I promise to laugh more, to not judge, to not take myself so seriously. To be more like Renee.

~GD Carey

The Visit

Just a thin veil between this world and that world of
beauty and love. Just a thin veil that hides the
view of our Spirit loved ones above.
~Gertrude Tooley Buckingham

On Christmas Eve, Dad struggled a bit while holding the front door open to welcome us, his smile half-hearted after months spent mourning Mom. With each hug from me, my husband, and the kids, his melancholy seemed to lift. We followed him into the familiar living room, and it immediately struck me that the traditional decorations Mom always loved to display were nowhere in sight. My throat tightened.

My two sisters and their families were already sharing the latest family gossip over Dad's blaring television set. After Dad got himself settled back into his well-worn easy chair, everyone milled around sipping the rich eggnog Trish served. The aroma of Kelli's cookies baking made my stomach rumble, and I hurried to get my version of the Christmas chili simmering on the stove the way Mom always had. We, each in our own way, rallied to reproduce Mom's epic Christmas cheer, but trying to recreate our past merriment without Mom was exhausting. We all ended up going to bed early.

I'd been sound asleep for most of the night when I looked up to see my mother, as real as though she were alive, hovering above me. I was filled with love, peace, and joy.

Mom wore a flowing robe with colors streaming away from her center.

White clouds hovered around her, filled with what seemed to be a galaxy of beings. Floating among them, I basked in their affection. Harmony and wellbeing enveloped me. I was no longer aware of my physical body. I wanted it to last forever.

Still tingling with awe, I was confused when I saw a regular ceiling above me. I felt the firm mattress beneath me and realized I was lying in bed, dawn's light edging through the bedroom window. Beside me, my husband slept, unaware of my incredible epiphany.

I closed my eyes, yearning, almost aching to continue the encounter. Instead, I lay awake, savoring my new serenity, then watching through the gap in the curtains as yellow and pink rays strengthened into daylight.

As soon as I heard my sisters awaken, I hurried to tell them about Mom's visit. Trying to use mere words to describe something incomprehensible, I finally stopped talking and took a breath.

Kelli, my younger sister, said, "Well, here's what happened to *me* last night. I dreamed I was back in our old church, watching the memorial lamp flicker. Didn't the pastor tell us it would stay lit forever to honor our departed loved ones?"

"Yes, I remember him saying that," I said.

"Well, in my dream I was so worried the light would go out, I started to cry. I kept sobbing, almost getting hysterical, shouting over and over in the empty church, 'Who will keep the lamp lit? How can it work?' Standing there so upset, I heard Mom's voice. She said, 'You will be okay. All will be well. Everything will go on.' I remember I wanted more. I wanted to see her, to hug her. Instead, there was a special silence, like she knew I would believe her. And I did."

Glancing from Trish to me, Kelli added, "Then all of a sudden, I realized I was in the bed facing Gary, and I knew Mom was standing behind me. I felt her rubbing my shoulder, like she always did. And... that's all I remember."

We stared at each other for a second, until Trish, my older sister, took a deep breath and released it with a light "whew." Then she said, "Oh, my gosh. Wait 'til you hear!"

"Last night, a pressure, like when someone sits on the bed, woke me

up. It felt so normal, I wasn't worried or scared. And there was Mom, sitting on the side of my bed with a small suitcase on the floor beside her. She was happy, very serene, and said, 'Dear, dear Trish, always my little worrywart. There is nothing at all for you to worry about... but I have to go now.' She smiled, as if she knew I would understand. And I did."

I found it hard to breathe, and felt goose bumps up and down my arms. I started to say, "So, we all..."

"Yeah, I wasn't accepting Mom's death. Seeing her last night, well, I'm okay now. I get it," Trish said.

Kelli said, "I've been missing her so much, wondering how I can get through life without her. It seemed so unfair. Now I know for sure she's always going to be with me."

Each time I recall Mom's visit, decades ago, I marvel at the gift of faith I received that Christmas Eve. Mom's visit woke me up spiritually. Where before I doubted, I now believe. Where before I was drifting, I now have a life filled with purpose and meaning.

All I have to do is close my eyes to remember that night. And, eyes wide open, I am filled with gratitude for life on this earth and for Mom's visit, which showed me the glimpse of eternity that changed my life forever.

~Wendy Keppley

77

Dancing into the Future

*The future belongs to those who believe
in the beauty of their dreams.*
~Eleanor Roosevelt

So many questions filled my mind. Why was I in so much pain? Did it have to do with my recent cancer surgery? Did it mean the cancer was worse than they thought or was it from some other cause? Even at best, I would be followed for years and not fully know if my cancer was eradicated for a very long time. And now I lay on a hospital table with a fever and excruciating abdominal pain. Soon I would have a scan to see what was causing the pain, but for now I was hooked up to an IV and had pain meds pouring into my arm. I was beginning to get some relief… and I was beginning to get sleepy.

The next thing I knew, I was on an old hospital bed in Nigeria, the country of my birth and childhood. As a missionary kid whose father worked as a pharmacist in the city of Ogbomoso, my surroundings were familiar. I was outside of a medical clinic of some sort waiting to be admitted.

The clinic was of the typical Nigerian sort: mud walls, thatched roof, open windows, dirt floor. It must have been during the dry season as things were dry and dusty. I was lying on an old, rusty metal bed and could see down a little embankment where a street was busy with people, motorcycles, and vehicles. The noise of the motorcycles and vehicles was loud and constant, along with the smoke from outdoor kitchen fires, burning trash and vehicles. Flies were a nuisance, as were the sweat and heat.

Then I woke up. I was relieved to see that I was actually lying in a clean hospital bed in a large hospital in my hometown near Dallas, Texas, with my wife sitting in a chair beside me. I told her about my dream and soon dozed off again.

I was back at the old Nigerian clinic, but this time I was inside. The room was large and dusty and only lit with natural light, so it wasn't very bright. Around the room were old, worn, wooden benches. I don't recall seeing anyone sitting in them. In the center of the room, a long aisle led to two different places. One was down an even darker, eerie looking area, and the other seemed to lead back out to a brighter area outside. As I came into this large room, someone was leading me by the arm. It wasn't clear to me if the person was male or female, but he or she seemed to be a dark, foreboding presence. The person started to lead me down the aisle toward the dark area.

Then, out of nowhere, someone intervened and took me by the other arm. Though it was also unclear if this person was male or female, he or she was lighter and brighter. The bright person kept telling the other person that I was not meant to go down that dark hall. There was a little tugging back and forth, and I was pulled in both directions. The dark figure eventually let go and gave in to the light figure, who led me back outside.

I woke up. I was back in my hometown hospital, with my wife still by my side and an IV still in my arm. I looked at the clock and saw that only a few minutes had passed since I had last checked the time. I told my wife about this dream, too. My eyes were still heavy, and I must have dozed back to sleep.

Suddenly, I was back outside the old, dusty clinic, waiting to be admitted, or perhaps I was being discharged. Someone was standing beside me, but I don't know who. All the familiar scenes from the first dream were there.

Then I woke up and described the scene to my wife. And once again, as quickly as I had woken, I seemed to be transported back to Nigeria.

This time (the fourth), it was a more pleasant experience. I was with a Nigerian hospital driver shopping for handcrafted sandals in downtown Ogbomoso. We entered the small shop that had sandals, handbags, and other leather goods hanging for display on the walls. Two Nigerian men were sitting behind a wooden desk and greeted us in their usual friendly way.

After exchanging greetings, the driver explained what I was looking for. He must have mentioned that I used to live in Nigeria years ago because they asked me to speak in their tongue. So, in my best Yoruba accent, I introduced myself and said I was OmoOgbomoso, which translated means "a child of Ogbomoso." That drew a huge response as they began to smile and laugh. Then I continued with my demonstration that I was from Ogbomoso by singing some native songs and dancing Nigerian style!

The two men literally fell out of their chairs with laughter and joined in dancing, as did the driver. We were all having a joyous time singing and dancing! I'm not sure if they were laughing more at my singing or the fact that I was dancing with them.

Then I woke up. I don't know if I ever bought those sandals or not.

This time when I told my wife, she teased me, telling me not to go back to sleep again. I didn't because the scan was about to begin.

I do not recall having any other dreams like that, before or since. In fact, I seldom have dreams that I remember. But those four short dreams will stay in my memory the rest of my life. I was diagnosed with an abscess at the surgery site and sent home with a PICC line through which I administered antibiotics for the next six weeks. But I no longer doubted my healing or my future. My dreams had assured me it was not my time. I had been led out of the dark, and my fears had turned to dancing.

~Ron Wasson

78

Strength in Numbers

Nothing in life is to be feared.
It is only to be understood.
~Marie Curie

n the night I found myself waking up on the bathroom tile of my parents' bathroom, I tried to remember how I got there. My left cheek was on the cold floor, and I felt almost soothed by it, as the rest of my eleven-year-old body was in a cold sweat. I closed my eyes and had a distinct vision as I laid waiting for someone to find me.

In my mind, I was lying in a bed that wasn't my own and, like in real life, I couldn't move. I could see my family and friends standing around me, looking at me fearfully. I wanted to ask them what was wrong, why they were all looking at me with such worry, but I couldn't speak. They touched my hands, my dad cried, my mom covered her mouth, and my grandmother muttered prayers, but all I could do was lie there and look at them.

I drifted back to sleep soon after, and I was shaken awake hours later by my mother. I told her that I'd gotten up to use the bathroom, but I'd felt too weak to walk, so I'd lain down. This, of course, was a lie. I had gotten up to use the bathroom, but I'd passed out in a cold sweat. However, I didn't want to worry her more than she already was.

Mom knew that I was sick — too sick to go to school, too sick to eat, too sick to stand. She would help me to the kitchen to get the gallons of water I was desperate for. But she didn't know that I also had to pee seven times each night. I didn't want to bother her, even if I had to crawl to the bathroom.

After four missed days of school, my mom finally phoned our family doctor. He told her I probably had the flu, that I needed more Gatorade and rest. We did that for a day, but she finally took me to the doctor's office after I threw up all of the Gatorade and soup she'd been trying to fill me with.

At the hospital, I was tested for every type of disease while my parents sat next to me, holding hands for the first time in years. When the doctor came in to tell them that I had Type 1 diabetes, I pretended to be asleep facing the wall with my eyes closed. I listened intently, confused, and I heard my dad asking questions while my mom sat next to him, sniffling back tears. Dr. James explained to them what my days would now look like: I would be checking my blood sugar, counting carbohydrates for everything I ate, taking insulin shots to cover said carbs, and on and on and on. I was eleven years old at the time, and while I knew everything would be different and more difficult, I didn't feel afraid. As I heard the door shut behind my parents, I turned over and stared at the ceiling.

Am I going to die? I wondered. My mom and dad came into the room a few hours later with a bag of supplies I would need for the next week in the hospital. My mom had packed my toothbrush, pajamas, and Winnie the Pooh. They told me what the doctor had told them, and I nodded, pretending it was the first I'd heard of it all. "We're going to go home and do some research," Mom said, "but everything will be okay. You're okay." My dad's face was turned, pretending he was looking at my monitor so I wouldn't have to see the expression of doubt he wore on such occasions when he was worried and unsure.

"Dad," I whispered. He looked at me. For some reason, I felt like this was my fault, like I had done something wrong. He wore the face I had been seeing in my dreams for months. The same anxious eyes looked back at me as I lay in the hospital bed, frozen with fear for my dad, not for myself. I realized that I would be fine, but my parents were going to be a mess. "I'm okay, Dad. I dreamed all of this before, and everything was fine. In my dream, I was alive and not even a little sad."

He stared at me for a while, and then he smiled, leaned down to hug me, and whispered into my ear: "You're my hero, little lady."

When the diabetes educator came in later that day, I was determined to learn everything, to control something that wasn't tame so that I could protect my parents from worrying about me.

For the next few days, I learned how to prick my finger to test my blood glucose, count how many carbohydrates were in a banana or a potato, and determine how I would feel when my blood sugar was high (tired, thirsty, a need to pee), or how I would feel when it dropped (shaky, confused, hungry). I learned how to give myself shots, and how to track my entire life, recording blood sugars, carbs, units of insulin, and exercise on an Excel spreadsheet my dad created and faxed to my doctor weekly. I grew up a lot in that one week.

The day before I was released on December 20, 2000, my mom arranged for a Christmas party in my hospital room. Friends from church and school showed up. My entire family was present, and even Santa Claus came with a gift of play make-up and fingernail polish. People brought balloons and flowers. One friend even brought a gallon jar of pickles as he knew they didn't have any carbs.

At one point during the celebration, I lay in my bed, attached to tubes and beeping machines, and I felt the love from all of these people spreading across the room. I realized I was living the same dream I'd envisioned the night I'd fallen on the tile. People had been looking at me with worry and concern, but here, in real life, in my non-dreamy struggle, I had people supporting me, trying to learn about my new way of life, and holding my hands unconditionally. This reality filled me with joy.

Worry had been replaced with understanding, compassion removed concern, and I was not anxious about this new way of life thanks to the people around me. This was simply a new routine. My dreams had prepared me, and my family and friends were here to help me through the rest of my life as an independent, adventurous, and optimistic person living with Type 1 diabetes.

~Lauren Dyer

79

Saying Goodbye to Daddy

We cannot destroy kindred: our chains stretch a little
sometimes, but they never break.
~Marquise de Sévigné

J ust before Easter in 2004, I was driving home from work. I was tired from the long day I'd had and my mind was drifting. Suddenly, it was as if someone were sitting next to me in the car. I couldn't see anyone, of course. But in my mind, I heard a voice speaking to me. I recognized it from several years before when it had told me that my great-grandmother was going to pass away right before she did.

This time, in a flat, non-emotional tone, the voice said, "Your father is going to kill himself. He's going to shoot himself."

My dad was a happy-go-lucky guy. He was filled with laughter and lightheartedness. I didn't want to believe that this could happen. My dad and I weren't very close. He and my mother divorced when I was little, and aside from Christmas, I didn't really see him or talk to him much. I had always wanted to be closer to him, but he wasn't an easy person to get close to.

I pushed away the voice immediately. My dad was a gunsmith. I couldn't imagine him doing something so awful. And yet, even though I couldn't wrap my head around it, something inside me felt it was the truth.

I told my sister. She and I bought him an Easter card and signed it with our phone numbers, asking him to call us. We left it on his porch, hoping he would get in touch. We didn't hear from him all through April that year. So I made copies of the photographs we had taken together at Christmas just a few months earlier and framed them. I took them to his house and visited with him. I don't know if I was trying to make myself feel better by seeing him and making sure that he still seemed stable, or if I was using the whole thing as an excuse to be close to him and try one more time to connect as his daughter. He did seem to be a little more distant than usual, but he still laughed and joked. So, I left his home, dismissing my scary premonition.

A few months later, I was staying over at a friend's house. I had a terrible feeling that night. The voice came again and said, "You're an orphan now. You no longer have a father." I have anxiety, so I dismissed it as just being my imagination. After all, the movie my friend and I were watching was about a father trying to save his daughter from a kidnapper. So I figured I was just being emotional. We went to bed that night, and early the next morning I received a phone call telling me that my father had shot himself in the head at around 9:30 p.m., which was when I had heard the voice.

Of course, it was a horrifying experience, and it still hurts me today. But I'm thankful for the premonition that urged me to try one more time so I don't have any guilt. That voice sent me to visit my father. It pushed me to have those pictures framed and they sat atop the closed casket at his funeral. Later, they were given back to me. I still have them in the same frames.

I got to give my father a last hug that night as I left his house. He knew how I felt, and I am at peace.

~Betty Jane Coffman

80

Dream Traveller

*And above all, watch with glittering eyes the whole
world around you because the greatest secrets are
always hidden in the most unlikely places.*

~Roald Dahl

All the kids saw when they looked at the little block I'd received as a Christmas present from my sisters-in-law in Canada was a delightful painting of a girl flying through the sky over a rather surreal landscape. What I saw, however, were the major plot points of four vivid, life-affirming dreams that I had two nights earlier. And yet this block of wood had been wrapped and sitting under the tree for the past week.

We were living in Egypt at the time, having moved there from Toronto a couple of years before. Our marriage was on the rocks, but at that point we were still together, heading into our second Christmas in our new home. We hadn't yet made any plans for returning to Canada, but it was clear that when we got back we'd be going our separate ways.

A couple of days before I opened that Christmas gift, I dreamt I was being nudged from behind while underwater in the ocean. I spun around to find a killer whale who obviously wanted to be stroked.

I've loved whales from the time I was a child. Topping my personal list of good-luck symbols, in times of stress, I'll sometimes see the vanishing tail of a diving whale when I close my eyes, and know everything's going to be okay.

With the whale's smooth, pliant skin gliding by under my palms, I couldn't have felt luckier if I'd won the lottery. She switched from a horizontal position to a vertical one so I could stroke the full length of her belly. A vicious-looking shark came into our vicinity and swam in circles around us, but I understood, as scary as the shark looked, he posed no threat. The shark left, and eventually so did my whale. After a few seconds, the whale came back.

Opening my eyes, I lay there trying to recapture the joy and relief of that dream. More tangible and visceral than any dream I'd ever had, I knew this was a message of some kind. It meant that everything was going to be fine. My worries (the shark) looked scary, but wouldn't actually pose any threat. Making a pact with myself to remember this dream, I fell back asleep, never suspecting I would wake four more times with the same imperative to remember before the night was through.

The next thing I knew, I was with Meiko, my childhood best friend. It had been a long time since I'd seen Meiko, awake or asleep, but she always appeared in my dreams when I needed help, advice, or love. In this dream, I told her about my previous dream. She asked if I was scared. When I said I wasn't, we dove into what I perceived to be a giant coffee cup. We were shooting down, headfirst, for so long that it was as if we would never reach the bottom. Then suddenly we were hanging onto the round ball of the earth. I slid off and shot out into the stars on my own.

I will never forget the sensation of speeding through the universe like a shooting star. My heart still racing when I woke up, I knew this was a repeat of the same message. Everything was going to be fine, better than fine. My spirit was going to soar with the stars even when I let go of the familiar — earth.

Next, I was on a train with my friend, Tamer. Still sleeping, I realized this dream was picking up where the other two had left off, adding travel and change to the message. With the world passing by out the window, I repeated the details of the previous dreams to Tamer to firm them up in my memory.

Finding myself in the driver's seat of a car, I understood this was a repetition of the travel message. I reminded myself again how important it was to remember these dreams and repeated the details of the previous three to my grandmother in the seat beside me. In the waking world, my grandmother had recently had a stroke, but sitting there, she was healthy and happy. And I was in the driver's seat, not exactly a hard fact to analyze.

In the final dream of the night, my mother and mother-in-law came to our apartment in Egypt to tell me it was time to leave. Walking from room to room, deciding what to pack, we came to several beautiful vases we all recognized as precious. They advised me to send those home early because they were breakable.

When morning finally came, I felt deeply loved and cared for. Rather than being alone in a foreign country in the middle of a deteriorating marriage, I felt like a cherished, cared-for thread, carefully woven in the immense web of life. I wrote out the details of the dreams so I would never forget.

Two days later, those messages were repeated and underlined in a dramatic, impossibly concrete way when I unwrapped that block of wood on Christmas morning. The block featured a girl soaring high above the town below. In the pattern of blue in the sky was what looked like a whale flying alongside her. There was a train track in the forefront and a lone car on the road. The caption at the bottom said "Dream Traveller." It was as if I'd dreamed that block into existence.

I once had a conversation with a friend about the nature of time. He thought time was like a horizontal line with each moment following the other in succession. I imagined it more like an undulating brick wall, with all moments happening at once, each one distinct yet part of an already complete whole. So many disparate moments went into my experience. When my sisters-in-law bought the picture. When the artist made it. When it was already sitting under the tree, and I was having the dreams. When I opened the gift that depicted my dreams. Each moment, perpetually transpiring in its place, until a time when the swimming whale, the shooting star, the traveling train and the car would all converge at a single point. It was as if a conductor was pointing her baton at each section of the orchestra to set the music playing, until with a final sweep of her hand, they all came together in a resounding crescendo.

The one thing I never fully understood from my dream-night was the vases. Sixteen years later, reliving the experience as I wrote this, I had a revelation. The kids were the precious vases who I needed to take back to Canada, making sure they were okay before their father and I split up.

The painted dream sits on my desk, as it has since the day I unwrapped it, for inspiration and comfort, and as a reminder of the magic of life.

~Maissa Bessada

There for Me

*Those whom we have loved never really leave us. They
live on forever in our hearts and cast their radiant
light onto our every shadow.*
~Sylvana Rossetti

S ome years of our lives are clearly more difficult than others.
Those are the years of struggle and loss and hurt we never
forget, and look back on, shaking our heads, wondering
how we found the strength to live through them.

1978 was one of those years for me. I was thirty-four, a divorced,
out-of-work art teacher, supporting my children by selling beaded
jewelry to tourists on San Francisco's Fisherman's Wharf. My dearest
friend, Stuart, had died that February. A car ran a red light at a city
intersection, colliding with his motorcycle as he drove to work, knocking
him to the ground and killing him instantly. He was thirty-nine. He
was the first man I'd loved and trusted since my divorce three years
before. Reeling from my loss, I struggled to accept what had happened
and to be strong for my sons.

Then in late May, two drug-crazed intruders broke into our apartment, and we jumped to the back yard from a second floor window to
escape them. Thankfully, my sons were unharmed, but I landed on a
concrete step, breaking and dislocating the bones in my ankle. "Looks
like one bad break to me," I heard one paramedic say to the other.
They loaded me into an ambulance, and sirens screaming, rushed me
to the hospital, where my leg was immobilized in a full-length cast.

Oh, God, what am I going to do? I thought. *I won't be able to walk, at least for a while, or drive to the supermarket to buy groceries, or go to work. My leg hurts, and I'm so scared. How will I get through this without Stuart?*

And that's when I heard Stuart's calm, low voice whisper in my ear. *No worries. I'm here for you. We'll get through this together.*

Stuart's presence stayed with me after that, sustaining me throughout the long summer, fall, and winter of healing — not only the bones in my ankle, but my battered spirit, and the spirits of my sons, as well. Sometimes, I heard Stuart's voice in my head. Other times, I saw him standing or sitting nearby, dressed in jeans and his favorite brown jacket. He was watching me; his surprisingly blue eyes crinkling at the corners as he smiled, letting me know I wasn't alone.

With Stuart's help, I found my strength again. My ankle not only healed, but I walked without limping. I returned to work. My family recovered. I found a sunny new apartment in another neighborhood and moved us in. We made a fresh start.

One night, soon after our move, while asleep in my peaceful new bedroom, I had a dream about Stuart and me.

It was daytime. We stood together on an unfamiliar San Francisco street, facing the corner of a tall building. From this position, we could look down along the sidewalks on either side of that corner — they appeared in sharp perspective, like in a drawing — each leading off into the foggy distance. Stuart wore a brown suit, a tie, and a crisp white shirt.

"You're all dressed up. What's the occasion?" I asked. I'd never seen him in a suit before. The whole time I'd known him, he'd worn only jeans, and a leather or denim jacket.

He was tall and stood smiling down at me, creating the dimples that had charmed me from the day we'd met. A breeze came up, ruffling his neatly combed, sandy-brown hair.

"I came to say goodbye," Stuart said, and indicated the sidewalks to our left and to our right with gestures of his hand. "Our paths diverge from now on," he said, sounding sorry, but matter-of-fact about it. "You need to go in one direction, and I, the other. I hope you understand."

Tears filled my eyes as I stared at him silently. Stuart and I shared the bond of belief in reincarnation — and somehow I understood that he'd remained close to me because of my need for him and his love for me. But now it was time for him to continue on with his journey — and for me to continue on with my life. Stuart smiled, and his big hands stroked my face gently. He bent and kissed me.

"I gave you my love. You'll never be without it." Then he turned and walked away, disappearing into the fog.

I was crying in the dream, and my face was wet with tears when I woke up. I never saw Stuart's face or heard his voice again after that night, but I remain grateful to know that miracles do occur when we need them. As long as we love, we are never alone.

~Lynn Sunday

82

Lasagna and the City of Love

A walk about Paris will provide lessons in history,
beauty, and in the point of life.
~Thomas Jefferson

The entire ten-hour flight from San Francisco to Paris, I was a jumble of emotions. *I can't believe I am doing this. How am I going to make it through this? How can I go to Paris when she is not there anymore?*

You see, this trip had been in the works for more than a year. I was headed to France with my boyfriend to celebrate his stepmother's seventieth birthday with his entire family. But first, we made plans to spend a few days in Paris visiting my dear friend, Celine.

Celine and I met in the dorms our freshman year of college, and we lived together all four years. After graduation, Celine moved to Paris — her lifelong dream — and attended Parsons Paris, the European branch of Parsons School of Design, to study fashion. She stayed there after, working for the school's admissions office. Hers was a glamorous life, living in the City of Love and traveling the world. Meanwhile, I stayed in the U.S. for graduate school. Now, I was building a career in the Bay Area as a teacher and writer.

Celine's family lived in Los Angeles, so we saw each other once a year or so, usually during the holidays when she came home to the States. Whenever we got together, it always felt like no time had passed.

We slipped right back into our everyday friendship, those college days when we saw each other morning and night, when we spent hours chatting and laughing in the tiny living room of our college apartment.

I was so excited to visit Celine in Paris — to meet her friends and introduce her to my boyfriend; to see her apartment and her office; to go to her favorite restaurants and attractions; to get a glimpse of her life in the city she adored.

But on January 26th, a phone call shattered my world. Celine was traveling in India for a friend's wedding. She was in a taxi that was broadsided by a bus. She was killed instantly.

My amazing, vibrant, funny, kind, fearless, beautiful friend… was dead? *How could that be?* Suddenly, nothing made sense anymore.

The only activities that gave me a little solace were writing and cooking. I found comfort in the routine of writing word after word and the rhythm of chopping vegetables. I wrote an essay about Celine in the format of a recipe: "How to Make Spinach-Artichoke Lasagna Three Weeks After Your Best Friend's Funeral." Something about the linearity of a numbered list enabled me to access, and write about, my overwhelming grief in a way nothing else could. I showed the essay to no one, but it was a comfort to write it.

Our plane tickets were booked, but I knew that I could not go to Paris. *How could I go to Paris if Celine were no longer there?*

And yet, I also knew that I needed to go to Paris. Celine would be furious with me if I canceled my trip.

And so, with a heavy heart, in June I boarded the plane I had booked the previous October.

I had previously been to Paris twice to visit Celine: once, during our junior year of college, when she studied abroad at the Sorbonne, · and I was a Chunnel ride away in England. My second visit had been during the summer while I was in graduate school. But with this visit, there was no Celine waiting at the airport arrivals gate. My boyfriend and I took the train to the Metro and navigated the narrow streets to our hotel by ourselves. It felt as if my dear friend would round a corner at any moment and surprise us. I kept looking for her in every young woman's face. I had to remind myself constantly—*She is not here; she is not here; she is not here.*

And yet, she was everywhere. I felt like I had been transported through time, back to the last time I had visited her in Paris. Memories flooded my mind and heart. That time she took me to the Japanese quarter and we slurped ramen noodles at a crowded bar. That time she took me to the Sacré-Coeur, and we watched the sun set over the city. That time we wandered around the Rodin Museum garden for twenty minutes, then spent two hours talking and laughing on a bench beside "The Thinker," more interested in each other's lives than in the world-famous sculpture ten feet from us.

Everywhere, I felt her presence. I lit a candle for her at the Sacré-Coeur. I bought two bright-colored daisies—her favorite flower—and threw the petals into the Seine for her. Outside the Notre Dame cathedral, the bells rang for no reason I could discern. It was a beautiful sound. With a flash of insight, I knew that she was ringing the bells for me. I went inside Notre Dame, thinking of her as I slowly walked down the aisle of the magnificent church. Celine was raised Catholic and was very devout in her faith. I always found comfort in her comfort, and even more so since her death. As I gazed up at a remarkable stained-glass window, a rainbow of colors flooding with light, I heard Celine's voice.

I love you, Dal, she said. *I am with you still.*

I began to cry, but they were not just tears of sorrow—they were tears of joy, too. I truly did feel Celine with me. I realized that I might not be able to call her on the phone or hug her or hear her laugh, but I could still share my life with her. Our friendship was not over because she had died. Our friendship still existed, and she still existed, in my memories and in my thoughts.

"I love you, too," I whispered. "Always."

The next day, we left Paris and took a train to join my boyfriend's family in the south of France. I still missed Celine and grieved her death, but I felt more at peace than I had in a long while. We enjoyed a delicious dinner with my boyfriend's family, and then, exhausted from travel, everyone retired to bed.

Comfort and Closure |

The next morning, my boyfriend's stepmother — one of the most no-nonsense people I have ever met — surprised me at breakfast by bringing up her dream from the night before. "You were there, Dallas," she said. "I don't remember much, except you were making lasagna, and you seemed so happy."

Lasagna. My essay. "How to Make Spinach-Artichoke Lasagna Three Weeks After Your Best Friend's Funeral." No one else but me knew about the essay.

Well, perhaps one other person did — Celine. I could feel this dream was a message from her. She wanted me to know she was okay. She wanted me to be okay, too. She wanted me to be happy.

I still miss Celine every day. But we visit in my dreams sometimes. And whenever I make lasagna, I think of her and smile.

~Dallas Woodburn

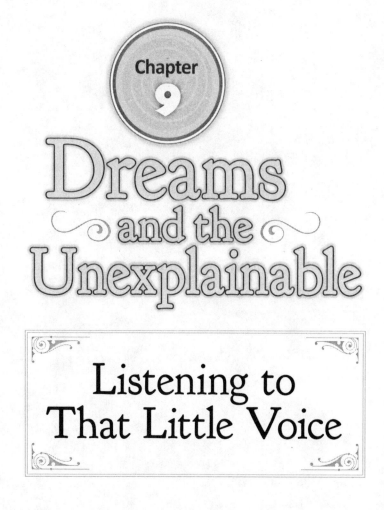

Chapter 9

Dreams and the Unexplainable

Listening to That Little Voice

83

Finding Mrs. Whitebread

*An effort made for the happiness of
others lifts us above ourselves.*
~Lydia M. Child

n a chilly late afternoon in March 1993, my two oldest children, Tyler and Emily, waited in the car while I
quickly retrieved my three-year-old, Jeremy, from his
daycare. As he happily chattered about his day, I buckled him in his car seat and prepared to head toward home. Through
the chatter, though, I heard a very clear voice in my mind, "Go to the
ball field."

My mental response was something on the order of "Huh?"

A moment later, I heard the same words, "Go to the ball field."
So strange, I thought, *but so very definite.* It wasn't a request; it was a
command.

The older kids were soon to start their T-ball season at a field just
a block from where I sat in my idling car. *Well, okay,* I thought, *that's the
only ball field I know of, and it's only a block away.* "Do you want to see
where you'll be playing ball?" was met with an enthusiastic response.

We turned in the opposite direction from our usual route home. In
this previously industrial, urban neighborhood, this block was deserted
and lined with boarded-up, brick buildings. As we went around the
corner, I noticed an elderly woman walking slowly on the sidewalk
past the old buildings, pausing and looking back and forth, up and

down the street. As I slowed a bit to see her more clearly, she appeared to be somewhat bewildered.

I slowed the car and hesitated, yet continued to the field. After I showed the kids where they would be playing, I decided to turn the car around and see if the woman still appeared to be confused. As I pulled the car next to the curb, and before I had even fully stepped out of my car, she said, "Can you help me? I'm trying to go home."

"Yes, ma'am, I'll be happy to help you."

After getting her settled in the front seat of my station wagon, I introduced myself and my children. She told me her name was Mrs. Whitebread. She wore an old overcoat that I suspected had once been her husband's, and a flowered scarf covered what I could see was a tidy bun. I guessed that she was probably in her eighties. She gripped an old, black handbag and a small paper sack. I asked her where she lived, and she gave me an address on a street I didn't recognize. She was sure she was very close to home, but I knew there was no street by that name in the immediate vicinity. She'd left home that morning around 10:00, she said, and walked to a hardware store that had tomato plants for sale.

When she told me where she had gone, I felt my breath nearly leave me. Judging from the house number she gave me, I knew that she had to have walked a few miles just to get to that store, and where I found her was at least a couple more miles beyond that. It was now about 4:00, and she had been walking all day. Having had no lunch, she must have been exhausted and hungry.

This was long before I had a cell phone and GPS, so I did the only thing I could. From the address she'd given me, we drove to the numbered cross street that would be closest to her home and then past block after block of named streets, most of them familiar to me. But I didn't recognize hers. Surely I just hadn't noticed the name of her street before. Block after block we went, and my concern grew that perhaps she didn't know exactly where she lived, even though she had seemed so certain about her address. We continued on, driving slowly to enable both of us to get a good look at each street as we passed. We traveled much farther east than she thought we needed to, but she suddenly began to get excited. "Yes, we're almost there." We crossed a major street, and she looked relieved. "It's right up here," she said. I turned onto her street and pulled to a stop in front of a small, red-brick bungalow. Her clearly panicked neighbor rushed out of the house next to hers.

"Mrs. Whitebread, where have you been? We've been so worried about you!"

"I went to buy tomatoes," she replied. And with that, she turned and walked into her house.

We never saw Mrs. Whitebread again, but my now-grown children still talk about that day more than twenty years ago when "Mom heard the voice" to go to the ball field.

~Kimberly Ross

84

Something Told Me

Don't let the noise of others' opinions
drown out your own inner voice.
~Steve Jobs

omething told me I shouldn't be going out that day, but
it was the first Saturday in a while that my husband and
I would have the entire day to ourselves. After running a
couple of errands, we'd do whatever fun things we wanted
to do: visit the Farmers' Market, have lunch out, go to a movie or
maybe the zoo.

"See you later," I said to my eighty-year-old mom who lived with
us. "Remember! Don't let the cat out."

"Don't you worry!" said my sweet and sometimes spicy mom. "I'll
take good care of Milot."

I'd heard that before! It's not that she wasn't responsible, but she
was getting older and less careful about letting our indoor cat sneak out.

As I opened the front door to leave, some opposing force seemed
to be holding me back.

Strange, I thought.

My husband, who was behind me, gave me a slight push.

"Go," he prompted. "What are you stopping for?"

"I don't know," I said.

I had an uneasy feeling. But we went. We ran our errands and
then drove downtown to the Farmers' Market.

We perused the stalls for over an hour, sampling some fruits, filling our bags with fresh tomatoes, oranges, cucumbers, lettuce, and such. I noticed beautiful, ripe figs on display. Mother used to love figs so I called home to see if she wanted any. There was no answer, but that wasn't unusual. On such a fine day, she was probably out in the back, tending to her plants.

We got her some figs and packed all the bags into the car. Then we drove to a popular Tex-Mex restaurant for lunch.

That was always a special treat. I could have those spicy frittatas any time of the day or night. Larry had his beloved chile rellenos. Then we topped it off with some Mexican sopapilla cheesecake and a second cup of cinnamon coffee.

"What shall we do next?" I asked. I was cheerfully enjoying doing "nothing" with my husband.

We decided to skip the zoo and take in a good movie at a nearby theater. Larry purchased the tickets while I observed the posters of the coming attractions. I couldn't take my eyes off Julia Roberts' photo.

When Larry joined me, he asked, "What are you staring at so intently?"

"Julia Roberts," I answered. "Doesn't she look like a younger version of Mom?"

He squinted as he studied the posters and said, "Actually, not at all. They both have their beauty, but in different ways. Your mom used to resemble Elizabeth Taylor."

Yet he had a hard time convincing me. He also had a hard time pulling me away from the poster. It was as if something was holding me there. I kept seeing my mother's face. As we walked to our seats in the dimly lit theater, a shudder went through me. As soon as I sat down, I jumped up again.

"We have to go home!"

"Why?"

"I don't know, but we have to go *now*."

I started rushing out, and he trailed behind me, protesting, "What happened? Are you worried about the cat? I thought you wanted to see this movie."

I couldn't explain it, but I had a horrible feeling that something was not right.

When he realized how serious I was, he went along without any further protest, as if he had sensed I knew something he didn't.

We couldn't get home quickly enough. As soon as we entered the front door, I called out, "Mother!"

No answer. "Mother, where are you?"

Larry headed toward the kitchen, calling, "Florence!"

It wasn't my mother who answered, but Milot the cat, with a loud yowl coming from my mother's room. I ran in there and experienced the shock of my life. My mother was in the middle of her room, flat on her back, silent and motionless. Though her eyes were wide open, she didn't look at me. She just stared up at the ceiling. The color had drained from her face, and she looked helpless.

"Oh, Lord, please let her be okay," I prayed.

Milot was meowing and kneading on my mother's chest.

I gently removed the cat, and by that time, Larry had come in.

"Mother, what happened? Answer me."

Something was very wrong because my mother was never, ever calm or silent if anything at all was amiss. Hardly a shrinking violet, she'd usually be yelling and screaming at the slightest provocation. But this time, there was not a peep out of her. That's what scared me the most. I leaned in closer, and she finally uttered two words in a whisper, "I fell."

She couldn't move, and we dared not move her. She looked like she was in shock! Without hesitation, we called 911, and the paramedics arrived almost immediately. Gently and mindfully, they did their preliminary examination and then promptly laid her out on a stretcher and rushed her to the hospital. We followed the ambulance in our car.

She had broken her hip. A broken hip is serious for anyone, but especially for a woman her age. But we were still thankful it was not a stroke or a heart attack. We learned later that she had fallen earlier in the day and could not get to the phone when I had called. Luckily, she had the presence of mind to remain still and not injure herself further. Or maybe she had been in a state of shock.

The wonderful doctors were able to repair her hip, and she healed completely. She lived another ten years.

To think that she had been lying there powerless for hours! And had we stayed for the movie, it would have been even longer. I was so grateful that I had finally listened to that inner voice warning me that something was wrong, and I wished I had done so sooner. I don't know if it was a premonition, or just that invisible, powerful bond that sometimes exists between mothers and daughters.

~Eva Carter

85

Every Hair on My Head

Courage is fear that has said its prayers.
~Dorothy Bernard

My family lives and breathes dirt track racing. Every Friday night, we race home from work to load up our cars, our kids, and my elderly in-laws so that we can get to the track for the best seats. We've been doing this for eighteen years.

Some races are bigger and better, especially on holiday weekends, and July 4th weekend in 2000 was no exception. Path Valley Speedway was packed, and I realized it was going to be a very long night. At one point, I happened to look over and noticed that my son, Justin, was sleeping. His dad had already raced, so I leaned over and asked him if he wanted to go home. He replied, "No, I want to watch them all tonight."

I sat there for a while thinking about whether we should stay or leave when, all of a sudden, I was overcome with this thought: *You need to leave and go home now!* I sat there for a couple more minutes thinking, *Why rush?* But when the thought got stronger and just wouldn't let up, I leaned over and asked my mother-in-law, Bessie, "Do you mind if we leave now?"

She said, "No, let's go. Justin is sleeping anyway."

As I was pulling out of the speedway, I was once again overcome with an urgency to get home right away. I was running all these reasons through my head when Bessie said, "Look, is that a car on fire?"

I said, "Maybe, but I can't tell. We will have to get closer."

As I pulled closer, I realized that we must be the first people on the scene, so I told Bessie to stay in the car with Justin. As I started running toward the fire, a gentleman screamed at me to stay back, that he had called for help, but I didn't stop. I just kept running until I could feel the heat. When I stopped, I could see two people in the Chevy Blazer. I looked up in the air and said, "God, what do you want me to do?"

Without a moment's hesitation, I started yanking on the passenger door. It flew open, and I realized that an unconscious child was inside. I started pulling on the seat belt, and the gentleman kept yelling at me to get away from the car. I ignored him and finally got the child unhooked. I picked him up and carried him to safety, laying him on the ground away from the car.

I ran back to the car and said, "God, I can't do this." And I heard him say, "Yes, you can." I ran around the vehicle, but realized immediately that I couldn't open that door, so without thinking I crawled into the blazer through the passenger side door. I started pulling on the woman inside and realized that her foot and leg were crushed between the seat and the door. I asked God to give me strength, and then I crawled over the console into the back seat and started yanking on her seat as hard as I could. All the while, I could feel the flames getting closer and closer to us. Finally, after the fourth or fifth yank, the seat broke. I flew backward, but as I leaned forward I realized she was free, so I started pulling her sideways.

The man was still screaming at me to get out of the car, so I screamed back, "Help me or shut up!" That seemed to rattle him into action, and he grabbed her by her jeans and yanked her across the seat. I jumped out of the burning vehicle just as the fire trucks and ambulances rolled onto the scene.

I leaned down over the lady and told her that she would be okay. I would be praying for her and her son. Then, in my shock, I walked away without talking to anyone. As I crawled into my car, Bessie asked if I was okay and if the people in the car were okay. I told her "Yes," and we drove home.

When I got home, I showered the blood off of me. Only then did I sit down and cry. All I could think of was, *Did I hurt her? Did I do more damage to her leg by yanking her out of that car?* I was so upset that when my husband arrived home and asked me if I knew about the accident at the turnpike entrance, all I could say was, "Yes, and I hope they are okay." I went to bed that night never telling him that I crawled into that burning car. The next day, both my son and my mother-in-law told him what I did. Needless to say, he was a little upset because I could have been hurt.

The next week when we arrived at the races, everyone was talking about the accident and how badly injured the lady was. They told me that she was in critical condition with a head injury, as well as severe leg and foot injuries. They also told me that the boy was fine. Just as they were telling me this, my husband walked up to me and said, "You are never going to believe this, but the lady whose life you saved is my cousin Regina. What are the odds of that happening?"

Regina was in the hospital for almost four months, but when she was released she had her husband bring her to the races to find me. We both started crying right away when we met. Regina said, "I have something to show you, but I want to ask you something first. Why did you risk your life to save me?"

I shrugged my shoulders and said, "I really didn't think about it."

Regina said, "I don't remember much about the accident, but I remember you talking to God as if he was right there in the burning blaze with us. I remember you saying, 'God, you put me here, so you better help me right now to get this lady out.' Then you said the funniest thing. You said, 'God, please don't let my hair burn.'" As she said that, tears rolled down my face. All I could think was how vain I was to think that my hair was that important!

Regina handed me pictures of the accident and said, "I've never believed in God, and yet I know you do with all your heart."

As I looked at those pictures, I could not believe my eyes. The steering wheel was melted together into a U-shape. The driver's side door, dash and inside roof were completely melted. Basically everything was scorched and burned except the front seat where Regina had been sitting. There was no way that either of us should have crawled out of that car without being burned. Yet I knew that we did. Then and only then did I truly realize that God really did care about every hair on my head.

~Annette Rasp

86

A Clear Connection

There is no surprise more magical than the surprise of
being loved. It is God's finger on man's shoulder.
~Charles Morgan

My wife and I dated in high school, then went our separate ways. Several years later, we reconnected with some help. What God gave Theresa and me, in my view, was a very clear message — a message that we both understood and trusted.

Theresa and I both grew up in Louisville, Kentucky. She attended an all-girls Catholic high school, Mercy Academy. I attended an all-boys Catholic high school, St. Xavier. Theresa became friends with my older sister, who also attended Mercy. Several weeks after we met, I got up the nerve to call Theresa on the phone and ask her out on a date. We were both in our junior year of high school. We continued to date and became very close over the next two years.

We discovered that we had similar core values and morals. Our strengths and weaknesses were such that we could tackle just about any project together. We were an example of "opposites attract" in the best possible way. We complemented each other. Completed each other. Everyone told us that we were destined to be married to each other. But we were still very young.

After high school, I started at the J.B. Speed School of Engineering at the University of Louisville, which also meant alternating semesters in Middletown, Ohio during my last two years. Theresa began taking classes at Jefferson Community and Technical College in Louisville and then transferred to Western Kentucky University in Bowling Green. We went our separate ways and started dating other people, but we still kept in touch.

Sometime during my junior year of college, I started hearing a kind, gentle voice in my head. It kept saying, "You are going to marry Theresa." I found myself getting into these mental conversations. *How can I possibly marry Theresa? We are not seeing each other. She is dating some guy who keeps asking me to help him fix his Ford Pinto, and I have been seeing a young lady in Ohio and another in Louisville.* But I kept hearing that voice. "You are going to marry Theresa." I prayed and thought about it, wondering why I was feeling like this.

Finally, one night, about four months since I had talked to or seen Theresa, I heard it again: "You are going to marry Theresa." I thought to myself, *Okay, I give up. I will call her up and talk to her.* I wasn't even sure if she was in town.

So I picked up the old rotary phone in my parents' kitchen to call Theresa, but I did not hear a dial tone. You see, I had picked up the phone at that split second between when an incoming call is connected and the phone actually rings. It was Theresa on the phone.

It seems she had been hearing a similar nudging voice for some time and decided to call me at the exact same time I had decided to call her!

Six months later, we were engaged. A year after that, we both finished college and got married. God had a plan for us and I am so happy we both said, "Yes."

~Mark J. Thieman

87

Laboured Breathing

Intuition is a spiritual faculty and does
not explain, but simply points the way.
~Florence Scovel Shinn

I doused my cloth in bleach and began to feverishly polish the handle of the door. I didn't care if I took off the brass finish as long as it killed the germs.

"Carrie," my husband said, "what are you doing?"

I couldn't respond to his question because I was in the throes of a panic attack. The only sound I managed to make was a pathetic whimpering. *What else needed to be disinfected?* I had cleaned the railings, light switches, and door handles. Then my gaze settled on the source that promised to be the most compromised: the bucket of toys my nephew had touched. I dragged them upstairs to the waiting tub and poured a bath hot enough to disinfect a sewer. I threw the toys into the steaming water by the armful. My husband had followed me and was just as hastily plucking out the toys that shouldn't be submerged.

"Please tell me what's wrong," he pleaded.

I didn't know how to respond. The truth was I believed my son's life was in jeopardy. This feeling had begun to take root before his birth, and I couldn't seem to shake it. I began to see everything as a threat, from his umbilical cord to his feeding habits. Now even my nephew's cold seemed like a harbinger of doom. So I made up some lame excuse about being tired and rushed my family out the door, all so I could scrub my house as though they'd exposed us to Ebola.

I knew I had to explain my actions, but what was I supposed to say that wouldn't sound ludicrous? I was just an ordinary, stay-at-home mom. I didn't have any psychic gifts. I had never so much as predicted the correct sex of one of our three children. And now I was supposed to convince my husband that my premonition was accurate? I took a deep breath and said, "I'm scared that something bad is going to happen to our baby."

My husband chuckled with relief. "That's all?" his expression seemed to say. He patted me reassuringly on the back. "Nothing bad is going to happen," he promised.

I wasn't convinced, and the feeling only grew more intense. It was starting to affect my appetite and sleep. I tried to reason with myself, but no logical argument could force the premonition to subside. So I had to choose to accept the warning and risk how others perceived me, or ignore it and risk my son's life. When I thought of the feeling in those terms, I had no choice but to acknowledge the premonition as real and inevitable. So I remained hyper vigilant and disregarded the concerned murmurings from my family, who were now wondering if I was suffering from postpartum depression.

When my son was two weeks old, the panic revealed itself as justified. My newborn suddenly had a hard time catching his breath. We took him to a doctor immediately, and I got the validation I never wanted — my son was very sick. At the emergency room, they performed a battery of tests. I expected to be told that my son had caught the respiratory syncytial virus (RSV) from his cousin, a cold that can cause pneumonia or respiratory distress in infants. Instead, we were told that my son had been born with a congenital heart defect; more specifically, multiple ventricular septal defects. He had holes in his heart — so many that they had put him into heart failure. The doctor praised the observations that caused us to seek medical care. "If you hadn't noticed his laboured breathing when you did…" She never finished her sentence, but the insinuation hung around me like a lead blanket.

My husband stared at the doctor with a stunned expression on his face. "My wife knew there was something wrong," he tried to explain. The doctor nodded and gave me a kind smile. It was obvious to me that she didn't understand what my husband meant. In her mind, I was just an observant mother, not a psychic one.

That day, we were sent home with hope as thin as spider filament. It might have been a frail thing, but I clung to it as fiercely as the spider himself. Eventually, I settled into a routine that included twice-daily medications, cardiology appointments, and feeding routines. I did everything the doctors asked and prayed it would be enough. When he was six months old, we were given amazing news: The holes in my child's heart had spontaneously closed, and he would never require open-heart surgery. I was astounded. Not only had a premonition saved his life, but now a miracle had healed his heart. He ended that year every bit the phenomenon he began — a wonder in so many ways.

~Carina Middleton

The Lucky One

To a father growing old, nothing
is dearer than a daughter.
~Euripides

My parents lived on a quiet country road. After almost fifty years of marriage, my mom passed away from a rare cancer, leaving Dad, a trim carpenter and part-time farmer, extremely lonely—with no one to talk to, no more home-cooked meals, and no idea how to take care of a household.

My husband and I had just moved next door. At first, I assumed Mom's domestic duties, but gradually coaxed Dad into doing his own laundry. He enjoyed telling everyone he knew about his pink "tighty whities" that he'd washed in hot water along with a red flannel shirt.

Next, I suggested we concentrate on cooking, but Dad never got further than using the microwave. Instead, he ate with us a few nights a week and took home leftovers.

Juggling the demands of a job, husband, kids, grandkids, house-work, and a lonesome father kept me busy. Every evening, no sooner had I walked in the door from work than I received the inevitable phone call—Dad just calling to chat.

Once in a while, when I had the day off from work and lots of chores to do, I kept the garage doors closed to hide from his watchful eye.

Dad was on his own during deer season while my husband and

I went to our cabin in the woods. We'd planned on staying the entire week, but my better half cut his hand to the bone one evening while skinning the ten-point buck he'd shot. Since his injury required stitches, we came home a few days early.

The next morning, after going through a stack of mail and newspapers, I told my husband I needed to attack the mountain of dirty clothes we'd brought home.

My next sentence came out of nowhere. "Think I'll call Dad and see if he needs anything from town."

A look of surprise crossed my husband's face. "What happened to playing catch-up from deer camp?"

"That can wait. I need to see Dad."

Dad beamed when I walked in the back door of his quiet kitchen just as he'd finished his bowl of cold cereal.

"Thought you guys weren't coming home until the weekend."

After I explained what happened, he jumped at my offer to shop and rode along. First stop, the hardware store for a fluorescent light-bulb, and then the bank. And oh, could we pick up milk and bread at the grocer? I chuckled, wondering what he'd think of to lure me over the next day.

Another sense of urgency sent me back to his house that same afternoon. With Thanksgiving the following week and family gatherings still held at our parents' home, I needed to do some serious housecleaning.

Dad was looking forward to the huge banquet.

Trying to be heard over the vacuum cleaner, he hollered, "I'm glad you learned how to make your mother's rolls."

As I continued cleaning, my eyes teared, recalling the week before Mom had passed away. She'd called early one morning and offered to teach me how to prepare her signature yeast rolls, a family favorite.

As I finished cleaning and trudged outside to leave, Dad came to the door and called out, "Thanks for all you do for me."

Dad's sister, who visited him almost daily, phoned the next morning. Her voice faltered as she delivered the devastating news.

"Your dad passed away during the night. He must've had a heart attack."

Absorbing the sobering truth, my first thought was, *What if I hadn't gone to see him?*

Tears fell as my mind replayed the last twenty-four hours, especially the way Dad's face lit up at my unexpected visit. I will be forever grateful for the inner voice that guided me to his doorstep the previous morning, giving me one final, precious dad-daughter memory.

On the fifth anniversary of his passing, loving thoughts of Dad flooded my mind. He was in every childhood recollection, whether it was coaching my softball team, teaching me and my siblings to play ping pong, or taking us fishing, sleigh riding, ice skating, and bowling. As I walked into the family room, my eyes were drawn downward. I almost stepped on a card that had sat on the bookshelf for years, but somehow landed open on the floor.

As I bent to pick it up, I spotted Dad's scrawled handwriting. "Thanks for all you do. I am so lucky."

"You're wrong, Dad," I said out loud. "I'm the lucky one."

~Alice Muschany

89

Like an Elephant

Elephants can sense danger. They're able to detect an
approaching tsunami or earthquake before it hits.
~Jennifer Richard Jacobson

It was a typical cloudy Atlanta day and I was killing time in the school cafeteria, nursing a coffee and looking forward to my late photography class. After class I would walk through downtown Atlanta at precisely 7:25 p.m. to catch the Peachtree Center subway. That's what I did every Friday to connect with my husband farther north.

So why did I suddenly feel this acute sense of dread, and why did the words "anywhere but here" start running through my head?

I often think about the Indian Ocean tsunami of 2004, which was, if not the most destructive or dramatic natural disaster to have occurred, at least the most memorable for one particular reason: the elephants. I remember hearing in the news how, despite thousands of human casualties, few animals suffered injury. Locals and tourists saw the animals run to higher ground a good few hours before the disaster struck, leaving all witnesses to ask themselves, *How did they know?*

I wasn't even thinking about the elephants of Thailand that late winter afternoon in 2008 when I felt this acute need to get out of school and downtown Atlanta at all costs — even if the cost was skipping out on my photography studio class yet again and risking a reduction in my grade for excessive absences. I actually enjoyed my photography class and had no desire to avoid it. Still, that need to flee persisted. I tried to shrug off the feeling and continue my usual routine, but the mounting anxiety was becoming so overpowering that I finally forced myself to sit down, look up at the gray sky, and ask myself: "Where do you want to go?"

Anywhere but here.

Anywhere but the downtown Atlanta campus or any of my usual coffee shops and hangouts inside "the perimeter." I went through the list in my head, trying to find a coffee shop that didn't make me uneasy. I finally hit upon one at Lindbergh Center Station that I frequented maybe once a year. It was as far away as I could get from the downtown area while still being on the MARTA line.

Do it! Now!

So I headed to MARTA at an unusual hour and to a place I rarely frequented, but every step of the journey took me farther away from Georgia State, Woodruff Park, Peachtree Street, and my anxiety. At some point, it began to rain very heavily. By the time I got to Lindbergh Center Station, the rain was serious, though the magnitude of the storm didn't register until I caught wind of the news. A giant, unprecedented tornado was tearing through downtown Atlanta that very minute. It shut down electricity, tore through buildings and barreled through the very park I always crossed on my way to Peachtree Center at precisely 7:25 p.m. on Fridays. On foot. In the dark. All alone.

When I had phoned my husband hours earlier, I had been unable to give a concrete reason for my change of plans. But by the time he arrived to pick me up that night, at that faraway coffee shop, I just looked at him and said, "Remember the elephants? I think that just happened to me."

~Alicia Araya

90

The Boots That Saved My Life

We want to feel we are in control of our own existence.
In some ways we are, in some ways we're not. We are
ruled by the forces of chance and coincidence.
~Paul Auster

I've never hunted and have never been interested in the sport, but my friend, Matt, became a devoted hunter. Matt and I were college friends. He lived in the New York City area and I lived in upstate New York, and he would often come stay with me to hunt in the woods around my house. On the days he hunted, he would be up and out well before dawn. He would leave me a note about where he was heading—longitude and latitude—and where and when he expected to emerge from the woods.

My job was to find him there and bring him back to my place. This routine worked well every time, and I liked the challenge of working from numbers on a map to pinpoint where I'd find him, reading whatever book I had until I heard the snap of a twig under his boot.

He called me one time, though, and said he'd be bringing along his friend, Kevin. I knew Kevin and liked him, but as soon as I heard Matt's voice on the phone telling me this, I felt uneasy. I had no idea why I should feel that way. Matt asked if I could meet them at a certain spot—longitude and latitude—some distance from my place and pick them both up to drive them back to their hotel. I agreed, but, even as

I did, I felt an odd tightening in the pit of my stomach.

The day of the hunt, I went about my usual business and then got into my old clothes for hiking, including my old boots. I was just about to leave, my hand on the doorknob, when I felt the very strong — and strange — sensation that I should change my boots. I'm not big on fashion and don't spend much time thinking about what to wear, so I couldn't understand why I was feeling this way. My wife, Betsy, had recently bought me a new pair for work — not for stomping around fields or woods — and the ones I was wearing were my traditional go-find-Matt boots. There was no reason to change my boots, but when I tried to shake off the feeling and leave the house, the sensation was so strong I couldn't resist it.

New boots on, I drove the forty minutes to the pickup spot I'd calculated and pulled in by the tree line off a back road. I grabbed my book and walked down the road, consciously keeping from the sides where my boots might scuff on rocks. Scanning for a suitable reading spot, I noticed a green hill and wandered over to it. This hill overlooked a ravine lined with stones of various sizes and shapes. The sun was dropping down low, and the small valley was illuminated with a bright orange glow that sparkled among the large granite and smaller quartz far below me. Looking around, I figured this was pretty much the perfect spot since they would see me on the hill from whatever direction they came. I sat down and read my book.

It wasn't long before I heard a shout and saw them coming down the road. They weren't carrying any deer or any other game, just their rifles. I called out, "No luck?" Matt shrugged and smiled, but Kevin was clearly angry and shouted, "Nothing! Out all day and — nothing!" Matt just shrugged again, saying, "Next time," and we all sat down on the hilltop, Matt to my left and Kevin to my right.

Matt was talking about the day while Kevin checked his .30-06 rifle and kept shifting the bolt. Kevin was complaining about how he wanted to shoot something, had come on the silly trip just to shoot something, and hadn't had a chance all day. Matt told him to calm down. Kevin continued on — he'd been ripped off, the stupid deer had it in for him, the day just wasn't right for deer hunting anyway — and all this time I looked across the ravine and down at the last light of the day sparkling among the stones.

Suddenly, as I was looking down, I noticed a splotch of mud on the toe of my left boot. And here I'd been so careful! As I noticed this mud, I heard Kevin's voice louder beside me as he yelled, "I don't care. I don't care! I'm shooting something, whether it's living or not!" As he said this, I leaned forward to flick the mud from the boot and heard the loud crack of his rifle fire next to me — heard the *ping* of the bullet hitting stone. And as I leaned down, my finger touching my boot, I felt the bullet whiz through the top of my hair in ricochet. If I had not leaned forward at that precise moment, the bullet would have gone right through my forehead and, with the hollow points Kevin had in his weapon, would have completely blown out the back of my head.

He couldn't apologize enough, but my heart was beating so fast and loud that I could hardly hear him. Sure, I was angry, but the main sensation I had was awe. I thought of Betsy, waiting for me back home, of my mother and my brothers and sisters and friends and all the lives that could have been changed in a moment if I hadn't bent forward to brush some mud off my boot — a boot I shouldn't even have been wearing that day. Something, somewhere, had saved my life, and ever since I have been quite conscious of that fact and always very grateful.

The memory of that day has come back to me many times since — every anniversary with Betsy, when my daughter Emily was born, and so many days with them both since. When a friend or student or anyone else has thanked me for some assistance, or when I publish another story, the memory stirs. All the years since that day have been possible because of one single moment when I listened to and trusted what I felt, even though it made no earthly sense at the time.

~Joshua J. Mark

91

Listen and Learn

When you listen, it's amazing what you can learn.
When you act on what you've learned, it's
amazing what you can change.
~Audrey McLaughlin

I t was unusual for me to drive without children in the vehicle. But on this sunny, autumn afternoon, I had an appointment and left them in the capable hands of their grandparents. While driving, I enjoyed listening to music on the radio and felt calm, relaxed and a bit carefree. It was a welcome little break.

As I sat at a red light, admiring the yellows and oranges of tree-lined Center Avenue, dotted with its well-preserved Victorian mansions, I noticed that I was alone at this normally bustling intersection. Eerily, not one other car was in sight.

My confusion with the lack of traffic faded as the light turned green. But when I began to go, a very clear voice became present in the left side of my head.

It said, "Look farther down the road."

Unable to process this, I ignored the voice and started to move forward.

The voice returned, firm and insistent. "I SAID, LOOK FARTHER DOWN THE ROAD."

I stopped. This time there was no denying it.

Just then, a double-trailered truck plowed in front of me at about sixty miles per hour. I felt the displaced air as it passed. It had run the light at twice the posted speed. I sat frozen, my mind stunned.

Had I gone when the light turned green, my minivan and body would have been splattered all over historic Center Avenue. My two little sons would have instantly lost their mom, my husband his wife.

The voice, that inexplicable voice, did not allow disaster to unfold. Soon, traffic was filling the corner. A horn honked at me.

I wanted to shout, "Stop. Don't you people know what just happened?" But, of course, they didn't know. Life kept moving, and I had to go with it.

In the years since this incident, I have frequently traversed the intersection of Center Avenue and Trumbull. Traffic is always present. I cross with a reverent respect for the voice that allowed me to still be here today. And, in a profoundly comforting way, I know that I am not alone… ever… anywhere.

As an aside: Today, I was struggling with whether or not I really wanted to share this story.

I prayed, "Lord, if it is okay with you, I'll send this. If not, somehow let your answer be evident."

As I returned from the grocery store and pulled my car into the garage, a song came on my Christian radio station, the repetitive chorus playing, "Write your story, write your story." I found myself singing along, as I have heard this song many times. I turned off the car, not realizing what I was singing. Then, it hit me. I turned the radio back on to confirm. Sure enough, Francesca Battistelli, was still singing "Write Your Story."

This answer was also crystal clear.

~Ann Marie

Chapter 10

Dreams and the Unexplainable

Messages from Heaven

92

A Father's Gift from Beyond

I cannot think of any need in childhood as strong
as the need for a father's protection.
~Sigmund Freud

The scream started from somewhere deep within my soul—a low, guttural growl that intensified with each passing second. I was a wounded child, and my heart was raw with pain.

"Had they gotten him here earlier, we could have saved him." For over fourteen hours, my father had bled into his brain when an aneurysm burst. He lay on a gurney in the hallway of the local hospital, left untreated until 6:00 the following morning when a doctor decided to ambulance him to a hospital a few hours away. My father died at 9:10 a.m. on September 21, 1976. He was fifty years old.

My life and that of my two younger brothers had just imploded. We were now without the guidance of both parents. My mother had been ill for several years—unable to walk or care for herself—and had lived in a nursing home for the past year. At the age of twenty, I had just become responsible for them all.

During my father's funeral, my mother casually mentioned she expected me to marry as soon as possible so my brothers would be cared for. Already disoriented from medication an aunt had given me in hopes of staving off hysteria, my head was spinning, and my body flashed hot and cold as I struggled to comprehend what my mother was asking of me in the crowded room of mourners.

"You'll still be allowed to live in the house, but I won't have you living in sin! You'll be married as soon as possible. I'll give you a little money for groceries every few weeks, but you're the oldest, Judy. It's your responsibility to take care of your brothers!"

I'd stopped listening after "married as soon as possible." *I wasn't ready for marriage yet! I'd only been engaged five months!* I screamed silently. *I don't want to be a wife, mother, or caregiver. I just want to run and hide.* But that wasn't an option.

The two weeks after my father's funeral were a blur. I went on with life, pretending I was fine, but really I was trapped inside a windowless bubble. Black. Bleak. Frightening. Surreal.

Daily visits to my mother became increasingly more strained. Every visit began with, "Have you decided on a date yet?" She was worried, she said. Worried that I'd leave my brothers behind and go off on my own and have a "wonderful life." Her words, like the rest of my world lately, bounced against me and fell away dully.

My mother, paternal grandmother, and paternal aunt were against a traditional wedding so soon after my father's passing. Out of respect for my father, they wanted a simple Justice of the Peace gathering. Yet something inside me screamed resistance while another part of me cowered with guilt and shame. How could I be so selfish as to want a "white-gown wedding"?

I wanted to hide. But, instead, one evening after a particularly stressful day of visits with my mother, grandmother, and aunt—listening to the same arguments and feeling the same guilt and shame—I sank down on the bed and, with tears streaming down my face, begged for a sign. I needed to know what to do because, at that very moment, I was done trying to please everyone. I was done with talking about marriage. I couldn't be sure I even wanted to be married. Not now. Not ever.

I had no idea what I wanted—except for my father to be there in the room with me right then. Alive. Well. But, that wasn't going to happen, so I needed an answer from somewhere. The answer I received, however, was not at all what I expected.

The next morning, I jumped out of bed and raced to the kitchen table with scenes from the dream I'd had the night before still vivid in my mind. But the large Swiss Army Knife with the emerald-green cover my father had placed near the edge of the table wasn't there. It had been so vivid. So real, but it had only been a dream. How could I show anyone a dream?

Then a small inner voice whispered, "Show it by telling."

First, I drove to my paternal grandmother's home, then to my aunt's, and finally to the nursing home, relaying my dream each time.

Dad had been sitting at the kitchen table talking to my brothers. He told them he loved them, and then waved for me to sit across from him as they left the room.

"I know how difficult this has been, Judy, and I am so sorry. But I want you to have your wedding your way. If no one believes that I've been here tonight, show them this." He placed a large Swiss Army Knife with a beautiful emerald-green cover on the table and pushed it toward me.

"They'll know without a doubt that I was here, and I support you. Had I lived, I would have given you the biggest wedding I could afford. But I didn't, so this knife will be all you need to convince those you need to that you have my blessing."

Every time I finished relaying my dream, the response was the same: "Have your wedding your way."

We married October 30, 1976, in a wedding that fell together as though orchestrated to perfection. People offered their services for free or gave us price breaks. Our wedding is still talked about today by friends and family as one of the best weddings they've attended.

Three weeks after our wedding, I sat down with my grandmother to ask her a question. "Why did you change your mind about how we had our wedding? Why did you change it so quickly after I told you my dream?"

Her response stunned me. "Your father was sixteen and had joined the Army. Before he left for training, your grandfather gave him a Swiss

Army Knife with an emerald-green cover. You couldn't have known what this knife looked like because it was lost before you were born, yet you described it perfectly."

Her eyes misted.

"During the reception, your aunt and uncle were with me. We were facing the front doors looking out at the night, and a man appeared in the doorway. He just stood there with a big smile on his face. He watched everyone in the room. Then he looked right at us, smiled broadly, and nodded." She drifted away in thought, falling silent.

"Who was it?"

"Your dad." A single tear fell. "He was wearing the same suit he was buried in. He was just so happy that everyone was enjoying themselves. It was as though he had just stepped outside for a bit. It felt like he was really there."

She chuckled suddenly. "He drove me to drink, you know! I had my first beer that night."

~Judith Richardson Schroeder

I Just Needed to Say Goodbye

*Don't be dismayed at goodbyes. A farewell
is necessary before you can meet again.*
~Richard Bach

In 1977, my sixteen-year-old brother, Jimmy, was killed in a car accident. He died on my sister's birthday and was buried on my birthday. Two days later, my two younger sisters were scheduled to have a double wedding. In fact, Jimmy had died after the stag party for one of my future brothers-in-law. He was the designated driver for the party and he took a corner too fast and hit a pole.

There was no time to cancel the wedding, and more than 500 guests came out two days early to attend Jimmy's funeral. It was bizarre and surreal that something so tragic should be followed by something that should have been so happy. I can't remember the wedding ceremony at all. I was twenty-two years old, and my heart ached so badly that I finally understood the expression "dying of a broken heart."

One month after my brother's death, I was still broken and cried myself to sleep every night. I couldn't remember if I'd told him how much I loved him. I couldn't remember our last conversation. I couldn't remember his voice. I desperately needed to talk to him and tell him I loved him, and especially to tell him goodbye. Thoughts of my brother filled my head every waking moment, and every night I would toss and turn, trying to find respite from my grief in sleep. When exhaustion overtook me, I'd sleep a dreamless few hours, and in the morning I would wake to find my pillow wet from tears. Even in my sleep, I was crying.

One night, I gave up completely. I said, "God, I cannot live with this pain. I just want to die. I want to see my brother again!" I cried myself to sleep feeling as though I was drowning in waves of grief, and that night I had a dream that changed my life forever.

I dreamed a lady came to me. She felt like a sister, but she wasn't, and yet I felt I knew her. She was dressed all in white with beautiful, long blond hair, and she motioned for me to follow her. She took me to an "elevator of light," and we rose to a place that I can only describe as a waiting room. She told me to wait there for my brother.

When he appeared before me, the tears flowed down my face as we hugged each other hard. I told him how happy I was to see him and how much we all missed him. He told me he missed us too, but that he was busy! He said he was learning patience.

In life, Jimmy was the most impatient sixteen-year-old I'd ever known — he wanted to do everything, and his motto had always been, "I'm here for a good time — not a long time!" So when he told me he was learning "patience," I understood exactly what he meant! He also told me to tell Mom to quit crying so much.

It felt so good to talk to him again and to tell him how much I missed him and loved him. He told me to remember that he would always be there for us when we really needed him, but to quit bugging him for the little everyday things. I desperately wanted to stay with him, but he said I couldn't go beyond the "waiting room" because I wasn't ready yet.

We hugged goodbye, and he told me to tell Mom that whenever she heard the bird, she would know it was him saying hello. I had no idea what that meant, but he said, "Just tell Mom. She'll know what it means!" Then my beautiful guide appeared and took me back through the elevator of light.

I woke up, but this time I had tears of happiness on my face. A weight had lifted off my heart. Being with my brother in that dream felt more real than any other experience I'd ever had in my life, and he'd said things I had never heard of before.

I had no idea what he meant about the bird, but my mom knew. When I told her about the dream, she told me that Jimmy had learned to mimic a certain bird's call. He would often stand on the sundeck and call to it, and it would answer back. She was immediately comforted by the message.

Jimmy's words, "I'll be there when you really need me…," came back to me as I was driving through a snowstorm less than three months after his death. I heard his voice say to me, "Do up your seatbelt!" It was an order, not a suggestion. I fastened my belt, and a few minutes later the car slid, as if in slow motion, off the slippery, snow-covered mountain road and rolled two and a half times down an embankment. If I hadn't had my seat belt on, I would have been dead. Thanks to the words he spoke in my dream, I knew that what was about to happen was important enough for him to "be there," and I'm glad I listened.

When I told Mom that Jimmy had saved my life, she looked at me, and a wave of understanding passed through her. She said, "I understand now. It was Jimmy's time to leave, but it wasn't yours." She is now ninety-two years old and still patiently waiting for her time to leave because she expects to see her son again.

Sometimes, we get to say goodbye in life. And sometimes, if we are really blessed, we get an opportunity to say goodbye in a dream that is more than a dream. It is a gift.

~Glenda Standeven

Here and Now

Life is available only in the present moment. If you
abandon the present moment, you cannot live the
moments of your daily life deeply.
~Thich Nhat Hanh

My granddaughter, Kaitlyn, opened a cupboard door and reached for a white porcelain mug. "Do you want sugar or milk?"

"Thanks, honey, but this is just fine." My flavored coffee required only hot water. Super swift. Just like my life. I rushed through most mornings in a hectic routine. Get up, get dressed, get to work. Rush home, do chores, go to bed. Get up and do it all again.

Now here I stood in my granddaughter's kitchen. Little Aubree, just two, played in the other room. This was a visit for me to relax and enjoy time with loved ones. But I couldn't turn off my brain. After spending all day with Aubree and Kaitlyn, my mind automatically reviewed a to-do list of everything that needed to be done when I returned home. I crawled into bed at 10:30 in the upstairs guest room.

I woke up with a sudden start. After I took in where I was, thin tendrils of memory converged into a vision. There was a dream, and it had seemed so real. I sat in bed, closed my eyes, and let the wispy thoughts merge in my mind.

The dream begins with me in my dad's house. It's a nondescript ranch home with two smallish bedrooms, a large kitchen, and a big living room. I'm in Dad's closet, looking for one of his favorite sweaters. There's a door at the back of the closet — a door I've never seen before. I turn the metal knob and find a long string cord just inside the doorframe. When I pull on it, a bare bulb illuminates a set of wooden stairs, very dusty and old.

Stepping gingerly on the stairs, which creak but hold strong, I journey down. What I find is a hallway with a maze of corridors going in many different directions leading to many rooms.

There's one filled with posters of actors and actresses covering the walls, standing up in frames and taped to the ceiling. In another are all varieties of coins, big, heavy, round silver dollars and silver certificates. In yet another are baby clothes, tiny little outfits in all colors of the rainbow.

In yet another room are turntables and record players along with stacks of vinyl 33s, 45s and 78s, as well as console televisions — big boxy things with the numbers worn off on the knobs from hand-flipping the channels. And still another room is filled with wooden carved objects: spinning wheels, birdhouses, and wooden toys like a duck that quacks when you pull him on a string.

Each room is crammed full. I squeeze past one table, then another, touching some items, afraid to touch others for fear they will disintegrate before my eyes. After a while, I delicately pick up and cradle two objects. One is a carved mahogany dresser bowl like the one Dad deposits his coins into from his pockets after work. The other is a porcelain mug that declares "World's Best Dad" on the front.

I enter another room to my right, this one filled with service station memorabilia like a big, round, white sign with a red flying horse and the words "Mobilgas SPECIAL" underneath. There are old stand-up pumps with round lighted signs on top, and cans of Quaker State and Pennzoil.

I happen to look toward the doorway. Seated in a chair is a man. I look once, then again.

"Dad, is that you?"

"Yes. Come and sit down here by me," he says.

As I sink into the chair next to his, I can't take my eyes off him.

He tells me that when he started to collect things, people were surprised and wondered why he'd collect items that were brand new and had no value.

Dad looks me straight in the eyes. "You don't realize how valuable something is until much later."

I glance at the coffee mug and wooden bowl in my hands. When I look up, he's gone. Carrying my two treasures, I slowly go back upstairs, walk through the closet, and into the kitchen.

"Miss," a woman says, holding a clipboard in her hand. "You can't keep those."

"Why not?" I clutch my treasures to my chest.

"They're part of the estate and must be sold at auction."

I look around. The counters brim with Dad's kitchen items, tagged and ready for sale. Then I remember: Dad passed away eighteen months ago.

That's when I woke up. I burrowed under the covers and let my thoughts take me back. It felt so real, like I could touch my dad's face, the rough stubble on his chin, see his eyes crinkle when his face lit up in a wide smile. He said something about not realizing how valuable something is until much later. I sighed. *Didn't I rush through each day? Often with a long to-do list of chores and errands? Wasn't I already worrying about work when I still had three wonderful days left with my loved ones?*

I shrugged off the blanket and almost jumped out of bed. *Instead of thinking about all the things I had to do when I got back home, what if I were present, really present, in the here and now?* I crept down the creaking stairs and into Aubree's room. She stood in her crib, arms outstretched, bright eyes shining.

My dad would have loved Aubree. And he would have cherished every moment he could be with her. I would do the same.

What's most valuable is what I have right now, right here in front of me. It was a lesson from my dad, my angel in heaven. One I would never forget.

~B.J. Taylor

95

Anastasia's Ghosts

The more enlightened our houses are,
the more their walls ooze ghosts.
~Italo Calvino, The Literature Machine

lbert Anastasia was a ruthless and feared Cosa Nostra mobster; he ran Murder Inc., and, later, the Gambino crime family. On the morning of October 25, 1957, as he sat in the fourth of twelve barber chairs, leaned back, and allowed the barber to place a hot towel on his face, two masked gunmen burst in and unloaded their handguns.

I shared two things with the famed mobster: our birthday and that I lived the first seven years of my life in the graceful Mediterranean home he built on the bluffs of Fort Lee, overlooking the Hudson River and New York City skyline.

Two years after Anastasia's death, and shortly before my arrival, my father, Buddy Hackett, asked Anastasia's widow to sell him the home. Years later, after moving our family to California, my father would recount first-person experiences with the spirits that inhabited Anastasia's house.

Often Buddy would go to the kitchen in the middle of the night for a snack, and as he held open the refrigerator door, he would feel and hear breathing on the back of his neck. He'd ask, "Who's there?" He saw nothing, but would hear footsteps run down the long corridor away from the kitchen.

The finished basement housed the laundry area, kids' playroom, furnace room, and bar with screening room. Each year, on the coldest night, and always in the middle of the night, the furnace pilot light would blow out. Wakened by the chill in the house, Buddy would tell of going to the basement in his robe, kneeling down on ice-cold floors, and coaxing the furnace to re-ignite, all the while feeling a warm breath on the back of his neck.

Tina, our nanny for many years, reported one of the oddest experiences. In the playroom, there was a green chalkboard on wheels, encased in a pine frame with a wood ledge for the chalk and erasers. Tina told my parents that while doing the laundry, she heard a voice in the playroom. She entered the room to find a nun in full habit kneeling at the ledge, praying. Tina asked the nun how she got in the house; but the apparition fizzled and disappeared.

My bedroom had aquamarine walls with hand-painted cherubs reclining on clouds in two decorative scenes. I was sure that one of those cherubs' arm positions would change, at the elbow, back and forth between head-in-hand and hand lying flat on the cloud.

It started with the ghosts in Anastasia's house. Those moments were the jumping-off point for many discussions with my father about spirituality and afterlife. Those conversations led Dad to comment, "If I can find a way, I will connect with you after death."

I know Kabbalah by belief and experience, not lifelong study. My father was my conduit to this thinking; he studied Jewish mysticism. He guided me: "Tap in. It's available to you always. Just believe and be open." At the same time, he taught his children that Kabbalah was not to be studied until you are of "a wisdom-filled age," and have enough life experience under your belt to piece together concepts and apply them to your life.

My dad's life-ending heart attack occurred sometime between nightfall and the following morning of June 30th in 2003. I was living in Montana, hiking daily and feeling fit and strong in all ways. I went to bed on the 29th feeling good, but I awoke several times that night. The morning of the 30th, I felt horrible. In my head, nothing was right. I couldn't start my day; I was off, *way* off. I abandoned my planned activities and stayed in the house.

My mother phoned later that morning to say she was home fighting the flu. At her urging, my father had gone to our beach home to hopefully avoid getting ill. She went on to say that she had been trying to reach him since the previous evening; he wasn't answering the phone.

I felt it as soon as she started to speak. We hung up, and I phoned the firehouse four doors up the beach. My mother arrived to be met by paramedics blocking her from entering the home. She would phone an hour later to confirm what I already knew: Buddy had left this world.

Three months later, the night before my 43rd birthday, I was driving up the California coast to meet my husband. Throughout my life, I have spent many fine days on the Big Sur coast. It has always been one of my favorite places to go and think things through. It was late in the afternoon, and my plan was to pull out at one of the scenic overlooks, light Shabbos candles, and watch the sun set.

The Pacific Coast Highway was empty. I pulled off and parked. I had the scenic overlook to myself. I set my candles on a boulder, lit them, and recited the prayer to welcome the Sabbath into my heart and mind. It was a beautiful, warm September evening, no fog, and just a few wispy clouds high in the sky.

I was looking out over the ocean when it happened.

A brilliant light flashed through the sky. As quickly as it appeared, it disappeared. The light was accompanied by a sound, like tearing a sheet of paper in half, amplified tenfold. The light started high in the sky and fell straight toward the sea, stopping just above my position on the sea cliff, exposing and concealing itself in an instant.

I looked to the highway. Was there oncoming traffic with bright lights that cast this illumination out over the sea? No, no one there. I was alone. I looked back to the light. It was gone. I could not deny what I had just experienced. I felt my father in that moment, and I felt he would be with me always. No matter what came to me in life, he would protect and watch out for me.

A month later, I was with a dear friend, a teacher of Hasidism and Kabbalah. I told her of my experience on the Big Sur cliff, and the sound that accompanied the incredible light. She said I must be very spiritual; what I described is in the book of Tanya. It is called the Kav.

I searched for a definition: "The vector of Divine light which emanated after the initial concealment of Divine light." The sound is described as the force it takes to create and conceal.

There are individuals who study these concepts their entire lives: man's fall into darkness and his quest to access the light. For me, I was introduced to this energy in my childhood home. I learned at a young age to trust my intuition and to accept rare but undeniable moments. There are energies that dwell elsewhere and make their presence known to those who listen. These moments have informed me throughout my life.

~Lisa Hackett

96

Chicken Soup for the Soul

The Recipe

Cooking is like love. It should be entered
into with abandon or not at all.
~Harriet Van Horne

L
ike all widows, I've slowly and painfully made the transition from two to one. Since Tom's passing, the kitchen has been quiet. Dinner preparations for one are modest and quickly finished. The exception is Christmas, when our daughter Kathleen arrives to take over the kitchen in her father's place.

My husband had learned to make pasta sauce as a child in Brooklyn at the knee of his Italian grandmother. Several times a year, he would come home laden with garlic, onion, anise, oregano, tomatoes, and several bottles of wine — "A little for me, a little for the sauce." The well seasoned "spaghetti pot" would make its appearance, Italian tenors would burst onto the sound system, and the house would fill with steam and tantalizing scents. Sauce making was an event, so for many years I dutifully operated as sous chef. I chopped, stirred and sautéed as specifically directed, and was always thanked with a kiss and a waltz around the kitchen.

This dynamic changed when Kathleen, the youngest of our six children, arrived. Always her father's shadow, she was squeezing tomatoes and measuring spices while still in diapers. As she grew, I quietly stepped into the background, leaving the two of them to bond while perfecting their art. Vigorous Sicilian-style discussions sometimes emanated from the kitchen: "No, no, no! You have to use whole nutmeg and grate it yourself!" "San Marzano tomatoes, nothing else!" Appropriate adjustments were evidently agreed upon, and the sauce evolved. Nothing was ever committed to writing, however. In fact, the word "blasphemy" was used to describe the very idea. One daughter-in-law was insistent, though. Grumbling, Tom finally scribbled out the recipe by hand, with many verbal embellishments. "Sauce is an art!" he warned her. "We don't clone, we create!" Amused, she gave him a copy. I never saw it again.

Every time we moved, the spaghetti pot moved with us. And even while he was battling three bouts of cancer, Tom still created his masterpieces with Kathleen. She was staying with us, finishing her graduate work, when Tom passed in December 2012. Her personal memorial to him was, of course, a large pot of pasta sauce, prepared for her siblings for Christmas dinner a few days after the funeral. She stepped forward to take Tom's place as the guardian of tradition, the keeper of the flame, and suddenly the pasta sauce meant more than just a meal. It was now the link between the children and their father. It was a celebration of love and remembrance, repeated every Christmas, even when Kathleen, too, had married and moved away.

Last year, however, the phone rang the week before the holiday. "Mom? Catastrophe! Work has gone crazy. I won't be in until the night before Christmas, and the sauce has to cook for several days!"

Like any mother, I jumped right in. "Don't stress, honey. Give me a shopping list. I can get the sauce going, and you can do the final spice adjustment when you arrive."

I could hear the concern in her voice. "Are you sure? You've never done it before."

"Never done it before? Who do you think assisted Dad before you came along? I've helped with the sauce many times! I can manage." And then I remembered. "Besides, I think Dad wrote out the recipe way back when. He scanned a lot of his papers into his old laptop if I can find it. I'll look in the attic tomorrow."

After jotting down the shopping list, I sat down to think about what I had just done. I was about to make Tom's pasta sauce — for

Christmas, from scratch — on the strength of my experience in stirring and tasting. *You're out of your mind!* I told myself. My heart began to pound. *This means so much to the children. It's their link with their dad, the day each year that he would have wanted them to be together and remember him. I can't mess this up, I just can't.* I looked around the empty kitchen. For a dizzying moment, I almost heard the music and laughter, smelled the spices, felt myself twirl in a dance spin — but no, there was nothing but me and the silence, as always.

"Tom," I whispered, trembling. "Please. Please help me. I've done so many things alone since you've been gone. I'm tired. Tired and nervous. I want to do this for the children. I want to do it for you. I just can't do it alone." I took a deep breath, then another, and began to feel a sense of peace stealing over me. *It's okay,* I thought. *I just need rest. Tomorrow I'll feel better. I'll hunt down the laptop and find the recipe. I've got this.*

Quietly, I moved around the house, straightening up and turning out the lights. At the bedroom doorway, I turned to let the dog into the room before shutting the door. As usual, I read for a bit before turning off my light. I slept soundly.

At 3:30 a.m., I snapped awake. The dog was scratching at the closed bedroom door. I sighed. Evidently, I was about to make a long, chilly trip through the empty house to the kitchen entry so that he could go outside. I snapped on the light, thrust my icy feet into my slippers, and reached for my robe while the dog danced in anticipation.

Throwing open the bedroom door, I looked down to avoid tripping over the dog and stood rooted in astonishment at the sight of an object lying white against the wooden floor. My heart reacted, leaping wildly in my chest, before my mind recognized that it was a sheet of paper, folded several times. It looked so much like a note deliberately meant for me that I froze.

Could someone have left this here on purpose? I wondered, in rising panic. *No, I know I'm alone in the house.* I mentally retraced my steps of the night before. *Don't be silly,* I scolded myself. *It's plain you dropped something when tidying up before bed.* Shaking my head at my foolishness, I scooped up the folded paper from the floor as I followed the dog to the kitchen. I opened the trashcan, but something made me pause.

I looked down at the creased note in my hand. Surely, surely if it had been lying outside my door when I went to bed, I would have noticed. Good heavens, I would have had to step right over it! I knew I must not throw this message away without reading it. So in the dim kitchen, I slowly unfolded it. The creases in it were heavy, as though it had been folded for many years, as in fact it must have been. It was a page I had not seen in twenty years — nor thought of until that evening.

It was the pasta sauce recipe.

~Loreen Martin Broderick

97

Reaching Out

I've learned that people will forget what you said,
people will forget what you did, but people will
never forget how you made them feel.
~Carl W. Buehner

I started volunteering for hospice because I wanted to give back. When my dad was sick, hospice helped him and my family through it. Nearly ten years after he passed away, living in a new city, I found myself searching for something to feed my soul. The local hospice residence was only five blocks from where I worked, so I signed up as a volunteer. A couple of times a week, I'd leave the office at the end of the day and head over there, never knowing what to expect from my visits with the dying patients. Talking with a dying person has always come easy to me, and it's an honor to be a part of something so sacred.

Making my rounds, I'd stop into six or eight rooms per shift. If the patients felt like talking, I'd pull up a chair and chat a while. If they needed help with a meal, adjusting their bed, or making it to the bathroom, I'd do what I could for them. And if they wanted to just sit in the quiet, I did that, too. Some people aren't comfortable in the quiet, but I spent many evenings simply "being there" for several hospice patients. Sometimes, there's no need to talk. Sometimes, there are no words.

In high school, I cared for several children as a way to earn spending money. I grew really attached to Kimberly, a ten-year-old with muscular dystrophy, who had to have several surgeries and was often wheelchair bound. And, in recent years, I've helped raise a boy who has Down syndrome and is autistic. He's non-verbal, but he has no problem communicating. He has his own language.

I've always felt comfortable providing care for others, and I enjoy it. And that's why I came to a crossroads in my life. I was wondering if I should pursue a new job working in suicide prevention training. It would pay much less than my current office manager position, but I would be doing worthwhile work. And I was wondering if I should continue my hospice work, because I found myself spending more and more time there.

I'd been praying for a sign for weeks, looking for guidance for the next step in my life. And then one Saturday morning, I awoke from a dream about my dad.

He was lying on the couch where I'd seen him so many times during his illness. His hand was outstretched, reaching for me. As I drew closer, he said, "I want you to continue to reach out…"

I tried to pull myself together after that emotional dream. That day, I was scheduled to go to the home of a weekend client, Patricia, to work on some financial reports. Working with numbers would be a welcome distraction.

Knowing that Patricia is an empath and highly sensitive to others, I purposely avoided her when I got there. I knew she would feel my sadness. So I spoke to her briefly, and then headed straight into the office. The desk faced the corner of the far end of the room. When she stood in the doorway to tell me she had to go shower and then to a meeting, I was relieved. I wasn't in the mood to make small talk. Never turning around to face her, I simply said, "Okay."

I tried to get lost in my work, but in what seemed like only moments later, she was in the doorway again. Still facing the computer, I was confused when she said, "I think I got a message for you last night."

I couldn't imagine who would call her house, looking for me. Without turning around, I simply asked, "What?"

She came into the office and sat in the other chair. Out of the corner of my eye, I noticed that her hair was wet. She apparently had taken her shower and come right back downstairs. She said, "I got a message for you, and I think it was your dad."

Instantly, I turned around, and facing her, again I asked, "What?"

She explained that as she was lying in bed the night before, she sensed a male energy in the room, and she knew that it was attached to me somehow.

My head was spinning as I tried to wrap my mind around what she was saying.

She explained further. "I sensed that it was your dad, and he wanted me to give you a message. He said that you are to continue to reach out."

I was stunned. Her words took my breath away. Tears filled my eyes at the thought that my daddy could reach out to me through others, and that the message was identical to what he'd told me in my dream that very morning. The answer to my questions about my life and career came through loud and clear, from my dad, twice in the same day!

~Sunny Stephens

98

Here for You

My home is heaven. I'm just
traveling through this world.
~Billy Graham

"I t doesn't look good," Kim, my sister-in-law, said over the
phone. "But then again, how many times have we said
that?" she said with a small chuckle.

My mother-in-law, Gloria, seemed to have nine lives.
It had been nearly eleven years since Jim, her husband, had passed
away. All the years of taking care of him after his stroke had taken
a toll on Gloria's health. Since his death, she had survived a heart
attack, ovarian cancer, more than one stroke, two hip replacements,
and a seizure. She had been in hospice care, but was dismissed when
her death didn't come in the expected six-month timeframe. She just
always seemed to bounce back. Her tiny, eighty-nine-year-old body
just kept on ticking, no matter what life threw at her. In fact, while we
did not get to see her often due to the distance between us, we had
all commented when visiting last summer that she seemed healthier
and more vibrant than she had in years.

Even so, the toll was enormous. She could no longer get out of
her wheelchair. She had a very hard time hearing, despite hearing aids
in both ears, which made conversation frustrating for her. This led
to occasional bursts of inexplicable anger. Her doctors said that her
eyesight was too poor for her to read, but she insisted on "reading"
her newspaper every day.

The most difficult loss was not physical. She was often confused. She had periods of lucidity, but she frequently mixed up her children and grandchildren, calling us by each other's names. Although she had lived with Kim since shortly after Jim's death over a decade ago, she would complain that she was ready to go "home," to the house that had been sold years before.

She now required round-the-clock, in-home nursing care. She hated the medical fuss, and hated the hospital even more. She often tried to get out of bed on her own, or thrashed to try to release the medical apparatus she was attached to when in the hospital. Once young, beautiful, and lively, this was not the way she wanted to live.

We used to joke that Gloria was too ornery to die, but I believe that fear kept her here. She was a strong Catholic, but once confided that the unknown of death terrified her. So she lived on for years, in a sort of a halfway zone, partly here and partly gone.

Now Gloria was back in the hospital, which we knew she hated, and Kim told us that this might be it. Life had been so hard for her over the past years that my other sister-in-law, Jean, said she didn't know what to pray for — was it better for her to recover, or was it her time?

"What makes this time different?" my husband Jeff asked.

"She said Daddy's been visiting her," Kim replied. "He has told her not to be afraid, that he's here for her. She seems very happy to see him — she's not so agitated."

This wasn't the first time that Jim had shown himself since his death. Shortly after he died, Kim had a very vivid dream — he sat at the foot of her bed and told her not to be sad. He was fine. He wanted her to be happy. Kim awoke and could have sworn he had actually been there.

And on the day of his funeral, Devon, my then four-year-old, asked Grandma why she was crying. Gloria explained that she was missing Granddaddy. Devon, with an innocence that can only be possessed by a small child, replied, "But Grandma, Granddaddy's right beside you. He's holding your hand!"

This was the first time we had heard of Jim visiting Gloria, and Kim said that his visits had been frequent. After the call, Jeff and I talked about whether he should fly home to see his mother. We agreed that he would book a flight in the morning.

Very early the next morning, before anyone else was up, the phone interrupted my early morning quiet. Even the ring sounded different. I knew. Kim said Gloria had died early that morning. It had been very peaceful.

Gloria died on November 15th, the eleventh anniversary of her husband Jim's death, in the early morning, just as he had.

We no longer had to wonder what to pray for. She had gone home — and Jim was there for her.

~Bridget McNamara-Fenesy

99

Thanks, Mom

Death ends a life, not a relationship.
~Jack Lemmon

One Sunday afternoon during a visit at my parents' house, my mother led me into her bedroom. "Suzanne, I have something I want to give you." She pulled open her top dresser drawer, lifted out a small box, and handed it to me.

"What is this, Mom?" I asked and tugged at the lid. The interior, lined by royal-blue velvet, held a gold wedding band. A continuous leaf pattern had been etched on the surface. I glanced at her and smiled. "Really?"

"This ring belonged to your grandmother, given to her by Grandpa in honor of their 50th anniversary. She bequeathed it to me when she passed away. Try it on and see if it fits."

"But, Mom, don't you want to wear it? There's no hurry to give it to me."

"I want to be sure you have this. I made a promise to my mother to pass it down to you."

I slipped off my diamond wedding ring and slid on the shiny band. It fit my finger perfectly. Butterflies fluttered inside my chest as I admired the new piece of jewelry. My thoughts couldn't make sense of the gift, but it held a very special meaning for me. The family connection brought tears to my eyes.

"It does fit me well," I said and smiled.

"The ring's too tight on me. I'm so glad you're able to wear it in her memory. Take a look inside. He had their initials engraved in there, too."

I slid it off, squinted and saw the tiny letters inscribed in the gold.

"How unique. Thank you very much, Mom." We hugged.

Three months later, we buried my mother at age sixty-eight. She had found out she had pancreatic cancer in May, and there was nothing the doctors could do. At her funeral, I reminisced about the day she gave me that ring. She had already known her fate. She was a brave soul.

Since the moment I'd put on that ring, I'd never taken it off. It meant so much to me, and I now wore it in memory of my mother *and* grandmother.

A year later, I decided to color my gray hair. I had to remove the ring to put on the rubber gloves. That next morning, I couldn't find my precious ring anywhere. I retraced my steps. Had I set it on the bathroom sink or tossed it on my dresser? I searched each place thoroughly. I couldn't find it.

I berated myself. That ring stood for so much. How could I have been so careless?

Six months later, I still hadn't found Grandma's wedding band. How could it have just disappeared? I vowed to keep looking.

One night at 2:00 a.m., when I was sound asleep, I heard my mother's voice in a dream. She said, "Suzanne, move the dresser." My eyes opened wide, and I bolted to a sitting position. I'd know her voice anywhere. Chills traveled through me. I searched the corners of my dark bedroom. *What had just happened? Was it really her?*

Nothing was amiss. My husband snored away on his side of our king-size bed. I dropped back to my pillow. First thing tomorrow, I'd check the floor beneath the triple dresser.

After morning coffee, I borrowed a wooden yardstick from my husband's tool rack. I squeezed my body into a tight corner beside my dresser and stared. Total blackness greeted me. I rose and grabbed a flashlight, returned and peered in again. In the illuminated area, I saw a glint of something metal. I stood and crammed that yardstick in as far as I could. Then I swept the carpet toward me. Dust bunnies came out. No ring.

I swiped again and dragged out a lost earring — one of a pair that had recently been misplaced when I was in a hurry to insert it. *Was that what she meant?* I sighed. Thinking positive, I gave it one more try and raked the floor even harder. A gold item flashed as it rolled by. My heart did flip-flops. I knelt and scooped it up.

My grandmother's ring.

I'd found it. Immediately, I slipped the band back on. Joy flowed through me. I glanced up to where my mother resides now. And after she spoke to me in that dream, I know she watches over me. Thanks, Mom.

~Suzanne Baginskie

Strength through a Dream

Grandma always made you feel she had been waiting
to see just you all day and now the day was complete.
~Marcy DeMaree

"Kelly, settle down! Can't you just sit?" I was eight, and most adults couldn't handle my hyperactivity. Mom was worn out from trying to make me behave while we visited my grandparents.

"She's okay; just let her be." My grandmother was my best friend and advocate. "Here, chickadee, come help Gramma repot these plants."

Gramma embodied unconditional love, radiating warmth and patience as she welcomed my hyperactive visits throughout her life, continually encouraging my creativity.

Always giving, she and Grampa coordinated my wedding when I became pregnant at eighteen. They gave us the tiny apartment adjoining their garage.

My husband's abuse started almost immediately. I learned to duck his swings and cry quietly. Gramma was unaware of my suffering but she poured hope into me each day as she tenderly put her arms around me. Telling me she loved me made me feel safe somehow. She was my rock.

My grandfather was hospitalized during my second trimester. My uncle came from Georgia to support Gramma, with hopes that my grandfather would recover and return home.

Early one morning, my uncle banged on my door, yelling, "Mother's dead! Mother's dead!"

I followed him into Gramma's house and… he was right. The morning was a blur of visits from neighbors. Dad arrived, and soon the mortician took Gramma away.

I was pregnant and miserable. I'd lost Gramma — my best friend, neighbor, and confidante.

The house filled with relatives, and I closed myself in my grandparents' bedroom. Sitting on the edge of their bed, I hung my head and wept. *What would I do now? Who would love me?*

As I cried alone quietly in her bedroom with the doors closed, I felt an arm around my shoulders. The soft, warm, reassuring hug felt familiar. I looked up to see who was comforting me, but I was still alone. I gasped, then relaxed and allowed her love to console me, as my Gramma had done so many times before.

Two weeks later, Grampa died in the hospital. My husband and I moved into the house until the estate was settled.

Weeks rolled by, and my belly grew. We were always broke. When Gramma and Grampa's food was gone, we had nothing to eat. When their heating oil ran out, we froze. With no money, I relied on Gramma's bras and big "granny panties" for coverage.

The month before my nineteenth birthday, I had a beautiful baby girl. Being in Gramma's house was comforting; I felt her presence with me daily. I never doubted my ability to care for my newborn while I was in that house.

Soon, however, the house sold, and we had to move. Without the support of Gramma's memories, I felt weak. The abuse escalated, and I grew anemic and frail.

Within months, Baby Number Two was conceived. Soon after his birth, I realized that the babies were in danger; we *had to* escape. But I was so timid and fragile!

Twice, I left my husband, but returned after he promised to change. Of course, there was no improvement.

I couldn't break out of the cycle I was in though. That is, until

Gramma helped me make the final, irrevocable break from my abuser.

One night in a dream, I was facing a thick wall made of stone. Light rays showed through a narrow aperture — a rectangular passage two feet wide and four feet tall. In my dream, I crawled up into the opening and, on my hands and knees, made my way through it. It was like a tunnel. The stones were smooth, but they hurt my knees.

The crawl was short, and the sunlight on the other side of the wall was warm and welcoming. I saw emerald green trees and grass — and my grandmother! There she stood, welcoming me with her bright smile and outstretched arms. She gave me a much-needed hug.

"Oh, Gramma, is it really you?"

"Well, yes, my little chickadee. It is me." She continued to hug me. The warmth was real, and the reassurance absolute. I allowed myself to melt into her arms.

"I miss you, Gramma. I love you so much." I felt overwhelming love for her. I also felt shame. I was ashamed of my weakness. I had always been a firecracker with whom adults struggled — that spunky eight-year-old had become a wimp.

My grandmother held onto my upper arms firmly. Looking into my eyes, she said with conviction, "Kelly, I am so proud of you. I love you. I always have."

Without further conversation, I knew I had to go. I had so many questions and wanted to stay, but knew it was time to leave. I entered the short, narrow tunnel to crawl back to my life. I paused to look back over my shoulder and I heard a voice: "You can't come back here."

While sad, I smiled at having been with my beloved grandmother. I awoke with a renewed resolve to meet the future with determination. I thanked God for allowing me a few precious minutes with Gramma.

Through my dream, my grandmother had given me the encouragement I needed. Mustering the courage that I knew I had inside me and the strength that comes from being her granddaughter, I gathered my babies and left — this time for good.

I called my parents and told them that I was leaving him forever. I don't know how they could have believed me, but they did and helped us move. Finally, I could mature as a healthy person, and my children could grow up in safety and peace.

Throughout the years I have used the power of my memories of Gramma. She was strong and upright. I think of her often as I wear her purple apron or serve food in her bowls. If ever I feel weak or unsure of myself, I just remember our last visit — the visit that changed my life forever.

~Kelly J. Stigliano

Birth and Death

Love knows no limit to its endurance, no end to its
trust, no fading of its hope; it can outlast anything.
Love still stands when all else has fallen.
~Blaise Pascal

She wore a white, cotton robe covered in tiny pink-and-green roses. Her short auburn hair was curled neatly, with a hint of gray showing at the edges, just as I remembered. We were in a house. I'm not sure whose house, but it was familiar and comforting to be there and to be with her. She walked, and I followed.

Although it felt odd that my Granny Miller was with me, since she passed away when I was a teenager, I was elated to be with her. We spent a long while just talking, being in one another's presence and catching up on the years of my adulthood we had been unable to spend together. Immediately before she left, she turned to face me and said in a confident, soothing tone, "Your daddy is going to die, but it will be all right."

At that moment, I awoke to the sound of my dog barking, signaling she wanted to go outside. I lay confused in bed for a few moments, listening to the dog. What a strange, vivid dream. My Granny Miller was my father's mother. Although I loved her very much, it had been many years since her passing and I didn't think about her very often.

I decided the dream was the result of my overactive emotions and hormones because I was twenty-eight weeks pregnant with our first child. All was well in my safe, full world, and I was happily awaiting the baby. I got up from bed and headed toward the dog, but as I stood,

I felt something warm and wet running down my legs.

I went to the hospital for evaluation by my obstetrician. My amniotic fluid had indeed broken, and by that afternoon I was in active labor. I was rushed to a hospital with a Level 1 neonatal intensive care unit ninety miles away from home. Three days later, my husband and I were the shocked, terrified parents of a new baby girl. Jordan Abigail was born weighing one pound, twelve ounces, and was fourteen and a half inches long. All of the expert healthcare professionals caring for her were optimistic and told us she was extraordinarily healthy. The hospital staff prepared us to expect that Jordan would remain in the neonatal intensive care unit until her due date, which was twelve weeks away.

For the first week after Jordan was born, I got absolutely no sleep. I blamed myself for her premature birth and could not stop thinking about what I did to cause my body to experience early labor. I was, after all, a registered nurse and should have been able to prevent what happened.

I kept thinking about that dream. It frightened me because I convinced myself that my grandmother had said my baby was going to die, not my father. Daddy was strong and healthy and took care of the entire family. Obviously, the dream was meant to warn me of an extreme complication that would take this tiny, precious being from our lives.

Largely as a result of the encounter with my grandmother, every possible moment was dedicated to soaking in Jordan's cries, her smell, the touch of her paper-thin skin, looking at every inch of her fragile, little body. I rarely left her side. Both our families were consumed with her wellbeing.

After six weeks she reached a milestone of three pounds, and we were all relieved. I decided the dream didn't mean anything.

A couple of weeks later, my mother reported that my father wasn't feeling well. His symptoms were vague. He reported he was weak and couldn't put his finger on exactly how he felt. I encouraged him to go to the doctor. Several days later, my mother called me and said she was taking him to the emergency room. He had been taking a bath and was so weak she could hardly get him out of the bathtub. At that point, I knew something was seriously wrong. My father avoided going to the doctor and had never been to the emergency room that I could recall. I asked Mother if she needed me to come home. Daddy told me to stay where I was needed — with Jordan.

My father ended up being rushed to a cardiac specialty hospital adjacent to where Jordan was hospitalized. I was able to visit him *and* my baby. Three days after that, he died as a result of heart failure caused by a heart attack.

I have always been comforted that my grandmother prepared me for the most difficult time in my life and also confirmed that she was with her son during his life transition. Sixteen years later, I watch my daughters, Jordan and Jessie, grow into the amazing human beings they were destined to be, and I feel my father's presence in our lives. Granny Miller was correct: It has been all right.

~Judy Ann Mitchell

Dreams
and the
Unexplainable

Meet Our Contributors

Meet Amy Newmark

Meet Kelly Sullivan Walden

Thank You

About Chicken Soup for the Soul

Meet Our Contributors

Adrienne A. Aguirre is a licensed minister with a Masters of Art in Theological Studies from Bethel Seminary San Diego. Chaplain Adrienne provides spiritual and bereavement counseling to hospice patients and their loved ones. She's also a freelance journalist and a prison-ministry volunteer. Reach her at 2240521@gmail.com.

John (Jake) Cosmos Aller is a novelist, poet, and former Foreign Service officer having served twenty-seven years with the U.S. State Department. He has completed three novels, and published his poetry in electronic poetry forums, including *All Poetry*, *Moon Café*, and *Duane's Poetree*, and literary magazines.

Monica A. Andermann lives and writes on Long Island where she shares a home with her husband Bill and their little tabby, Samson. Her work has been included in such publications as *Woman's World*, *Guideposts*, *Ocean* and many other *Chicken Soup for the Soul* titles.

Alicia Araya creates art through drawing, oil painting, printmaking, mixed media, and photography. Lately she has focused on collaborating on literary and artistic creations with her husband. She lives a stone's throw from the Appalachian Trail and invites you over for coffee anytime.

Love for the garden transformed **Barbara Blossom Ashmun's** life, inspiring her to become a garden designer, teacher, and writer. She's written seven garden books, most recently *Love Letters to My Garden*. Her greatest joy is gardening on a sunny acre in Portland, OR.

Suzanne Baginskie lives on the west coast of Florida with her husband, Al. Recently retired, she enjoys writing and has been published in various *Chicken Soup for the Soul* books. Her other interests include traveling, reading, and watching movies. She is currently working on an inspirational romantic suspense novel.

For the past twenty years **Maissa Bessada** has made her living writing promotional and marketing materials, but her heart lies with fiction. In 2013 she wrote and produced a six-episode satirical sci-fi audio drama about CSIS special agent, Ace Galaksi. You can meet Ace at www.acegalaksi.com.

D.E. Brigham has recently completed a forty-year career in secondary and higher education in the U.S. and abroad. He lives with his wife in a log house in Eastern Tennessee where he is starting a career as a writer. He is an avid pickle ball player, gardener, and kayaker. E-mail him at davidebrigham@gmail.com.

Loreen Martin Broderick holds a BS in Paralegal Studies, summa cum laude, and is pursuing an MA in Educational Psychology and Counselor Education at Tennessee Technological University. An avid reader, writer, crafter, and amateur genealogist, her greatest delights are her large loving family, dear friends, and beloved grandbabies.

Born and raised in Maine, **Heidi Campbell** is currently a high school English and journalism teacher in Georgia. She received her BA in English from Oglethorpe University, and her M.Ed from the University of Georgia. She is married with three kids and two dogs. She enjoys reading, writing, traveling, cooking, and antiques.

Peter Canova is a businessman/author. Two of his books, *Pope Annalisa* and *The Thirteenth Disciple* have won nineteen prestigious literary awards including Nautilus, Writer's Digest, and Eric Hoffer. He credits spiritual experiences for changing his life.

GD Carey is a writer and paranormal enthusiast from Southern California. When not writing or investigating the paranormal, she enjoys amateur matchmaking for friends and family. The song in her story can be found at soundcloud.com/voiceinthewilderness/make-some-good-and-pass-it-on.

Eva Carter has had a career in the entertainment field and finance. She is currently a freelance writer who enjoys Nia dance, (a combination of martial arts, dance arts and yoga). She lives in Dallas, TX with her husband, Larry. E-mail her at evacarter@sbcglobal.net.

Brenda Cathcart-Kloke lives in Denver, CO. Writing inspirational stories is a dream come true for her. An avid Broncos fan, she loves spending time with her family and reading *Chicken Soup for the Soul* books.

Christie Chu earned her BA from Wheaton College, IL. She is a military wife, mother of three, and writer. She spends most of her time getting ready to move or unpacking from the last move. Christie writes about family, expat life, and dealing with transition.

Laurel Clark has been keeping a dream journal for forty years, using dreams as a source for personal guidance and inspiration. She leads groups to assist other people to draw upon dream wisdom. Laurel teaches at the School of Metaphysics in Missouri and is a member of the International Association for the Study of Dreams.

Betty Jane Coffman is a certified massage therapist, therapeutic massage instructor and professional artist. She is also the author of several books, both fiction and nonfiction. Her most widely recognized titles are *From Blood to Blood*, *Blood Legacy* and *The Anatomy of Forgiveness*.

Heather M. Cook is a married mother of four children living in middle Tennessee. She is finishing up her degree in communications and plans to pursue writing as a career rather than the hobby it has been for many years. She enjoys reading and spending time with her family.

Lynn Darmon is an Evidential Medium living in Michigan with an international clientele. She has been featured on ABC's *20/20* and *The Dr. Oz Show* along with other appearances in television and radio. When not working, Lynn enjoys traveling to spend time with her two grown children — one in New York City and the other in Los Angeles.

Amy McCoy Dees is a mother, historian, and published novelist. She writes American history for young adults/children and loves traveling into the past to discover "hidden gems" to share with her readers. She recently traveled to Wales and adores the Welsh valleys, castles, and people there.

Stefanie DeLeo is a published playwright, actress, and teacher. She has a Master's degree in Theatre from New York University and was a Peace Corps volunteer in South Africa for two and a half years. Her published play, *Worth a Thousand Words*, jumpstarted her career as a writer.

Ralph S. Delligatti worked for forty-seven years in the Las Vegas casino industry. He is married to Paula and they have five sons, eight grandchildren, and one great-grandson. He published a book entitled *The Last Casino* and the screenplay *Deadly Defiance*.

Charlie Denison is a freelance writer, award-winning journalist and accomplished recording artist/singer-songwriter. A graduate of the University of Kentucky School of Journalism, Denison lives in Lewistown, MT with his wife and stepson.

Leslie Dunn's articles have appeared in *Redbook*, *Moody Monthly* and *Nashville Parent*. She was also a frequent contributor to the *Gainesville Sun*. Dunn is an ACA Certified Kayak Instructor and wrote the book, *Quiet Water Kayaking: A Beginner's Guide to Kayaking*, and a book about her hero, *Rudolf Virchow: Four Lives in One*.

Rita Durrett is a retired Family and Consumer Science teacher. She is mother to two boys and grandmother to five boys and a little girl. Rita blogs, sews, does needle art, and writes.

Lauren Dyer is a former school teacher, currently traveling around the U.S. with her dog West, kayaking, climbing, backpacking, and writing about her experiences. Follow her experiences on Instagram at the.rambling.woman or e-mail her for questions, comments, or job offers at Laurendyer1433@gmail.com.

Judy Dykstra-Brown is an artist and writer and has lived in Ajijic, Mexico, since 2001. Her recent work has appeared in *Veils, Halos,* and *Shackles, Felan* and *El Ojo del Lago.* Her books *Prairie Moths, Lessons from a Grief Diary* and *Sock Talk* are available online. She posts daily on her blog at judydykstrabrown.com.

Janice R. Edwards received her BAT degree in 1974. She taught English and Journalism before working at Texaco. She is a freelance writer for *Image Magazine* and has been published numerous times in the *Chicken Soup for the Soul* series.

Rachel Fort travels full-time in an RV with her husband and daughter. Rachel loves life on the road but looks forward to settling down someday, living off the grid, and having horses again. She plans to keep on writing.

Kelle Grace Gaddis's book, *My Myths,* was published in 2016. She earned her MFA from the University of Washington and has published numerous poetry and fiction works. She is honored to be a 4Culture "Poetry on Buses" winner in 2015 and 2017. She lives in Seattle with her partner Martin while working on a short story collection and novel.

Andrew Garcia was born in New York City in 1942. He served in the U.S. Navy from 1960 to 1964. Andrew attended California State University and graduated from Southwestern University School of Law. He practiced law in Los Angeles and Long Beach, CA for forty years and is now retired.

In 1999, **Lisa Garr** created *The Aware Show*, a transformational radio show featuring experts in the fields of mind-body-spirit and science. Lisa also hosts her show on Hay House Radio, KPFK, WBAI, Gaia TV and Coast to Coast AM and reaches millions globally per month. She is considered a pioneer in the field of Conscious Media.

The author of three poetry collections, **Joan Gelfand's** work appears in national and international journals. Her chapbook of short fiction won the Cervena Barva Fiction Award. Joan blogs for the *Huffington Post* and coaches writers. Her forthcoming novel, *Fear to Shred*, is set in a Silicon Valley startup. Learn more at www.joangelfand.com.

James A. Gemmell can be found most summers walking one of the Caminos de Santiago in France or Spain. His other hobbies are writing, playing guitar, drawing/painting, golfing and collecting art.

As co-founder of Mount Horeb House Ministries, **Annette Geroy** has spent the last fifteen years working with women who have experienced abuse or neglect. She writes and speaks with tender honesty, bringing hope for healing to wounded hearts. She is the author of two books: *Looking with New Eyes* and *Built with Stones of Turquoise*.

Dalia Gesser entertained audiences for twenty years with her delightfully original one-woman mime clown and mask theater shows. Since 2000 she has been bringing her theatre arts programs to children and adults. She lives north of Kingston, Ontario in beautiful lake country and can be reached at daliag@kingston.net.

Jessica Ghigliotti is a wife, homeschooling mother of three, children's author and parenting blogger, raising her family in beautiful Vermont. Learn more at JessicaGhigliotti.com.

T'Mara Goodsell lives, writes, and dreams in St. Louis, MO and has written for various anthologies, newspapers, and publications. She is working on a composite novel and a book for young adults.

Angelene Gorman was an elementary teacher for sixteen years and now owns a school photography company. She loves anything to do with the ocean, including boating, diving, fishing and collecting seashells.

Lisa Hackett enjoyed a twenty-five-year career as a production person in the film and television industry before she met and married cowboy poet Waddie Mitchell. They have traveled the road together for twenty years. In 2012 Lisa launched www.BuddyHackett.tv to honor and make available the life work of her father.

Michael Hausser is a proud graduate of Rutgers University and has been writing slice-of-life vignettes and short fiction for two decades. He lives in Central New Jersey with his lovely wife and four children. He is currently working on a series of short fiction stories. E-mail him at mikeyocy@comcast.net.

Christy Heitger-Ewing, an award-winning writer and columnist who pens stories for national, regional, and local magazines, has contributed to over a dozen anthologies and is the author of *Cabin Glory: Amusing Tales of Time Spent at the Family Retreat* (www.cabinglory.com). She lives with her husband, two sons, and two cats.

Award-winning author **Sallianne Hines** writes about home/family life, art, and craft. A former children's therapist, she's mom of three and grandma of eight. Besides playing "real" games and cards with the kids, she walks dogs, feeds cats, and rides horses. E-mail her at shineswriter@gmail.com or www.facebook.com/shinesWrites-1087439491334177.

Hanna Kelly has a Bachelor of Arts degree from Boston University and is a former corporate librarian for a New York City law firm. Originally from New York, she moved to Canada in 1985. She is the author of several essays, poems and short stories. Hanna has three adult sons and resides with her husband in Ottawa, ON.

Wendy Keppley, a Florida native, counseled troubled teens and taught college courses for high school honor students. She enjoys family, playing with her grandsons, and living in the woods near Tampa, FL. Wendy also loves writing, kayaking, reading, yoga, exploring waterfalls, and oneirology. E-mail her at wendykep@gmail.com.

M.D. Krider is a stay-at-home mom of two girls. She likes to express her creativity through writing, watercolors, drawing, and jewelry making. Melissa is currently working on her first novel.

Jocelyn Ruth Krieger is seventy-nine years old and a former model, singer, actress, and music teacher. Her writing has appeared in *Lessons from My Parents*, *The Detroit News*, *Detroit Free Press*, *Baby Talk*, and other publications. She resides in Boca Raton, FL. Since writing this story, Jocelyn has been blessed with another grandchild and great-grandchild.

Brenda M. Lane received an AS degree in Engineering Technology in 1998. Her passion is music and she is currently composing music for the film *Heaven, the First War* being done by Martoos Studios. Disney, Pixar, Walden, talent are on board. Three grown children call her Mom and three grandchildren call her Mimi.

Amanda Lee shows people how to live with ease as well as success in this chaotic world. She is happiest living, learning and teaching at the intersection between science and spirituality. She has two teenagers and lives in NSW, Australia. She loves being surrounded by nature and travelling to places that are food for the soul.

Janet Elizabeth Lynn was raised in Long Island, NY. Her first novel was published in 2011. Since then, she has published seven murder mysteries and joined her husband, Will Zeilinger, to write the *Skylar Drake Mysteries* series. Janet and Will are writing their fourth book in the series and yes… they are still married.

Ann Marie has enjoyed reading aloud to children in a school setting for the past twenty years. She occasionally writes short stories. She is married and the mother of two grown sons. She worked as a nurse for twenty-five years and enjoys playing tennis and sewing.

Joshua J. Mark is an editor/director and writer for the online history site *Ancient History Encyclopedia*. His nonfiction writing has also appeared in *Timeless Travels* and *History Ireland* and his short fiction in *Litro* and *Writes for All,* among others. He lives with his wife Betsy and daughter Emily in upstate New York.

Heather McMichael is a single mom of four living in Houston, TX. She enjoys nerd things such as Comic-Con and Superhero TV shows, which she guiltily watches without the little ones for now. She enjoys writing with sarcasm almost more than… nope. Sarcasm wins.

Bridget McNamara-Fenesy lives in Oregon, where she works as a business consultant when she is not writing. Her work has appeared in *The Sun* and *Fate* magazine, the *Chicken Soup for the Soul* series, as well as other publications. E-mail her at bridgetmcnamara@comcast.net.

At only eleven years old, **Kathryn Merz** wrote her first novel after her mother brought home the family's first computer. Three decades later, she still loves writing stories. Kathryn resides in Massachusetts with her husband, Brian, and their young son, Joseph. You can find more of her short stories and novels at KathrynMerz.com.

Carina Middleton is a stay-at-home mother and wife to an RCMP officer. She enjoys spending her time reading, writing, and trying to raise children who are functioning human beings.

Patricia Miller writes about the best emotion — love! She's a wife and mom of two, living in Bradford, Ontario. Patricia enjoys cottage life, pizza, and snowboarding. She studied creative writing at Durham College after earning her BA from the University of Western Ontario. Learn more at www.AuthorPatriciaMiller.com.

Ferna Lary Mills writes for her online encouragement ministry at www.rainbowfaith.com and posts weekly words of encouragement at www.facebook.com/RainbowFaith. She resides in East Texas and leads workshops on making sleeping mats for the homeless. You can find her on Facebook.

Judy Ann Mitchell has two daughters, holds a Master of Science in Nursing from Western Kentucky University, and is an Associate Professor for the Kentucky Community and Technical College System. She enjoys traveling, making memories with family and friends, exploring American history, and spirituality. Writing is one of her many passions.

Marya Morin is a freelance writer. Her stories have appeared in publications such as *Woman's World* and Hallmark. Marya also penned a weekly humorous column for an online newsletter, and writes custom poetry on request. She lives in the country with her husband. E-mail her at Akushla514@hotmail.com.

Rhonda Muir lives with her husband Tom in Stromness, UK where they're refurbishing a Georgian home and collaborating on writing projects, an upcoming Orkney-themed website (Orkneyology.com), storytelling adventures, and life. Rhonda's fantasy novel, *Grimmelings*, set in Orkney on the very beach where Tom proposed, is due to be published soon.

Alice Muschany writes about everyday life with a touch of humor. Her grandchildren make wonderful subjects. Her essays have appeared in numerous anthologies, magazines and newspapers. Her hobbies include hiking, swimming, and photography. E-mail her at aliceandroland@gmail.com.

Brian Narelle, a graduate of the USC School of Cinematic Arts, began his career writing for *Sesame Street*. After years of children's films and television he wrote his first book, *Living in Vertical Time*, the spiritual teachings of a donkey named Murray. His next book will feature the canine poetry of Warren Peace, his puppet alter ego.

Ela Oakland lives in Colorado.

Barbara A. Owens wrote professionally for many years before "retiring" to raise her four kids. She has learned much in the ensuing years, including how to put out grease fires and how to interpret (and pay attention to) dreams. She lives in Idaho with her family, two dogs, thirty chickens and eight sheep. Her life is never boring.

Jerry Penfold lives in East Aurora, NY, in a house he built with his own hands. He and his wife have four children and seven grandchildren. They enjoy camping in New York State Parks. Jerry has always been a dreamer.

Daniela Petrova is a New York-based freelance writer. Her articles and essays have appeared in *The New York Times*, *The Washington Post*, *Salon*, and *Women in the World*, among others. Her fiction has been published in literary journals and anthologies, including Best New Writing 2008. She is working on her first novel.

Lori Chidori Phillips resides with her beloved mate of thirty-two years in Southern California where they enjoy spending time with their grown children and learning new things every day. She invites readers to correspond with her at hope037@hotmail.com.

Ashley Previte is a senior copywriter and editor with clients spanning Fortune 100 companies to bestselling authors and Billboard musicians. She is a lover of Pugs, speed crossword puzzler, life-long vegetarian, avid reader, and mother to a fabulous six-year-old daughter.

Connie Kaseweter Pullen lives in rural Sandy, OR, near her five children and several grandchildren. She earned her Bachelor of Arts, with honors, at the University of Portland in 2006, with a double major in Psychology and Sociology. Connie enjoys writing, photography, and exploring nature.

Annette Rasp lives in Southern Pennsylvania. She has three children and three grandchildren. Annette enjoys spending time with her family and especially enjoys riding motorcycles with her husband, John.

Denise Reich is an Italian-born, New York City-raised freelance writer, dancer, and *Star Wars* museum and baseball geek. Recent credits include pieces in the Canadian magazine *Shameless,* TheMighty.com, and *The Santa Monica Review.* Her Broadway memoir, *Front of House,* was released in late 2015.

Donna L. Roberts is a native upstate New Yorker who lives and works in Europe. She is an Associate Professor and has a Ph.D. in Psychology. Donna is an animal and human rights advocate and when she is researching or writing she can be found at her computer buried in rescue cats. E-mail her at donna_roberts13@yahoo.com.

Kimberly Ross, M.Div., is a speaker, teacher, and energy worker. This is her third story to be published in the *Chicken Soup for the Soul* series and the second that deals with dreams and premonitions, a life-long interest. She lives in the Kansas City metro area and can be reached at kim@kaizenliving.org.

Judith Rost, a native of Minnesota, has been writing since junior high school. She initially gave up her love of writing to raise a family and continue in other careers. She now resides in Texas and writes Christian fiction and nonfiction including cozy mysteries. E-mail her at booksbyjarost@outlook.com.

Emily Rusch has her BSA in Health Science and currently works in the fitness industry as an instructor and coach. She is passionate about healthy living, traveling, tacos, and turquoise. She is a cancer survivor and lives life to the fullest every day alongside her husband and three boys.

Regina Schneider is currently on the staff of three cats: Bogie, Missy and Lulu. While her kitty Molly's passing left a huge hole in her life, her current cadre of fur-faced children keep her on her toes. Living in Marin County, CA, she spends her days as a legal support supervisor.

Judith Richardson Schroeder guides women 50+ to love and honor their goals and visions. She loves long road trips, airplane takeoffs, and grateful living, but mostly the love and support she receives from her family and friends. As a coach and mentor, she teaches, speaks, and writes to and for women exploring their limitless success.

Irene Spencer is a New York Times best-selling author of *Shattered Dreams: My Life as a Polygamist's Wife*. She was the second of ten wives, mother of fourteen of her late husband's fifty-eight children. To learn more and /or to order a copy of her books, visit www.IreneSpencerBooks. com.

Glenda Standeven is a bone cancer survivor, inspirational speaker and author from Chilliwack, BC. She is the author of *I am Choosing to Smile: An Inspirational Life Story of a Bone Cancer Survivor* and *What Men Won't Talk About… and Women Need to Know: A Woman's Perspective on Prostate Cancer*.

Sunny Stephens has always had a passion for the written word. EG Kight put one of her poems to music, and the song aired on an ABC family show. A song she co-wrote landed on Koko Taylor's *Royal Blue* album, which was nominated for a Grammy. Sunny lives in Nashville, TN, works in music management, and continues to write.

Kelly J. Stigliano lives in Orange Park, FL with her husband, Jerry. They have five children and two granddaughters. A member of Word Weavers International, she has been published in magazines and anthologies, and actively blogs at *Mentoring Moments for Christian Women*. Kelly travels extensively as an inspirational speaker.

In 1999, **Shannon Stocker** was derailed from pediatrics due to RSD/ CRPS, a life-threatening illness. Nearly a decade later, a coma saved her life. She and her husband Greg live in Louisville, KY with their little miracles, Cassidy and Tye. Shannon writes picture books, is currently working on her memoir, and is a musician.

Lynn Sunday is an artist, writer, and animal advocate who lives near San Francisco with her husband and two senior rescue dogs. Nine of her stories appear in eight *Chicken Soup for the Soul* books, and numerous other publications. E-mail her at Sunday11@aol.com.

B.J. Taylor knows her dad in heaven watches over her. B.J. is an award-winning author whose work has appeared in *Guideposts*, many *Chicken Soup for the Soul* books, and numerous magazines and newspapers. You can reach B.J. through her website at www.bjtaylor.com and check out her dog blog at www.bjtaylor.com/blog.

Steven Lane Taylor has a passion for teaching people how to recognize and cooperate with the divine flow of life. He has written three books on the subject, beginning with *Row, Row, Row Your Boat: A Guide for Living Life in the Divine Flow*. Steven lives in beautiful Sedona, AZ, with his lovely wife, Carol.

Sheila Taylor-Clark is a writer from Lewisville, TX. Her hobbies are fine dining, traveling, community service, blogging and watching reality television. Sheila is married to Nathaniel and has a daughter, McKenzie. She hopes to write a novel or collection of short stories soon and can be reached via e-mail at shaycpa@msn.com.

Mark Thieman and his wife Theresa have been married for thirty-two years and have two grown children. Mark has worked as a computer automation engineer for thirty-six years. Mark is considering a second career in church ministry.

A Georgia girl married to a Canadian biker/ship's captain, **Kemala Tribe** circled the world with husband and son before landing on a tiny island in British Columbia. A faith-based novel is in the works, as is a non-fiction book on divine healing subsequent to her husband's death. E-mail her at kemalawrites@gmail.com.

Teri Tucker is a writer and publisher of books on India. She received her MS in Vedic Studies from MERU in Switzerland in 1976. Born in California, she has lived all over the U.S., Europe, and Asia. Currently she is residing in the remote Himalayas.

Ron Wasson was born in Nigeria, West Africa, the son of missionaries. He now lives in the Dallas, TX area. He and his wife have two daughters and two grandchildren. He has published articles with *SEEK*, *Among Worlds*, *Power for Living*, *The Upper Room*, *The Secret Place* and is a guest blogger for www.whatHehasdoneformysoul.blogspot.com.

Mary T. Whipple is a fantasy novelist and folklore enthusiast. Her debut novel, *A Venom Vice,* was released on July 1, 2017. When not reading or writing, Ms. Whipple can often be found playing video games with her husband while their puppy, kitten, and bearded dragon look on dolefully and beg for treats and tummy scratches.

Mary Z. Whitney has contributed stories in over twenty-five *Chicken Soup for the Soul* books. She's heard from countless readers sharing just how much the stories mean to them. Mary also writes for *Angels* *on Earth* and *Guideposts*. She has written two books, *Max's Morning Watch* and *Life's a Symphony*.

Aurora Winter is a serial entrepreneur, trainer, and speaker. The author of five books, she is frequently featured on radio and TV. She currently trains entrepreneurs how to present their message powerfully. She founded the Grief Coach Academy. Her passion is to help people live up to their full potential.

Dallas Woodburn is a writer, editor, teacher, and literacy advocate living in the San Francisco Bay area. To date, she has been a proud contributor to more than two dozen *Chicken Soup for the Soul* books. She regularly blogs about simple, joyful, healthy living at DaybyDayMasterpiece.com.

Will Zeilinger was born in Omaha, NE. As a youth, he lived in Turkey for five years. He received a BA in Graphic Design. Now retired, Will lives and writes mystery novels in Southern California. He loves to travel the world with his wife, Janet.

Meet Amy Newmark

Amy Newmark is the bestselling author, editor-in-chief, and publisher of the *Chicken Soup for the Soul* book series. Since 2008, she has published 150 new books, most of them national bestsellers in the U.S. and Canada, more than doubling the number of Chicken Soup for the Soul titles in print today. She is also the author of *Simply Happy*, a crash course in Chicken Soup for the Soul advice and wisdom that is filled with easy-to-implement, practical tips for having a better life.

Amy is credited with revitalizing the Chicken Soup for the Soul brand, which has been a publishing industry phenomenon since the first book came out in 1993. By compiling inspirational and aspirational true stories curated from ordinary people who have had extraordinary experiences, Amy has kept the twenty-four-year-old Chicken Soup for the Soul brand fresh and relevant.

Amy graduated *magna cum laude* from Harvard University where she majored in Portuguese and minored in French. She then embarked on a three-decade career as a Wall Street analyst, a hedge fund manager, and a corporate executive in the technology field. She is a Chartered Financial Analyst.

Her return to literary pursuits was inevitable, as her honors thesis in college involved traveling throughout Brazil's impoverished northeast region, collecting stories from regular people. She is delighted to have come full circle in her writing career — from collecting stories "from the people" in Brazil as a twenty-year-old to, three decades later, collecting stories "from the people" for Chicken Soup for the Soul.

When Amy and her husband Bill, the CEO of Chicken Soup for the Soul, are not working, they are visiting their four grown children and their first grandchild.

Follow Amy on Twitter @amynewmark. Listen to her free daily podcast, The Chicken Soup for the Soul Podcast, at www.chickensoup. podbean.com, or find it on iTunes, the Podcasts app on iPhone, or on your favorite podcast app on other devices.

Chicken Soup for the Soul

Meet
Kelly Sullivan Walden
aka "Doctor Dream"

Kelly Sullivan Walden is on a mission to awaken the world to the power of dreams. She is thrilled to be joining the Chicken Soup for the Soul family once again after the debut of *Chicken Soup for the Soul: Dreams and Premonitions*. Kelly is also the author of several bestselling books, including *I Had the Strangest Dream*, *It's All in Your Dreams*, *Dreaming Heaven*, *Dream Oracle Cards*, *The Love, Sex & Relationship Dream Dictionary*, *Discover Your Inner Goddess Queen,* and *Goddess Queen Pearls of Wisdom Journal*.

In *First for Women* magazine, she is the "Dear Abby of Dreams," answering the inquiries of people worldwide in her, "Instant Insight: Unlock the Power of Your Dreams" monthly column.

Her approach to dreams is both reverent and zany, which may account for why she's rumored to be the lovechild of Carl Jung and Lucille Ball. Her empowering message has been featured on many national talk shows, including *The Dr. Doctor Oz Show*, *Ricki Lake*, *The Real*, *Bethenny*, *Coast to Coast*, and Hallmark's *Home & Family*.

Kelly is a certified clinical hypnotherapist, whose unique approach to dream therapy (dream alchemy) led her to become a trusted advisor, coach and consultant, enriching the lives of countless individuals, including Fortune 500 executives, UN ambassadors, celebrities, entrepreneurs, inner-city kids, and stay-at-home moms. She is known as an inspirational speaker/workshop facilitator and founder of Dream-Life Coach Training (an on-line training program to empower people to develop dream mastery). Kelly is also proud to be the program director/founder of CHIME IN — The Change Is Me International, a youth-driven, adult-supported initiative that supports the United Nations Sustainable Development Goals by empowering young leaders (age 16–24) by inspiring radical diversity and extreme self-responsibility.

Like John Lennon, Kelly Sullivan Walden is a dreamer, but she knows she's not the only one. She dreams that one day people will stop taking their dreams lying down, and instead, be excited to sleep, and inspired to wake up to the power of their dreams. She imagines water cooler conversations and international summit meetings that begin with, "So, what did you dream last night?"

Sign up for your free Dream Declaration Meditation at www.KellySullivanWalden.com. You can also find her on Facebook at KellySullivanWaldenDoctorDream, or on Twitter or Instagram as KellySWalden.

Thank You

We owe huge thanks to all of our contributors and fans. This book was a treat for us — a testament to the power of dreams and intuition and to the power we all have within our own minds to solve our problems... even while we're asleep! As very busy writers and editors, our team at Chicken Soup for the Soul loved reading these stories about how we can multitask even more — by assigning ourselves topics to dream about!

We had thousands of submissions for this book and there were way more than 101 great stories, so some of the submissions that didn't fit in this title will appear in other *Chicken Soup for the Soul* books in the future. Our editors spent months reading all the great choices, and we're grateful to Elaine Kimbler, Ronelle Frankel, and Susan Heim for narrowing the list down to several hundred semifinalists for Amy and Kelly to enjoy.

Susan Heim did the first round of editing for us, and Associate Publisher D'ette Corona continued to be Amy's right-hand woman in creating the final manuscript and working with all our wonderful writers. Barbara LoMonaco and Kristiana Pastir, along with Elaine Kimbler, jumped in at the end to proof, proof, proof. And yes, there will always be typos anyway, so feel free to let us know about them at webmaster@chickensoupforthesoul.com and we will correct them in future printings.

The whole publishing team deserves a hand, including Maureen Peltier, Victor Cataldo, Mary Fisher, and Daniel Zaccari, who turned our manuscript into this beautiful book.

Sharing Happiness, Inspiration, and Hope

Real people sharing real stories, every day, all over the world. In 2007, *USA Today* named *Chicken Soup for the Soul* one of the five most memorable books in the last quarter-century. With over 100 million books sold to date in the U.S. and Canada alone, more than 250 titles in print, and translations into nearly fifty languages, "chicken soup for the soul®" is one of the world's best-known phrases.

Today, twenty-four years after we first began sharing happiness, inspiration and hope through our books, we continue to delight our readers with new titles, but have also evolved beyond the bookstore with super premium pet food, television shows, podcasts, positive journalism from aplus.com, and licensed products, all revolving around true stories, as we continue "changing the world one story at a time®." Thanks for reading!

Chicken Soup for the Soul

Share with Us

We all have had Chicken Soup for the Soul moments in our lives. If you would like to share your story or poem with millions of people around the world, go to chickensoup.com and click on "Submit Your Story." You may be able to help another reader and become a published author at the same time. Some of our past contributors have launched writing and speaking careers from the publication of their stories in our books!

We only accept story submissions via our website. They are no longer accepted via mail or fax.

To contact us regarding other matters, please send us an e-mail through webmaster@chickensoupforthesoul.com, or fax or write us at:

Chicken Soup for the Soul
P.O. Box 700
Cos Cob, CT 06807-0700
Fax: 203-861-7194

One more note from your friends at Chicken Soup for the Soul: Occasionally, we receive an unsolicited book manuscript from one of our readers, and we would like to respectfully inform you that we do not accept unsolicited manuscripts and we must discard the ones that appear.

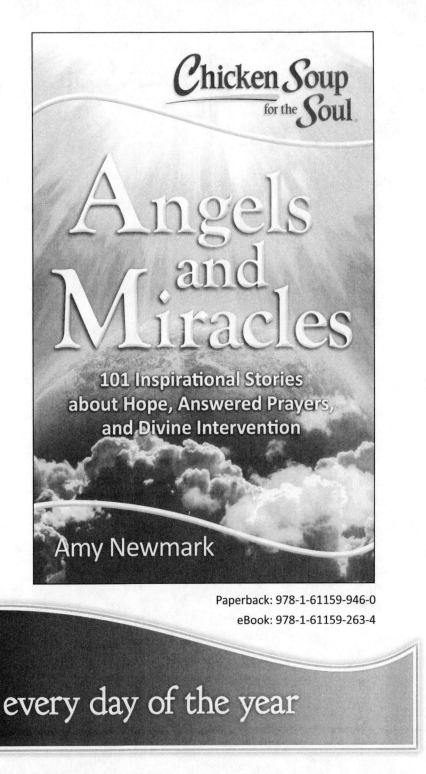

Chicken Soup for the Soul

Angels and Miracles

101 Inspirational Stories about Hope, Answered Prayers, and Divine Intervention

Amy Newmark

Paperback: 978-1-61159-946-0
eBook: 978-1-61159-263-4

every day of the year

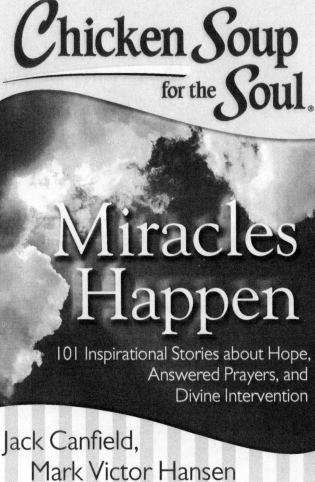

Chicken Soup for the Soul.

Miracles Happen

101 Inspirational Stories about Hope,
Answered Prayers, and
Divine Intervention

Jack Canfield,
Mark Victor Hansen
& Amy Newmark

Paperback: 978-1-61159-932-9
eBook: 978-1-61159-233-7

to good people every day